Regina O. Obe and Leo S. Hsu

pgRouting
A Practical Guide

loca e
PRESS

Credits & Copyright

pgRouting

A Practical Guide
by Regina O. Obe and Leo S. Hsu

Published by Locate Press LLC

Copyright © 2017 Locate Press LLC
ISBN: 978-0989421737
All rights reserved.

Direct permission requests to info@locatepress.com or mail:
Locate Press LLC, PO Box 671897, Chugiak, AK, USA, 99567-1897

Editor   Gary Sherman
Diagrams   Virginia "Vicky" Vergara
Ellie with tablet illustration   Gary Battiston
Cover Design   Julie Springer
Interior Design   Based on Tufte-LATEXdocument class
Publisher Website   http://locatepress.com
Book Website   http://locatepress.com/pgr

Contents

Part 1

Getting Started with pgRouting

1 *Introducing pgRouting*

pgRouting is a PostgreSQL extension for developing network routing applications and graph analysis. It relies on PostGIS, the PostgreSQL geospatial extension. This book will guide you through the installation and usage of pgRouting, along with exercises you can apply to your own area of interest.

http://www.postgresql.org

http://postgis.net

1.1 Code and Data for the Book

The code and data for this book are available as a single download file at `http://loc8.cc/pgr/pgr_1e_code_data`. We'll also point out links to where the original data was obtained if you wish to get an updated version.

1.2 Why pgRouting?

If you are reading this book, chances are that you are already using PostGIS, the spatial extender for the PostgreSQL database management system. PostGIS excels at storing and processing spatial data. Distance measuring functions in PostGIS let you answer questions of how close something is to another. However, PostGIS falls short when trying to find distance along constrained paths such as roads. It also won't help you if you need to apply costs and resource constraints to these travels.

Let's say you have a table of towns as points and highways linking the towns as linestrings. To find the shortest path between two towns, you could conceivably enumerate through all the linestrings using a recursive query to find all combinations of possible line strings, reject ones not starting and ending at your two towns, compute the distance of the remaining, and pick out the shortest. A quick back-of-the-envelope calculation shows that you have

$$\sum_{k=2}^{N} \frac{N!}{2(N-k)!}$$

possible paths. This brute-force approach to solving the shortest path problem quickly becomes unwieldy after the number of nodes exceeds about ten.

Many mathematicians and computer scientists have tackled this classic shortest path problem. They have accumulated numerical algorithms that will solve the problem without having to resort to naively counting. pgRouting is a PostgreSQL implementation of this body of work. By using pgRouting, your shortest path problem becomes nothing more than executing a function to arrive at the answer. pgRouting goes further than just giving you the answer. You'll find additional functions to validate your network and check for such conditions as completeness. For example, are there highways linking every town and do you have roads that lead to no towns.

In short, pgRouting eliminates the need for you to code numeric recipes from scratch. All the classic algorithms, and variants, are already at your disposal: Dijkstra, TSP, and others.

History

pgRouting is currently in version 2+. The latest stable release is 2.3. This book covers pgRouting 2.2-2.3. We built our examples using pgRouting 2.3, PostGIS 2.3, and PostgreSQL 9.5+. Some, but not all, may work in lower versions. We'll note cases where we are using features not available in lower versions.

http://www.camptocamp.com
http://www.orkney.co.jp

http://georepublic.info
http://imaptools.com

The predecessor of pgRouting was a product called pgDijkstra, a project started by Sylvain Pasche of Camptocamp. The Japanese company Orkney extended available routing algorithms beyond just Dijkstra, and rechristened the new product pgRouting. Daniel Kastl, formerly with Orkney, ventured out on his own and formed a new company Georepublic.. Georepublic inherited the mantle as primary maintainer of pgRouting. iMaptools, Virginia Vergara, and a broad user community round out the rest of the maintenance team.

Licensing

pgRouting is licensed under GPLv2 license, with some functions being MIT licensed. In addition, it relies on the following open source libraries, with varying open source licenses:

- PostGIS, GPLv2+ with dependencies on MIT and LGPLv2+ licensed libraries
- Boost, under Boost Software License
- Computational Geometry Algorithms Library (CGAL), under a GPL/LGPLv3 license

http://loc8.cc/pgr/gplv2
http://loc8.cc/pgr/mitlic
http://loc8.cc//pgr/lgplv2
http://loc8.cc/pgr/boostlic

http://loc8.cc/pgr/cgallic

1.3   Installation

To install pgRouting, start by visiting the download site at `http://pgrouting.org/download.html`. You'll find source code for pgRouting, ready for compilation, along with links to many precompiled binaries for various operating systems.

Binaries

The easiest way to get PostgreSQL extensions is from a binary distribution. To minimize dependency issues, you'll want to get the pgRouting distribution package from the same place you got your PostgreSQL and PostGIS. Appendix B, on page 269 details the most popular distributions for each OS at time of writing. Distributions change, so always check the pgRouting website for links to the latest.

Starting with version 2.1, the pgRouting team consolidated all the required binary files into one—`librouting-2.1`, with the version number included in the file name. You should have no trouble if you keep your pgRouting updated to within two minor versions of PostGIS. The current pgRouting version 2.3 pairs flawlessly with PostGIS 2.2 and 2.3. As far as installation goes, pgRouting does not have any binary dependencies on PostGIS itself. But like other C/C++ based PostgreSQL extensions, pgRouting has a binary dependency on PostgreSQL minor version. This means that if you have a pgRouting 2.3 compiled against a PostgreSQL 9.5 database, you would need to recompile against PostgreSQL 9.6 when you upgrade.

Source Code

If you want to scrutinize the source code, contribute to the pgRouting project, or can't find a binary distribution for your OS, you can download pgRouting from the GitHub repository: `https://github.com/pgRouting/pgrouting` and compile yourself. On GitHub, the `master` branch leads to the latest stable release. The `develop` branch leads to latest development version. Each released version has an identically named tag. For instance, if you're looking for 2.3.0, you want to traverse the branch tagged as `v2.3.2`. All released versions are listed on the `https://github.com/pgRouting/pgrouting/releases` page.

Each minor version also has a branch where bug fixes are applied before they are tagged for release. For example branch release/2.3 will have bug fixes slated for the next release.

Enabling pgRouting in a PostgreSQL Database

If you run into issues installing, verify your binary is in the `lib` folder and the corresponding `pgrouting.control` and `pgrouting-2.3.2.sql` files are in the `share/extension` folder of your PostgreSQL install. The PostgreSQL `lib` folder is where all extension libraries reside and the PostgreSQL `share/extension` folder is where the corresponding scripts for extensions reside. This step is normally done for you when you install the binaries from a distribution or compile and install the binaries from source using `make install`. Next, you must enable pgRouting in your database. (PostGIS must be enabled first if you have not already done so.)

For example, to enable pgRouting and PostGIS in a new database called `pgr`, follow these steps using the `psql` command line or pgAdmin SQL window:

Listing 1.1: Enabling PostGIS and pgRouting in pgr using psql

```
1  CREATE DATABASE pgr;
2  \connect pgr;
3  CREATE SCHEMA postgis;
4  ALTER DATABASE pgr SET search_path=public,postgis;
5  \connect pgr;
6  CREATE EXTENSION postgis SCHEMA postgis;
7  CREATE EXTENSION pgrouting SCHEMA postgis;
```

1. Create the database with *line 1*.
2. Connect to your new database with *line 2*.
3. Create a schema called postgis to house pgRouting and PostGIS extensions with *line 3*.
4. Add the new postgis schema to your database search_path with *line 4*.
5. Reconnect to the database so the new search_path is utilized.
6. Create the PostGIS extension in the postgis schema with *line 6*.
7. Create the pgrouting extension with *line 7*.

If you are using PostgreSQL 9.6 or above, you can replace *lines 6-7* with the following that uses the new CASCADE. Using CASCADE will force all dependency extensions, in this case postgis to be installed as well, and it will install it in the same schema as you chose for the pgrouting extension.

```
CREATE EXTENSION pgrouting SCHEMA postgis CASCADE;
```

Alternatively, you can use pgAdmin to click your way through the above steps. To create the extension in pgAdmin, use the Extensions->New Extension option as shown in Figure 1.1, on the next page.

> If you compiled PostGIS without raster support or are using PostGIS on a version of PostgreSQL earlier than 9.1, you will not be able to install PostGIS with the CREATE EXTENSION command. For PostgreSQL 9.0, you must use the contrib/scripts for both PostGIS and pgRouting. For PostgreSQL 9.1+ (with no raster), you must use the contrib/scripts for PostGIS, but you can use CREATE EXTENSION for pgRouting if you remove the line requires = 'postgis' from the file /share/extension/pgrouting.control.

Although you can just throw PostGIS and pgRouting extensions

Figure 1.1: Enabling pgrouting using pgAdmin

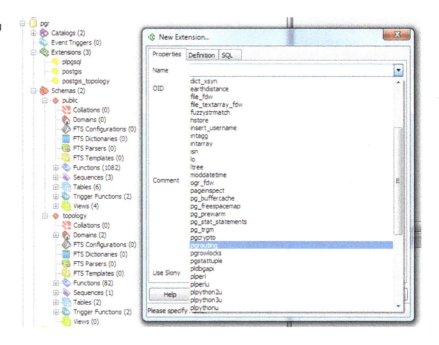

into your default schema (*public*), we advise you to create a separate schema to house extensions. Each extension could dump thousands of functions into your default schema—you'll want to avoid mixing these with functions of your own creation. Since pgRouting uses a lot of PostGIS functions, we like to install it in the same schema as PostGIS. Some applications, such as Ruby on Rails, by default install PostGIS in a schema called *postgis*. Installing `postgis` and `pgrouting` in the *postgis* schema is the convention we will follow in this book.

> Future versions of PostGIS may force it to install in a specific schema to resolve issues with database restore, foreign tables, and so that extensions like pgrouting and postgis_topology can schema-qualify their postgis function calls e.g. `postgis.ST_StartPoint` to prevent dependency issues during database restore. In PostGIS 2.3 the postgis extension was changed to not be relocateable which means once installed, you can not move it to another schema.

If you have multiple versions of PostGIS and pgRouting binaries available, you can specify which to use by appending the version number in CREATE EXTENSION as follows:

```
CREATE EXTENSION postgis VERSION "2.3.2" SCHEMA postgis;
CREATE EXTENSION pgrouting VERSION "2.3.2" SCHEMA postgis;
```

In pgAdmin, you will see more than one version available in the version drop down box.

pgAdmin has a drop down list from which to pick the schema. To avoid having to prefix functions with the schema name, add your new schema to the search path of the database as we did in *line 4* of Listing 1.1, on page 16.

> Changing the search_path of the database does not take effect in the current connection. You need to disconnect and reconnect to utilize the new search_path settings.

Always check that you have installed pgRouting correctly by running the query:

```
SELECT * FROM pgr_version();
```

If nothing is amiss, you will see output similar to the following:

version	tag	hash	branch	boost
2.3.2	V2.3.2	95c0a0643	release/2.3	1.59.0

Another new feature in pgRouting 2.1 is the ability to upgrade the extension. To upgrade from pgRouting 2.2.2 to 2.3.2 you would do:

```
ALTER EXTENSION pgrouting UPDATE TO "2.3.2";
```

To update to the latest version installed on your server:

```
ALTER EXTENSION pgrouting UPDATE;
```

> If you are upgrading from a lower version of pgRouting, or from an unreleased version, you can do `DROP EXTENSION pgrouting; CREATE EXTENSION pgrouting;` Doing a drop and recreate will work in most cases, unless you built functions against pgRouting types. In this case, you may need to drop your functions first and then recreate them after installing a newer pgRouting.

1.4   Where to Get Help

pgRouting provides several avenues for support. There is the bug tracker for reporting bugs, the user's mailing list, and GIS StackExchange for getting basic or advanced help.

If you are interested in getting involved in pgRouting development, you can subscribe to the pgRouting developer's list where you can get feedback about how to code algorithms.

In addition to public support, commercial support is also available.

All avenues of support are listed on `http://pgrouting.org/support.html`.

The pgRouting development team is very open to bug reports.

If you come across what you think is a bug in pgRouting, you can report this at `https://github.com/pgRouting/pgrouting/issues/`.

1.5   Routing Nomenclature

Routing problems and solutions have appeared in mathematical literature ever since the Renaissance. Diverse disciplines have incorporated them into their own field of study. Each discipline ascribed its own set of terminology. Before we go further, we want to present the terms that we will be using in this book.

Network, Graphs, and Topology

For our purposes, the terms graph, network, and topology are interchangeable. Of the three, network is the most generic term. Both graph and topology have rigorous mathematical underpinnings. We use both terms loosely—very loosely. Real world examples of networks abound: roads, Ethernets, genealogy trees, Facebook friends, the human circulatory system. In fact, any problem that can be modeled as interconnected relationships lends itself to being formalized as a network. Later in the book we'll present a network model of international exchange rates.

Edges and Nodes

A network is built from a patchwork of interconnected *nodes*. Nodes have many obvious synonyms: points, intersections, vertices, junctions. In this book we'll stick to using nodes over points—the latter is a PostGIS geometry. Connecting the nodes are *edges*. Edges are often referred to as segments, links, lines, or connections. We'll stick to referring them by the more common graph term of edges. The other synonyms could be confusing as they have special meaning in PostGIS and computer science.

Costs, Weighted vs. Unweighted Graphs

For real-world modeling, you can impute a value for each edge. We call these values *costs* or *weights*. For example, each edge on a network of highways could have costs that are a function of distance, speed limit, or surface (asphalt, gravel, turf, etc.). Each edge on an Ethernet could have a cost based on the maximum sustainable bandwidth, or the color of the physical cables (gray, orange, red, etc.) A network of an airline could have the "cost" of revenue miles assigned to each edge. From the passenger's perspective, the cost translates to fare price.

When edges have associated costs, the entire graph is *weighted* . If all edges always have the same cost or no costs, the graph is *unweighted*. The popular LinkedIn[1] network appears as an unweighted graph to its end user.

[1] https://www.linkedin.com

The end user could ascribe their own costs to each edge of the

Figure 1.2: Unweighted

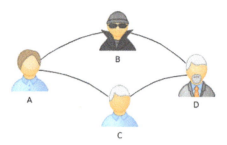

LinkedIn graph. Referring to Figure 1.2, let's say A is infatuated with D. To gain an introduction, A must implore B or C. Let's say C is the boss of D and B is the gardener of D. You can assign weights to represent degree of influence as in the following figure:

Figure 1.3: Weighted

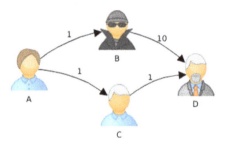

To get D to notice A, D is better off asking the boss than the gardener to make the introduction.

Directed vs. Undirected Graphs

When you ascribe directionality to nodes, your graph is *directed*, also know as a *digraph*. The classic example is a network of one way streets. Diagrammatically, directed edges are arrows. See Figure 1.4, on the facing page. Directed edges give rise to the concept of *source* nodes and *target* nodes. Edges can be *bidirectional*, with each direction having different costs.

Figure 1.4: Directed weighted

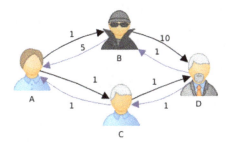

Matrix Representation

Matrices can represent networks. There are three common matrix approaches of representing graphs: *adjacency matrix, weighted adjacency matrix,* and *incidence matrix.*

In an adjacency matrix, both rows and columns correspond to nodes and the values in the cells are zeroes or ones to denote whether nodes are connected or not. An adjacency matrix doesn't consider costs.

In an adjacency matrix, both rows and columns correspond to nodes. Therefore, the matrix is always a square matrix. A matrix cannot contain empty cells, so you must have a convention of representing nodes that are connected versus ones that are not. An obvious choice is to use zero for disconnected nodes and unity for connected nodes. This convention leads to a binary matrix, one with only zeroes and ones.

We can represent LinkedIn graphs shown in Figures 1.2, on the preceding page and 1.4 as an adjacency matrix as follows:

$$
\begin{array}{c c}
 & \begin{array}{c c c c} \mathbf{A} & \mathbf{B} & \mathbf{C} & \mathbf{D} \end{array} \\
\begin{array}{c} \mathbf{A} \\ \mathbf{B} \\ \mathbf{C} \\ \mathbf{D} \end{array} &
\left[\begin{array}{c c c c}
0 & 1 & 1 & 0 \\
1 & 0 & 0 & 1 \\
1 & 0 & 0 & 1 \\
0 & 1 & 1 & 0
\end{array} \right]
\end{array}
$$

If you have weights between nodes, you can assign them to the cells, and then the matrix is referred to as a *weighted adjacency matrix*. You must have an exception in place to represent disconnected nodes. If you stick with using zeroes, you have to keep in mind that zero does not mean zero cost, so a more common pgRouting convention is to use -1 (or any negative number) or a really large number to designate disconnected nodes. The digraph of Figure 1.4, on the previous page can also be represented as a weighted adjacency matrix as follows:

$$
\begin{array}{c@{\quad}cccc}
 & \mathbf{A} & \mathbf{B} & \mathbf{C} & \mathbf{D} \\
\mathbf{A} & \begin{bmatrix} -1 & 1 & 1 & -1 \\ 5 & -1 & -1 & 10 \\ 1 & -1 & -1 & 1 \\ -1 & 1 & 1 & -1 \end{bmatrix} \\
\mathbf{B} \\
\mathbf{C} \\
\mathbf{D}
\end{array}
$$

In an *incidence matrix*, rows correspond to edges while columns correspond to nodes. The matrix will only be square if the number of edges is equal to the number of nodes. In the simplest manifestation, where you don't consider direction (an undirected graph), place a zero in cells where an edge does not connect to the node and a one in cells where an edge connects to the node.

In some definitions of incidence matrix, rows correspond to nodes and columns correspond to edge. This is the "node-edge" incidence matrix as opposed to the "edge-node" incidence matrix considered here.

The incidence matrix for Figure 1.2, on page 22 would look as follows:

$$
\begin{array}{c@{\quad}cccc}
 & \mathbf{A} & \mathbf{B} & \mathbf{C} & \mathbf{D} \\
\mathbf{A-B} & \begin{bmatrix} 1 & 1 & 0 & 0 \\ 1 & 0 & 1 & 0 \\ 0 & 1 & 0 & 1 \\ 0 & 0 & 1 & 1 \end{bmatrix} \\
\mathbf{A-C} \\
\mathbf{B-D} \\
\mathbf{C-D}
\end{array}
$$

Directions are easy to express in an incidence matrix, weights are not. If the arrow points into the node, use positive one. If coming out of the node, use negative one. We can represent our directed graph of Figure 1.4, on the previous page with:

$$\begin{array}{c c} & \begin{array}{c c c c} \mathbf{A} & \mathbf{B} & \mathbf{C} & \mathbf{D} \end{array} \\ \begin{array}{c} \mathbf{A}-\mathbf{B} \\ \mathbf{A}-\mathbf{C} \\ \mathbf{B}-\mathbf{D} \\ \mathbf{C}-\mathbf{D} \end{array} & \left[\begin{array}{c c c c} 1 & -1 & 0 & 0 \\ 1 & 0 & -1 & 0 \\ 0 & 1 & 0 & -1 \\ 0 & 0 & 1 & -1 \end{array} \right] \end{array}$$

In an incidence matrix a -1 or 1 denotes connectedness with the sign denoting directionality (coming into or out of the node). A 0 denotes no connection in both the incidence matrix and the adjacency matrix. In a weighted adjacency matrix a -1, some negative number, or a huge positive number can be used to denote no connection and 0 should be avoided entirely to minimize confusion with zero cost. The more interconnected your nodes, the fewer zeroes you'll have in your incidence/adjacency matrices. Relatively speaking, a matrix with few zeroes is considered *dense*, and with many zeroes, *sparse*.

Why Matrix Representation?

Many programming tools, such as R, MatLab, PostGIS raster, and even pgRouting itself, have numerous built-in functions to manipulate matrices.

Keep in mind that a matrix can be represented graphically as a heatmap[2]. You can use PostGIS raster, for example, for displaying this and to do other interesting operations on them.

You can also create new weighted adjacency matrices by overlaying several weighted adjacency matrices.

Adjacency List Representation

In road routing systems, representing connections as adjacency matrices can take up a lot of disk space, and in the end your matrix will often be filled with just negative ones or zeros to denote no connection. A more common way of representing these is with the use of lists, often referred to as an *adjacency list*. This is more commonly employed in pgRouting algorithms than matrices.

[2] https://en.wikipedia.org/wiki/Heat_map

An online tool that represents adjacency matrices, adjacency lists, and cost matrices graphically can be found at http://loc8.cc/pgr/galles.

Why so descriptive?

Let's review the attributes: weighted versus unweighted, directed versus undirected graphs, dense versus sparse matrices. You may be wondering if the attributes serve a real purpose other than adjectives—they do. To gain performance, algorithms avoid a one-size-fits-all approach. For example, if your matrix is highly sparse, an algorithm may do a first pass to pick out the connected nodes rather than naively iterating through all nodes.

1.6 Features provided by pgRouting

pgRouting comes packaged with numerous functions to implement optimization algorithms. On top of that, it includes functions to prepare your data. Let's take a look at the available functions.

Since pgRouting 2.0, functions packaged with pgRouting have the prefix *pgr* to distinguish them from other functions. The easiest way to see what functions and other database objects came with the pgRouting extension package is to run the following command in psql. (In pgAdmin, just expand the tree view in the schema where you installed pgRouting.)

```
\dx+ pgrouting
```

Running this provides output something like the following:

```
                        Objects in extension "pgrouting"
                            Object Description
-----------------------------------------------------------------------------
function _pgr_checkverttab(text,text[],integer,text)
function _pgr_createindex(text,text,text,integer,text)
:
function pgr_alphashape(text,double precision)
function pgr_analyzegraph(text,double precision,text,text,text,text,text)
:
function pgr_bddijkstra(text,integer,integer,boolean,boolean)
function pgr_createtopology(text,double precision,text,text,text,text,text,boolean)
function pgr_createverticestable(text,text,text,text,text)
function pgr_dijkstra(text,anyarray,anyarray,boolean)
:
function pgr_dijkstra(text,bigint,anyarray,boolean)
:
```

```
function pgr_dijkstra(text,bigint,bigint,boolean,boolean)
function pgr_drivingdistance(text,anyarray,double precision,boolean,boolean)
:
function pgr_drivingdistance(text,bigint,double precision)
:
function pgr_endpoint(geometry)
:
function pgr_kdijkstracost(text,integer,integer[],boolean,boolean)
function pgr_kdijkstrapath(text,integer,integer[],boolean,boolean)
function pgr_ksp(text,bigint,bigint,integer,boolean,boolean)
function pgr_ksp(text,integer,integer,integer,boolean)
function pgr_labelgraph(text,text,text,text,text,text)
function pgr_makedistancematrix(text)
function pgr_nodenetwork(text,double precision,text,text,text)
:
function pgr_trsp(text,integer,integer,boolean,boolean,text)
:
function pgr_version()
:
function pgr_vidstodmatrix(integer[],geometry[],text,double precision)
:
function pgr_vrponedepot(text,text,text,integer)
function pgr_withpoints(text,text,anyarray,anyarray,boolean,character,boolean)
function pgr_vrponedepot(text,text,text,integer)
function pgr_withpoints(text,text,anyarray,anyarray,boolean,character,boolean)
function pgr_withpointscost(text,text,bigint,anyarray,boolean,character)
function pgr_withpointscost(text,text,bigint,bigint,boolean,character)
function pgr_withpointsdd(text,text,anyarray,double precision,boolean,
  character,boolean,boolean)
function pgr_withpointsdd(text,text,bigint,double precision,boolean,
  character,boolean)
function pgr_withpointsksp(text,text,bigint,bigint,integer,boolean,boolean,
  character,boolean)
type pgr_costresult
type pgr_costresult3
type pgr_geomresult
(138 rows)
```

You should see around 35 functions and types listed for pgRouting 2.0, 138 for pgRouting 2.3.2, and 153 for pgRouting 2.4.0rc (soon to be released). All functions are well-documented in the pgRouting manual (http://docs.pgrouting.org).

In pgRouting, you will see some functions prefixed with underscores. These are developer helper functions, and you should ignore them for general use. Developer helper functions are useful for extending pgRouting.

The input API and output structure of Dijkstra and KSP has changed in pgRouting 2.1 and enhanced in later versions. Although for backwards compatibility the old API calls are supported, you should use the newer API calls since older API call argument syntax and output may be removed in pgRouting 3.0. We'll cover the differences between the two versions in later chapters.

We can categorize pgRouting functions and data types into four main categories:

- Builder - Functions to complete a network. For example, if you entered all the edges, the build functions will create a nodes table and fill in source and target columns of your edges table.
- Verification and fixer - Functions that point out trouble spots in the network. Functions that can fix the trouble spots automatically.
- Helper - Functions not directly related to routing, but useful nonetheless. Use these to compute matrices, generate isochrones, generate outputs to other formats, etc.
- Routing - Grand functions that implement routing algorithms. You'll find these to be heavily parameterized and overloaded to accommodate a wide array of uses.

pgRouting 2.0 has many set-returning functions that return cost types. These functions have since been replaced in 2.1 with functions that return tables with descriptive column names.

Builder Functions

A network has symmetries. For example, if you know all the edges, you can infer all the nodes. Builder functions complete a network by relying on predictable symmetries. Here are two notable examples:

- `pgr_createTopology` - Updates source and target fields in the specified edges table *<edge_table>*. It also creates a vertices table called `<edge_table>_vertices_pgr`.
- `pgr_createVerticesTable` - If you already have the source and targets filled in for an *<edge_table>*, this function creates the vertices table `<edge_table>_vertices_pgr` from this information.

> Don't confuse the pgr_createTopology function in pgRouting with CreateTopol-
> ogy in postgis_topology. PostGIS has its own topology objects that extend
> beyond the needs of pgRouting.

Verification and Fixer Functions

In a harmonious network, edges meet nicely at the same spot and
dead ends are non-existent.

Perfect harmony is a rarity when we work with real-world data.
Fortunately, pgRouting offers verification functions to sniff out prob-
lems in the network as well as fixer functions to repair automatically.
Here are some notable ones:

- pgr_analyzeGraph - After you've built your network, run this
  function to check for dead ends and disconnected gaps.
- pgr_analyzeOneway - Analyzes directionality, calls out edges that
  violate directionality rules.
- pgr_nodeNetwork - Ensures that all edges connect at nodes. Fix
  disconnected edges and edges that cross by introducing additional edges as necessary.

Additionally, don't forget that PostGIS itself includes hundreds of
functions to fix malformed geometries.

Routing Functions

The routing functions are the *pièce de résistance* of pgRouting. They
implement popular routing algorithms. Because they have many input parameters and overloads, we recommend that you refer to the
manual to make sure you have the correct signature for the variant
you're trying to use. The following is a list of routing functions.

Single-source Shortest Paths Algorithms

These functions take a begin node and an end node, generate all
possible paths, and return the one(s) with shortest path (least cost).

- `pgr_dijkstra` - Shortest path using the popular Dijkstra algorithm
- `pgr_bdDijkstra` - Shortest path using Dijkstra for bidirectional graphs
- `pgr_astar` - Shortest path using A* algorithm
- `pgr_bdAstar` - Shortest path using A* for bidirectional graphs
- `pgr_trsp*` - Shortest path with turn restrictions (TRSP), numerous signatures
- `pgr_ksp` - This returns the top K shortest path using Dijkstra

Pairwise Shortest Path Algorithms

These functions enumerate over all nodes, both connected by a single edge or multiple edges. For input, they accept a weighted, directed graph. For output, they return a square matrix of the shortest path for all pairs.

- `pgr_apspJohnson` - Pairwise shortest path using Johnson's algorithm
- `pgr_apspWarshall` - Pairwise shortest path using Floyd-Warshall algorithm

Multipaths Algorithms

These functions take a single begin node and multiple end nodes and return the shortest paths from begin node to each of the end nodes.

- `pgr_dijkstra*` - Multipath algorithm implemented using Dijkstra. Takes a single source node and an array of target nodes.

Optimization Algorithms

These algorithms try to find best sequence of travel given a set of nodes that need to be visited.

- `pgr_tsp` - The classic traveling sales person problem solved with heuristic and approximation algorithms
- `pgr_vrp*` - Vehicle route planner, a family of new and experimental functions unveiled in pgRouting 2.1

Proposed Functions

Also in pgRouting 2.1+ and above, you will find in the documentation what are called "Proposed Functions". These are functions that are prereleased in a version for experimentation and candidates for official support in the next version.

Although these functions are included, they may undergo structural changes and are not as stress tested as officially supported functions.

There are many of these you will find in pgRouting 2.2 - 2.4, slated for official support in a later version. Most notable of these are the `pgr_dijkstraVia` and `pgr_withPoints*` family of functions.

- `pgr_dijkstraVia` is very similar in purpose to `pgr_trsp` but utilizes the Dijkstra algorithm. It takes as input an array of vertices ordered in the order you want to stop at them and returns the least cost path that visits the stops in the requested order.
- `pgr_withPoints*` is a family of functions using Dijikstra that in addition to start and end vertices, takes an SQL statement that returns points along edges. These points are injected into the graph, constructing virtual nodes from them. The resulting travel path may then include these virtual nodes.
  If your path from start to end intersects any of the virtual points, they will be denoted by negative node numbers.
  You can think of this function as a vacation planner, the virtual points are points of interest, and your start and end is the path you are following, and if the route passes by any of the points of interest, they will be identified in the route.

2 *A Primer*

The techniques in pgRouting apply equally to networks large and small, so why not start small? In this chapter we look at a four-node network of airline routes. Once you master the example, you'll have earned your wings in pgRouting. You'll then be able to take flight to larger networks with thousands of nodes, limited only by your computing resources.

2.1 *Create a Network of Airline Routes*

As a starting point, we consider an undirected graph weighted by distance. The steps we follow to build our network are as follows: first create a table of airports, from which we derive the routes. The routes will serve as edges in the network. Once we have the table of edges, we use the function *pgr_createVerticesTable* to automatically generate the table of nodes.

To begin, we create a dataset of airports and routes. Airports will serve as nodes and routes as edges.

Airports: PostGIS Point Geographies

Listing 2.1: Create table of airports

```
1   CREATE TABLE airports (
2       id serial PRIMARY KEY,
3       city varchar(75),
4       iata char(3) UNIQUE,
5       geog geography(point)
6   );
7
8   INSERT INTO airports(city, iata, geog)
9   VALUES
10      ('New York', 'JFK', ST_POINT(-73.8893, 40.6975)::geography),
11      ('London', 'LHR', ST_POINT(0.0937, 51.5526)::geography),
12      ('Dubai', 'DXB', ST_POINT(55.3644,25.2528)::geography),
13      ('Mumbai', 'BOM', ST_POINT(72.8667,19.1583)::geography);
```

We chose PostGIS geography data type over the more common ge-

34 CHAPTER 2. A PRIMER

For those who need a brush-up or a complete treatment of PostGIS, please consult our book: PostGIS in Action http://www.postgis.us.

[3] Geodetic is a fancy word for measurement that treats the earth as round rather than flat.

ometry type.

Geography is geodetic with units in meters.[3]

Routes: PostGIS Linestring Geometries

Next create a `routes` table to serve as the table of edges.

We assume that routes exist between every airport pair. An SQL self join yields all pairwise combination of airports. We filter out pairs with the same airports and use the PostgreSQL `DISTINCT ON` construction to eliminate duplicates.

Listing 2.2: Create airport routes from airports

```
1   SELECT DISTINCT ON (least(X.city || Y.city, Y.city || X.city))
2       dense_rank()
3           OVER(ORDER BY least(X.city || Y.city, Y.city || X.city) )::integer As id,
4       X.city AS city_1, Y.city AS city_2,
5       ST_MakeLine(
6           X.geog::geometry,Y.geog::geometry
7           )::geometry(LineString,4326) AS geom,
8       ROUND(ST_Distance(X.geog,Y.geog)/1000) AS dist_km,
9       X.id As source, Y.id As target
10  INTO routes
11  FROM airports X CROSS JOIN airports Y
12  WHERE X.city <> Y.city;
```

Note that *line 10* performs an SQL `INTO` which creates the table named routes.

The generated table will have these records (geom column left out for brevity):

```
 id |  city_1  |  city_2  | dist_km | source | target
----+----------+----------+---------+--------+--------
  1 | London   | Dubai    |    5468 |      2 |      3
  2 | Mumbai   | Dubai    |    1925 |      4 |      3
  3 | Dubai    | New York |   11024 |      3 |      1
  4 | London   | Mumbai   |    7177 |      2 |      4
  5 | New York | London   |    5592 |      1 |      2
  6 | Mumbai   | New York |   12544 |      4 |      1
(6 rows)
```

We did not opt for the obvious choice of geography linestrings for our edges (we only used the geography data type to compute distance). Why not?

pgRouting edges must be PostGIS geometry types, not geographies.

In our code, we invoked the PostGIS ST_MakeLine function to create a linestring from two airports.

Although pgRouting will accommodate geometry multilinestrings, it will only consider the first string within the multilinestring. As such we suggest that you avoid multilinestrings altogether.

We used the typmod construct geometry(LineString,4326) to make sure that our linestrings have SRID of 4326 (WGS-84 Lon-Lat).

The PostgreSQL window function dense_rank provides a sequence of integers that we use to identify each edge. Our airports table assigned a serial integer id to each row. We use these ids to populate the source and target columns of the edges table.

From our edges table, we use the pgr_createVerticesTable function to derive the nodes table from the source and target columns:

Listing 2.3: Create routes_vertices_pgr table

```
1  SELECT pgr_createVerticesTable('routes','geom','source','target');
```

The first argument, the only one required, is the name of the edges table. The second argument names the geometry column of the edges. If you omit this argument, the function will look for a column named the_geom. The third and fourth arguments name the source and target columns respectively. Default names are source and target. The final argument to this function is an SQL WHERE condition to filter rows. Leaving it out instructs the function to consider all edges.

We show the result of running pgr_createVerticesTable below:

```
NOTICE:  PROCESSING:
NOTICE:  pgr_createVerticesTable('routes','geom','source','target','true')
NOTICE:  Performing checks, please wait .....
NOTICE:  Populating public.routes_vertices_pgr, please wait...
NOTICE:     ----->   VERTICES TABLE CREATED WITH  4 VERTICES
NOTICE:                                    FOR   6  EDGES
NOTICE:    Edges with NULL geometry,source or target: 0
```

```
NOTICE:                                 Edges processed: 6
NOTICE:  Vertices table for table public.routes is: ...vertices_pgr
NOTICE:  -------------------------------------------------
Total query runtime: 110 ms.
1 row retrieved.
```

2.2   Using pgr_dijkstra

With our network fully prepared, we move on to the problem of finding optimal routes. We begin with the Dijkstra family of routing functions. Most of the pgRouting routing functions take as input a desired set of start and end nodes, the edges table, or a subset thereof. The output is a set of records delineating the path to follow.

The input and output signature has changed between pgRouting 2.0 and 2.1. Though the old 2.0 syntax is still supported, you should adopt the 2.1 syntax for forward compatibility. In this chapter our examples incorporate the newer syntax. Refer to appendix A for examples using the 2.0 syntax.

Shortest Path

In this example, we will determine the shortest routes between New York (node 1) to Mumbai (node 4). We call the pgr_dijkstra function as follows:

Listing 2.4: Dijkstra shortest path from New York to Mumbai

```
1   SELECT X.*
2   FROM pgr_Dijkstra(
3       'SELECT id, source, target, dist_km As cost FROM routes',
4       1,
5       4,
6       FALSE
7   ) AS X
8   ORDER BY seq;
```

Most routing functions in pgRouting take a set of traversable edges as the first argument. The input must be in the form of a query (*lines 3-7*). For our example, we select all rows in the edges table, but you can easily feed in a subset by adding a WHERE filter. For networks that are large, you may wish to add a spatial filter that takes the form the_geom && ST_Expand(somegeom,dist).

The output columns from the query must be standard: id, source, target, and cost. So if you named your columns differently in the edges table, be sure to use AS to rename (as we do with dist_km). The next two arguments are the begin and end nodes (*lines 5-6*). The last argument in our example is a directed versus undirected flag, which we set to false because our graph is undirected.

If you specified true, meaning a directed graph, the function is going to expect an additional column, reverse_cost, in your query.

The output of this function is shown below.

```
seq | path_seq | node | edge | cost  | agg_cost
----+----------+------+------+-------+---------
  1 |        1 |    1 |    6 | 12544 |        0
  2 |        2 |    4 |   -1 |     0 |    12544
(2 rows)
```

Of no surprise, the above result tells us that the shortest path is a non-stop flight from New York JFK to Mumbai Shivaji. You'll notice that the output contains an extra summary row at the end to report the terminating node and the aggregate cost.

The simple output provides the path of traversal listing the id of the nodes. To make the output more user-friendly, Listing 2.5 joins in both the airports table and the routes to retrieve their English names and corresponding geometric path.

Listing 2.5: Dijkstra joined with other tables

```
1  SELECT X.seq, Y.city, ST_AsGeoJSON(Z.geom) As gson
2  FROM
3      pgr_dijkstra(
4          'SELECT id, source, target, dist_km As cost FROM routes',
5          1,
6          4,
7          FALSE
8      ) X INNER JOIN
9      airports AS Y ON X.node = Y.id LEFT JOIN
10     routes AS Z ON X.edge = Z.id
11 ORDER BY seq;
```

```
seq |  city    |                          gson
----+----------+--------------------------------------------------------
  1 | New York | {"type":"LineString","coordinates":[[-73.8893,40.6975...
  2 | Mumbai   |
```

We made an additional join with routes to retrieve the underlying geometry for the edge. We converted our geometry to GeoJSON, which is perhaps the most popular data format for rendering on web pages, at least at the time of writing.

Cheapest Path and Multiple Destinations

Let's suppose our measure of cost is airfare. Airlines typically price non-stop flights at a premium and shorter flights tend to be more expensive per kilometer flown to cover fixed costs. Let's price our legs as follows:

Three-letter IATA airport code

```
    leg  | fare
---------+------
 LHR-DXB |   300
 BOM-DXB |   400
 JFK-LHR |   600
 LHR-BOM |   700
 DXB-JFK |  1000
 BOM-JFK |  2000
```

Because we have only six fares, we'll hard-code them into the query instead of creating a separate table.

Using pgr_dijkstra to Compute Paths for Each Destination

In pgRouting 2.1, The `pgr_dijkstra` function can accept multiple target nodes.

To accomplish the same pgRouting 2.0, use the function called `pgr_kDijkstraPath`.

This means that with a single call, you can return multiple shortest path answers. Suppose a New Yorker is weighing the idea of taking a vacation to Dubai versus Mumbai and would like to find the cheapest ticket for each. We just vary our input to `pgr_dijkstra` by passing in the target as an array of nodes:

```
ARRAY('{2,4}'::integer[])
```

Or equivalently

```
ARRAY(SELECT id FROM airports WHERE iata IN ('DXB','BOM'))
```

The multi-destination variant of `pgr_dijkstra` returns a result set; the table below describes each column:

Column	Type	Purpose
seq	bigint	Sequential order of results. This is unique for the whole result. Starts at 1 (old 2.0 syntax started at 0)
path_seq	bigint	Sequential order of results for each end_v (this restarts numbering for each target vertex).
end_vid	bigint	Target vertex id this trip is for
node	bigint	Destination node id for this segment of the trip
edge	bigint	The edge id of the segment (terminal is -1 since it just has vertex node)
cost	double	Cost of this segment of trip in total path
agg_cost	double	Cumulative cost leading to this segment of trip in total path

Listing 2.6: Dijkstra using dynamic costs

```
1   SELECT
2       seq,
3       path_seq,
4       Y.city As destination,
5       z.city ||
6       COALESCE( '-' || lead(z.city)
7           OVER (PARTITION BY X.end_vid ORDER BY path_seq),'') AS segment,
8       X.cost,
9       X.agg_cost,
10      X.edge
11  FROM
12      pgr_dijkstra(
13          'SELECT id, source, target,
14              CASE
15                  WHEN source = 1 AND target = 2 THEN 600
16                  WHEN source = 2 AND target = 3 THEN 300
17                  WHEN source = 4 AND target = 3 THEN 400
18                  WHEN source = 4 AND target = 1 THEN 2000
19                  WHEN source = 3 AND target = 1 THEN 1000
20                  WHEN source = 2 AND target = 4 THEN 700
21              END AS cost
22          FROM routes',
23          (SELECT id FROM airports WHERE iata = 'JFK'),
24          ARRAY (SELECT id FROM airports WHERE iata IN ('DXB','BOM')),
25          FALSE
26      ) As X INNER JOIN
27      airports As Y ON X.end_vid = Y.id INNER JOIN
```

```
28       airports As Z ON X.node = Z.id
29   ORDER BY end_vid, seq;
```

Here's our result:

```
seq | path_seq | destination |     segment      | cost | agg_cost | edge
----+----------+-------------+------------------+------+----------+------
  1 |        1 | Dubai       | New York-London  | 600  |        0 |    5
  2 |        2 | Dubai       | London-Dubai     | 300  |      600 |    1
  3 |        3 | Dubai       | Dubai            |   0  |      900 |   -1
  4 |        1 | Mumbai      | New York-London  | 600  |        0 |    5
  5 |        2 | Mumbai      | London-Mumbai    | 700  |      600 |    4
  6 |        3 | Mumbai      | Mumbai           |   0  |     1300 |   -1
(6 rows)
```

pgr_dijkstra outputs the edges of traversal and then tags on an extra row to provide summary information. Because we have two paths, we have two rows containing summary information: rows 3 and 6. Within the summary row, the value for the edge field is -1 and the node field takes on the node id of the destination node.

The path_seq column shows the optimized path, sorted by destination. Don't confuse this with the unique seq column which serves merely as a row identifier.

2.3   Comparing travel options with Dijkstra

Many times, you may not care about the path of travel, but how much it'll end up costing you. This means you only need the summary rows. You probably don't need all the output fields either. Declutter your output by adding an SQL WHERE:

```
WHERE X.edge = -1
```

Skip display of other columns except destination and agg_cost. Your result now reduces down to:

```
destination | agg_cost
------------+----------
Dubai       |      900
Mumbai      |     1300
(2 rows)
```

Part 2

Working with Data

In this part we explore tools commonly used to load spatial data. Some of these tools are specifically geared for pgRouting and load data in a form already suitable for working with routing functions. Many tools you'll use will, at best, load data into PostGIS. In these cases you'll want to further massage the data so it's suitable for routing.

In addition to the basic routability of spatial data, there is the concern with costs you apply to routes. Tools specifically geared for routing, like osm2pgrouting and osm2po, apply costs as part of the loading process. However, you may not be satisfied with these costs and will need to apply your own. We'll cover costs briefly in here and get into more detail in later parts.

3 *Importing ESRI Shapefiles*

To this day, the most popular format for GIS is still the ESRI shape-file. PostGIS comes with two built-in tools for importing shapefiles: the command line utility shp2pgsql and, if you have a PostGIS distribution packaged with extras, you may also have shp2pgsql-gui accessible from pgAdmin via the plugins menu.

The official site of the London subway network is here: https://tfl.gov.uk/modes/tube/

In this chapter, we'll be using data from the London underground, aka "the tube." To retrieve the data, download and unzip the file named london.zip from http://loc8.cc/pgr/pgr_1e_london. The folder london_tube_lines contains the shapefile london_tube_lines.shp along with its customary entourage of an index file (london_tube_lines.shx), a textual data file (london_tube_lines.dbf), and a projection file (london_tube_lines.prj).

3.1 *shp2pgsql*

To import the shapefile use shp2pgsql:

```
PGDATABASE=pgr
shp2pgsql -D -I -S -s 4326 london_tube_lines london_tube_lines | psql
```

> If you are on Windows, you will need to prefix environment variables with SET, like SET PGDATABASE=pgr

shp2pgsql only dumps data to an SQL file that we then pipe to psql. To skip having to enter the connection information and credentials, you can set environment variables and customize your pgpass files. Visit http://loc8.cc/pgr/pgenvars and http://loc8.cc/pgr/pgpass for more information on how to do this.

Refer to http://loc8.cc/pgr/psql for psql usage.

Forcing Single Geometry

A myriad of switches allow you to fine-tune the import—we single out the -S switch. In PostGIS, all geometry types have a multi equivalent. For example, linestring as multilinestring, polygon has multipolygon, etc. Any geometry can cast to a multi type. The opposite is true only if the multigeometry contains a single constituent geometry. To speed up the import, shp2pgsql will by default treat all linestrings as multilinestrings. The -S switch tells shp2pgsql to import all geometries as single geometries (points, linestrings, polygons). The import fails if your data cannot be reduced down to single geometries.

pgRouting processes single features more efficiently than multigeometries, so whenever possible, choose single over multi.

For our tube data, each rail segment between two stations is an individual linestring. Therefore, we have no trouble using the -S switch.

Removing Elevation and Measurement

Another quirk of our tubes data is that it contains both a third dimension (Z) and a measurement dimension (M). You can see these by executing the following code:

```
SELECT ST_GeometryType(geom) FROM london_tube_lines LIMIT 1;
```

Perhaps at one time, the London transit authority did plan to distribute data with elevation, as subway tunnels do snake through the underground at differing depth. Perhaps it's an irrelevant artifact. In either case, execute the following SQL and you'll discover that all Z values are zero:

```
SELECT DISTINCT ST_ZMin(geom), ST_ZMax(geom) from london_tube_lines;
```

Even though the data contains a placeholder for the Z dimension, it was never populated. The M dimension is an extra set of non-spatial coordinates. You can use it to populate additional information about the geometry. For example, London transit authority might store the number of parallel tracks as the M coordinate.

pgRouting does not take kindly to data with Z or the M coordinates—we must flatten our geometries to have exactly two dimensions.

To do so, we use the PostGIS ST_Force2D function:

```
ALTER TABLE london_tube_lines
ALTER COLUMN geom TYPE geometry(LineString,4326) USING ST_Force2D(geom);
```

Check the geometry type again after execution to make sure you have succeeded.

> If you always want Z and M coordinates ignored, you can save some time by adding -t 2D to your shp2pgsql command to just load X,Y coordinates.

3.2 Routing Using Imported Data

Once we have prepared our data, we add the two requisite columns for pgRouting: source and target, followed by a call to pgr_createTopology.

Listing 3.1: Preparing London tube lines data for routing

```
ALTER TABLE london_tube_lines ADD COLUMN "source" integer;
ALTER TABLE london_tube_lines ADD COLUMN "target" integer;
SELECT pgr_createTopology('london_tube_lines', 0.00001, 'geom', 'gid');
```

The SRID of our data is 4326, WGS 84 Lon-Lat, hence our specification of tolerance must be in degrees. If all is good, pgr_createTopology returns a satisfying OK, and you should see the following transcript:

```
NOTICE:  PROCESSING:
NOTICE:  pgr_createTopology('london_tube_lines',1e-005..)
NOTICE:  Performing checks, Please wait .....
NOTICE:  Creating Topology, Please wait...
NOTICE:  ------------> TOPOLOGY CREATED FOR  497 edges
NOTICE:  Rows with NULL geometry or NULL id: 0
NOTICE:  Vertices table for table public.london_tube_lines is..
NOTICE:  --------------------------------------------

Total query runtime: 1560 ms.
1 row retrieved.
```

4 *Importing Textual Data*

Though not strictly a GIS technique, you'll often find yourself needing to load textual data. Data sources generally package descriptive data separately from the spatial data. For our London subway data, the packaged station data is provided as a CSV file.

4.1 *Importing Text File with psql \copy and SQL COPY*

The first step before you load the data is to create the table structure. This structure must match the structure of the file. After we load, we'll add additional columns.

There are two common ways for loading delimited data. You can use the `psql \copy` command or you can use SQL `COPY` construct. The `\copy` command is only available from within the `psql` command-line and has access to only files accessible from the local user's machine. The SQL COPY construct, has the benefit that you could call it from any stored function and use the pgAdmin SQL console. The shortcoming of SQL `COPY` is that it runs under the context (user id) of the postgres daemon process rather than the connected user. This means it only has access to folders that the postgres account has access to—furthermore, you need to be a super user to run it.

Using `psql \copy`, we load the stations file as follows:

Listing 4.1: Load stations data with psql

```
-- create stations table --
CREATE TABLE london_stations(station varchar(150), os_x float8, os_y float8,
    latitude float8, longitude float8, zone varchar(20), post_code varchar(20));

-- psql copy command approach
\copy london_stations FROM '/pgr/data/london/stations.csv' CSV HEADER;
```

The SQL COPY equivalent of `psql copy` we used is:

```
COPY london_stations FROM '/pgr/data/london/stations.csv' CSV HEADER;
```

If you are on Windows, your path file name should still use Unix style forward slashes. If your data is not on your default drive, you'll need to specify the drive letter: C:/pgr/data/london/stations.csv.

Once you've loaded stations, add a `station_id` field which will store the corresponding pgRouting node id as follows:

Listing 4.2: Map stations data to pgRouting nodes

```
ALTER TABLE london_stations ADD COLUMN geom geometry(POINT,4326);
ALTER TABLE london_stations ADD COLUMN station_id integer;

UPDATE london_stations
    SET geom = ST_SetSRID(ST_Point(longitude,latitude),4326);

UPDATE london_stations
    SET station_id = X.id
FROM london_tube_lines_vertices_pgr X
WHERE ST_DWithin(london_stations.geom, X.the_geom, 0.000001);
```

The station file includes extraneous maintenance stations. These don't line up with tube lines and have no corresponding node. We remove these stations with the following SQL:

```
DELETE FROM london_stations WHERE station_id IS NULL;
```

To improve join performance, we add indexes to our `source` and `target` columns.

Listing 4.3: Add indexes to london tube edges

```
1  CREATE INDEX ix_source_london_tube_lines ON london_tube_lines(source);
2  CREATE INDEX ix_target_london_tube_lines ON london_tube_lines(target);
```

For cost, we are going to use length of the edges and precompute the length of each edge since length will not change.

Listing 4.4: Store length of edges

```
ALTER TABLE london_tube_lines ADD COLUMN length float8;
UPDATE london_tube_lines SET length = ST_Length(geom::geography);
```

Now that the data is routable, we can use pgRouting functions to find shortest path between two train stops.

Listing 4.5: Use dijkstra to navigate train stops

```
SELECT seq, d.node, d.edge, cost,
    e.geom As edge_geom, n.geom As node_geom, n.station
FROM
    pgr_dijkstra('
        SELECT gid AS id, source, target, length AS cost
            FROM london_tube_lines',
        (SELECT station_id
            FROM london_stations WHERE station = 'Finchley Road'),
        (SELECT station_id
            FROM london_stations WHERE station = 'Piccadilly Circus'),
        false
    ) AS d
    LEFT JOIN london_tube_lines As e ON d.edge = e.gid
    LEFT JOIN london_stations As n On d.node = n.station_id
ORDER BY d.seq;
```

The resulting path would traverse four edges. Utilizing QGIS, we can overlay the london_tube_lines with our query. Using the Db Manager QGIS plugin, we can plot our query twice, once for the stations and once for the edge routes and arrive at a picture as shown in Figure 4.1, on the next page. For more information, refer to Db Manager Plugin, on page 219.

Figure 4.1: London tube lines travel route

5 Using ogr2ogr to Load Data

If you pulled the data straight from http:/loc8.cc/pgr/london_
stations, you retrieved a KML (Keyhole Markup Language) file.
KML is an XML-based format, *de rigueur* of all Google products.
To import a KML file directly, use the ogr2ogr command-line tool
found as part of the GDAL spatial data toolkit—often dubbed the
Swiss Army knife of GIS and a must-have for GIS practitioners. Visit
http://gdal.org to download the source code or find compiled
binaries.

GEOSPATIAL POWER TOOLS http:
//locatepress.com/gpt provides
a thorough treatment of GDAL.

To import our tube KML data, use the following syntax:

```
ogr2ogr -f "PostgreSQL" \
    PG:"host=localhost user=postgres port=5432 \
    dbname=pgr password=whatever" \
    "london_tube_lines.kml" \
    -nln london_tube_lines \
    -lco GEOMETRY_NAME=geom \
    -lco fid=gid
```

> The -lco fid=gid layer creation option will change the autogenerated pri-
> mary key name from the default ogc_fid to gid. This renaming switch is
> available at GDAL 1.9 and later.

5.1 Using ogr2ogr to Convert from KML to ESRI Shapefile

ogr2ogr is versatile. You can use it to convert data between different
formats. If you're offering data to the general public, you may wish
to have a version of your data downloadable as shapefiles due to
their wide acceptance. In the following code snippet, we convert
our tube data from KML to shapefile.

```
ogr2ogr -f "ESRI Shapefile" \
    london_tube_lines \
    "london_tube_lines.kml" \
    -nln london_tube_lines
```

6 *Importing OSM Data*

OpenStreetMap (OSM) data is a popular and free source for routing data.

It's expansive, covering the entire globe. It's diverse—not just roads, but bike paths, hiking trails, and even fault lines.

There are two common tools used for loading and preparing OSM data for pgRouting: osm2pgrouting and osm2po.

osm2pgrouting is a rudimentary command-line tool whose sole purpose is to load OSM data into pgRouting. It only supports the OSM XML (.osm extension) uncompressed format, and doesn't support the newer binary compressed .pbf format. It is planned for the 2.3 version of osm2pgrouting to support compressed .pbf format as well.

osm2po is an extensive Java toolkit. Loading data is but a small role in its overall offerings. osm2po comes with its own routing functionality as well as a web server and an interface based on OpenLayers. osm2po does not directly connect to PostgreSQL databases, but instead creates an SQL script from an .osm or .pbf file. You then execute the script to load the data. The table below highlights the differences between the two OSM tools:

Feature	osm2pgrouting	osm2po
Licensing	GPL	core (Freeware), plugins such as pgRouting loader (open source)
OSM (.osm format)	Yes	Yes
OSM (.osm.bz format)	No	Yes
OSM (.pbf)	No	Yes
Utilizes pgRouting and PostGIS functions, can write directly to database	Yes	No
Not memory bound (can write large files like whole continent)	No	Yes
Operating System	Requires compilation	Java 6+

osm2pgrouting has precompiled binaries for Ubuntu and Windows, otherwise, you'll need to compile for your OS. osm2po only requires that a Java Virtual Machine version 6 or higher be present on your machine.

6.1   osm2pgrouting

Latest Version

At time of writing, the latest version of osm2pgrouting is 2.2.0. Both osm2pgrouting 2.1 and 2.2 are designed with pgRouting version 2.1+ in mind.

osm2pgrouting 2.1 added the following major improvements:

- Nodes import as bigints, no longer limited by the upper bound of integers
- Additional columns for referencing back to the OSM source
- Costs are still in degrees, but new cost_s and reverse_cost_s for time based costing
- New fields length_m for length in meters
- Incremental loads. You can load multiple files relying on pgRout-

ing to skip over data already loaded.

- Supports loading data into a designated schema
- Faster processing
- Ability to store nodes with details if desired. This adds a lot of time to the load and populates another table called osm_nodes

osm2pgrouting 2.2 was a minor improvement over 2.1 and added:

- mapconfig_for_bicycles.xml
- A progress bar
- Addition of foreign key constraints

Installation and Help

If you are on Windows and took advantage of the Application Stack Builder to install PostgreSQL and PostGIS, you should already have osm2pgrouting present in your PostgreSQL bin folder. Should you need to compile, visit http://loc8.cc/pgr/osm2pgrouting_21 for the source code.

Once installed, launch osm2pgrouting from your command-line.

Help is always available via osm2pgrouting --help. To serve as a handy reference, the help for osm2pgrouting-2.2.0 follows:

```
Allowed options:

Help:
  --help                          Produce help message for this version.
  -v [ --version ]                Print version string

General:
  -f [ --file ] arg               REQUIRED: Name of the osm file.
  -c [ --conf ] arg (=/usr/share/osm2pgrouting/mapconfig.xml)
                                  Name of the configuration xml file.
  --schema arg                    Database schema to put tables.
                                     blank: defaults to default schema
                                            dictated by PostgreSQL
                                            search_path.
  --prefix arg                    Prefix added at the beginning of the
                                  table names.
  --suffix arg                    Suffix added at the end of the table
                                  names.
```

```
    --addnodes                            Import the osm_nodes table.
    --clean                               Drop previously created tables.

Database options:
  -d [ --dbname ] arg                     Name of your database (Required).
  -U [ --username ] arg (=postgres)       Name of the user, which have write
                                          access to the database.
  -h [ --host ] arg (=localhost)          Host of your postgresql database.
  -p [ --port ] arg (=5432)               db_port of your database.
  -W [ --password ] arg                   Password for database access.
```

> Some of the switches changed between osm2pgrouting 2.0 and
> osm2pgrouting 2.1.0, but 2.1.0 and 2.2.0 switches are the same. Make
> sure to refer to help screen for your version.

Configuration Files

Fine tuning of osm2pgrouting depends on configuration files. You
can specify the configuration file when you start osmpgrouting.

If you don't specify a config file, osmpgrouting looks for the file at
/usr/share/osm2pgrouting/mapconfig.xml.

The default installation includes two configuration files. mapconfig.xml
is the one intended for general use, whereas mapconfig_cars.xml is
more suitable for driving applications. You are free to customize or
create your own configuration files.

Using osmp2grouting

For our examples, we will import street data for Washington DC.
We sourced our data from GeoFabrik.de using the

district-of-columbia-latest.osm.bz2

version and extracted it to a .osm file and then renamed it dc.osm.
Because their data updates daily, your particular extract could differ

http://loc8.cc/pgr/osm_dc_
data

from ours.

For better organization, we begin by creating a separate schema:

```
CREATE SCHEMA ospr;
```

Here's our first load:

```
osm2pgrouting -f dc.osm -d pgr --schema=ospr -c /pathto/mapconfig_for_cars.xml
```

> We left out --host, --port, --user, and --passwd. You may need to pass these in
> if they are not the default values.

If your `mapconfig.xml` is in the default location and you want to use
that one, you can safely leave out the `-c` switch and the subsequent
path. You may need to specify the full path to the `mapconfig.xml`
file—we omitted it here for brevity.

After import, use the `dt` command in `psql` to see what you ended
up with:

```
\dt ospr.*
```

You should see seven tables listed:

```
                List of relations
 Schema |       Name        | Type  |  Owner
--------+-------------------+-------+----------
 ospr   | osm_nodes         | table | postgres
 ospr   | osm_relations     | table | postgres
 ospr   | osm_way_classes   | table | postgres
 ospr   | osm_way_types     | table | postgres
 ospr   | relations_ways    | table | postgres
 ospr   | ways              | table | postgres
 ospr   | ways_vertices_pgr | table | postgres
(7 rows)
```

The osm_nodes table will be populated if you included `-s 0` in your command, otherwise it remains empty. If you are using osm2pgrouting 2.1, you might have an additional table osm_way_tags. This table was removed in osm2pgrouting 2.2 since it had redundant information already present in ways.

Before we continue, we need to create some indexes on tables for
optimal speed, if they do not already exist.

osm2pgrouting version 2.1 or higher will automatically create indexes as part of the import. The most crucial table to index is the
one storing edges. (The `ways` table in our example.) Verify that
indexes are in place using `psql` shell:

```
\d ospr.ways
```

You see indexes listed at bottom of table definition:

```
                                                Table "ospr.ways"
           Column      |          Type          |                          Modifiers
    -----------------+------------------------+--------------------------------
        :
     the_geom         | geometry(LineString,4326) |
    Indexes:
        "ways_pkey" PRIMARY KEY, btree (gid)
        "ways_gdx" gist (the_geom)
        "ways_source_idx" btree (source)
        "ways_source_osm_idx" btree (source_osm)
        "ways_target_idx" btree (target)
        "ways_target_osm_idx" btree (target_osm)
    Foreign-key constraints:
        "ways_class_id_fkey" FOREIGN KEY (class_id)
            REFERENCES ospr.osm_way_classes(class_id)
        "ways_source_fkey" FOREIGN KEY (source)
            REFERENCES ospr.ways_vertices_pgr(id)
        "ways_target_fkey" FOREIGN KEY (target)
            REFERENCES ospr.ways_vertices_pgr(id)
```

Should you find indexes missing, create them with the following
SQL commands:

Listing 6.1: Create indexes on ospr tables

```
1  CREATE INDEX idx_ways_the_geom
2    ON ospr.ways USING gist(the_geom);
3
4  CREATE INDEX idx_ways_source
5    ON ospr.ways (source);
6
7  CREATE INDEX idx_ways_target
8    ON ospr.ways (target);
```

After every load, you should perform analyze on the tables you
loaded, especially ones you use frequently or tables populated with
a large number of rows:

Listing 6.2: analyze ospr tables

```
analyze verbose ospr.ways;
analyze verbose ospr.ways_vertices_pgr;
```

To perform analyze on all tables, opt for analyze verbose. The verbose option provides details as to what is happening along the way.
If you recently deleted many rows in tables, you may wish to do a
vacuum analyze verbose instead to physically remove deletions.

Routing with osm2pgrouting

Now, let's take a test drive. We'll ask pgRouting to provide turn-by-turn directions from the Capitol to the White House.

Listing 6.3: Directed path from Capitol to White House using KNN

```
1   SELECT r.seq, r.node, w.name As street,  r.cost::numeric(10,4),
2     ( SUM(w.length_m) OVER(ORDER BY r.seq) )::numeric(10,2) As dist_m
3   FROM pgr_dijkstra('SELECT gid AS id,
4                       source,
5                       target,
6                       cost, reverse_cost
7                     FROM ospr.ways',
8   (SELECT id FROM ospr.ways_vertices_pgr ORDER BY the_geom <->
9       ST_SetSRID( ST_Point(-77.009003, 38.889931), 4326) limit 1 ) ,
10  (SELECT id FROM ospr.ways_vertices_pgr ORDER BY the_geom <->
11      ST_SetSRID( ST_Point(-77.036545, 38.897096), 4326) limit 1 ), true) AS r
12      LEFT JOIN ospr.ways AS w ON r.edge = w.gid;
```

seq	node	street	cost	dist_m
1	11280	Capitol Circle Northeast	0.0004	41.92
2	14678	Northwest Capitol Circle	0.0001	48.88
:				
9	10328	Northwest Capitol Circle	0.0001	405.03
10	12907	1st Street Northwest	0.0002	423.65
11	5201	1st Street Northwest	0.0002	443.25
:				
13	11112	Pennsylvania Avenue Northwest	0.0027	712.46
:				
53	14743	Pennsylvania Avenue Northwest	0.0001	2405.68
54	7864	E Street Northwest	0.0001	2418.16
:				
60	12104	E Street Northwest	0.0003	2782.89
61	14709		0.0001	2791.95
:				
63	21902		0.0001	2818.60
64	10998	State Place Northwest	0.0006	2888.11
65	18913	West Executive Avenue Northwest	0.0001	2895.77
66	6097		0.0001	2904.29
:				
72	14141		0.0000	3077.69

(72 rows)

The above code is worthy of closer examination. We started with two coordinates in longitude and latitude. For each of the coordinates, we need to find the closest node. This is one of the most common problems in PostGIS: given a point, find the closest something. You can go about a solution in a few ways—some more efficient than others. We've elected to use the KNN (K Nearest Neighbor) approach.

The PostGIS KNN `<->` distance operator returns the distance between two geometries. You should always use it with a LIMIT n, for the nth closest. The `<->` operator uses spatial indexes only if it is present in the ORDER BY clause, which makes for awkward syntax, but `<->` is superior to other distance-finding functions, such as ST_Distance when used in the ORDER BY clause.

For PostgreSQL earlier than version 9.5 and PostGIS earlier than version 2.2, the `<->` is a bounding box distance operator. In our case, the bounding box of a point is the point, so the difference is moot. For large distances, you'd still use ST_DWithin and then sort by ST_Distance(the_geom::geography,...) even for points since the degree distance ordering may deviate from true distance ordering and give you the wrong answer.

Finding the closest node to a point is such a common task that pgRouting 2.1 introduced a helper function to handle it. The function is `pgr_pointToEdgeNode` and takes two arguments. The first is the table containing nodes, the second is a point geometry. We'll rewrite our Capitol to White House query using this function. You'll appreciate the more succinct syntax.

Listing 6.4: Directed path from Capitol to White House using pgr_pointToEdgeNode

```
1   SELECT r.seq, r.node, w.name As street,  r.cost,
2     ( SUM(w.length_m) OVER(ORDER BY r.seq) )::numeric(10,2) As dist_m
3   FROM pgr_dijkstra('SELECT gid AS id,
4                              source,
5                              target,
6                              cost, reverse_cost
7                       FROM ospr.ways',
8     pgr_pointToEdgeNode('ospr.ways',  ST_SetSRID( ST_Point(-77.009003, 38.889931), 4:
9       , 0.01)  ,
10    pgr_pointToEdgeNode('ospr.ways', ST_SetSRID( ST_Point(-77.036545, 38.897096), 43
11      , 0.01) , true) AS r
12        LEFT JOIN ospr.ways AS w ON r.edge = w.gid;
```

pgr_pointToEdgeNode makes the assumption that you named the geometry column in the edges table the_geom. If you imported your data using osm2pgrouting, this would be the default name.

Another under-the-hood operation of pgr_pointToEdgeNode that you need to be aware of is: the function finds the closest edge first. Once it has identified the closest edge, it evaluates the distance to the two end nodes, returning the one that's closer. This is generally not an issue when you have a dense network of edges and nodes (such as city streets), but could be a problem when you have few nodes spanned by long edges (such as airline routes).

Here's a scenario where you'll end up with undesirable results. Suppose you live in the geopolitically interesting enclave of Point Roberts in Washington State and you're trying to find a short flight to Seattle. The closest node to you is Vancouver International, where you can catch a non-stop commuter flight to Seattle. So you use `pgr_pointToEdgeNode` to look for the lowest fare with your home as the starting point. Unbeknownst to you, your home just happens to underlie the flight path of a long-haul international flight from New York to Beijing. And all your results return fares from JFK to Seattle!

6.2   Using osm2po

To get started, download the osm2po Java binaries from `http://osm2po.de/`. For our examples, we used version 5.0. and pgRouting 2.1.

Importing data using `osm2po` is a two-step process. First generate a SQL script, saving it to a file. Second, execute the script using `psql`.

Here's the command for the first step:

```
java -Xmx1408m -jar osm2po-core-5.0.0-signed.jar prefix=ospo \
    tileSize=x,c dc.osm
```

As of osm2po version 5.1.0, the pgRouting loader plugin is not enabled by default. If you are using osm2po version 5.1 or above, you can edit the `osm2po.config` file and remove the # shown on the line below. This will remove the comment from the line, enabling the plugin.

```
#postp.0.class = de.cm.osm2po.plugins.postp.PgRoutingWriter
```

Alternatively you can add

```
postp.0.class=de.cm.osm2po.plugins.postp.PgRoutingWriter
```

at the end of the java commandline. Refer to the demo.sh and demo.bat for an example.

We specified ospo for the prefix—as a result the folder ospo was generated containing ospo_2po_4pgr.sql, in addition to others.

The second step is to execute the generated file using psql:

Listing 6.5: Processing osm2po sql file
```
psql -d pgr
\i ospo/ospo_2po_4pgr.sql
```

Unlike osm2pgrouting, osm2po does not automatically generate the table of vertices.

We add one additional step:

Listing 6.6: Processing osm2po sql file: create vertices table
```
SELECT pgr_createVerticesTable('ospo_2po_4pgr','geom_way','source','target','true
```

The osm2po script puts in indexes for you so you don't need to worry about creating them.

Finally we can test drive our data with a similar query we used for osm2pgrouting:

Listing 6.7: Directed path from Capitol to White House using osm2po
```
1   SELECT r.seq, r.node, w.osm_name As street,  r.cost::numeric(10,4),
2     (SUM(ST_Length(w.geom_way::geography)) OVER(ORDER BY r.seq))::numeric(10,2)
3     As dist_m FROM pgr_dijkstra('SELECT id,
4                         source,
5                         target,
6                         cost, reverse_cost
7                       FROM ospo_2po_4pgr',
8   (SELECT id FROM ospo_2po_4pgr_vertices_pgr ORDER BY the_geom <->
9         ST_SetSRID( ST_Point(-77.009003, 38.889931), 4326) limit 1 ) ,
10  (SELECT id FROM ospo_2po_4pgr_vertices_pgr ORDER BY the_geom <->
11        ST_SetSRID( ST_Point(-77.036545, 38.897096), 4326) limit 1 ), true) AS
12        LEFT JOIN ospo_2po_4pgr AS w ON r.edge = w.id;
```

```
seq | node |          street          |  cost  | dist_m
----+------+--------------------------+--------+--------
  1 | 1453 | Capitol Driveway Northwest    | 0.0008 |   30.74
  2 | 2517 | Capitol Driveway Northwest    | 0.0010 |   69.38
  3 | 1046 | Constitution Avenue Northwest | 0.0026 |  225.04
  :
  8 | 4972 | Constitution Avenue Northwest | 0.0015 |  783.16
  9 | 4966 | Pennsylvania Avenue Northwest | 0.0014 |  880.30
  :
 12 | 4968 | Pennsylvania Avenue Northwest | 0.0001 | 1113.37
 13 | 7304 | 6th Street Northwest          | 0.0003 | 1131.41
 14 | 6648 | 6th Street Northwest          | 0.0010 | 1201.53
 15 | 4399 | Constitution Avenue Northwest | 0.0025 | 1376.81
  :
 27 | 5863 | Constitution Avenue Northwest | 0.0039 | 2644.71
 28 | 7413 | 16th Street Northwest         | 0.0014 | 2700.60
 29 | 7414 | Ellipse Road Northwest        | 0.0072 | 2873.08
 30 | 3820 | Ellipse Road Northwest        | 0.0153 | 3240.14
 31 | 5210 |                               | 0.0000 | 3240.14
(31 rows)
```

If we compare the results to Google Maps, they are all within the ballpark. Google Maps gives a 2.1 miles driving distance, or 1609*2.1 ~= 3378.2 meters.

6.3 Recap

Both osm2po data load and osm2pgrouting (using map for cars config) are not too far off, even though the paths they take are different.

The QGIS map in Figure 6.1, on the next page show the osm2po route in transparent blue and osm2pgrouting path in red overlaid on top of OpenStreetMap.

As you can see from the map, though we gave the same point to both sets, the node that was picked up is different, thus their starting points are actually different and their paths also end up different. The differences are largely due to the set of edges loaded via osm2po config that are different from osm2pgrouting config.

The numbers should be different from Google for several reasons. We are lazy in our computation and just chose to find the approximate closest node to our locations of interest, and then instead of

Figure 6.1: osm2pgrouting path overlaid with osm2po on OpenStreetMap in QGIS

taking the fractional length of the street, we are taking the whole length. Google is optimizing for time (cost based on time) which also considers traffic conditions and we optimized for distance. Remember in the case of driving, especially when considering traffic conditions, time is not only a function of distance but also must consider speed limit, traffic, etc. In a production scenario we would take these into consideration.

As a sanity check, the routing distance length along a road network should never be shorter than the shortest distance between the two points and is generally significantly larger. All are larger by a good margin than the linear distance between two points of 2518.34 meters computed with:

```
1  SELECT
2          ST_Distance( ST_Point(-77.009003, 38.889931)::geography,
3          ST_Point(-77.036545, 38.897096)::geography );
```

7 *Foreign Data Wrappers*

PostgreSQL has another feature not specifically designed for importing data, but one useful for that purpose: *foreign data wrappers* (FDWs). Foreign data wrappers are interfaces to *foreign tables*. As far as PostgreSQL is concerned, foreign tables are any external data source that you can query using a FDW. A foreign table could be a table in another database on the same PostgreSQL server or a different server. It could be an Excel file, a table in Microsoft Access, a flat CSV file, a NoSQL database, or any other data source. The PostgreSQL community authors and shares foreign data wrappers so the list of possible foreign table types is continually growing.

Although some FDWs not packaged with PostgreSQL are listed on http://pgxn.org/tag/fdw/ many are not. Most can be found on https://github.com/ by searching for Foreign Data Wrapper.

With FDWs, you can treat disparate and external data sources as if they were native PostgreSQL tables—you're shielded from the intricacies of making the connection. The main difference you may encounter is that foreign tables are slower to return data. How slow will depend on your source. Querying another table in another PostgreSQL database on the same server should take no time at all, querying a tab-delimited file with ten million records located in the Himalayas on a dial-up server could test your patience.

Some, but not all, FDWs will allow data updates.

Most PostgreSQL installs come packaged with two foreign data wrappers. `file_fdw` that allows you to query delimited text files and `postgres_fdw` that allows you to query another PostgreSQL database. The former is read-only, while the latter is read and write.

7.1 Importing File Foreign Data Wrappers: file_fdw

Using the `file_fdw` foreign data wrapper you can query comma or tab delimited files. The account under which you're running PostgreSQL must have rights to read the file. This generally means that the file resides on the same server or the network.

Install the `file_fdw` extension using the following SQL command:

```
CREATE EXTENSION file_fdw;
```

You can also use pgAdmin by right clicking Extensions on the browse tree.

FDWs require that you first create foreign "servers," as in below.

```
CREATE SERVER fs_local_files FOREIGN DATA WRAPPER file_fdw;
```

As you can see in the above code, specifying the FDW that you'll be using to connect to the foreign server is part of the creation process. The term "server" is actually a misnomer. For `file_fdw`, our server is just a formality and doesn't point to anything in the physical sense.

Next, we will import the CSV file containing the stations on the London subway. We had previously performed this feat using psql copy and SQL copy. Let's make use of the `file_fdw` extension.

We begin by establishing a foreign table for `stations.csv`.

The file must be accessible by the account under which PostgreSQL is running.

To do so, we need to copy the file somewhere on the server accessible by the postgres service, then execute the following SQL:

Listing 7.1: file_fdw foreign table for london stations

```
CREATE SCHEMA fdwt;

CREATE FOREIGN TABLE fdwt.ft_london_stations (
    station varchar(150),
    os_x float8,
    os_y float8,
    latitude float8,
    longitude float8,
    zone varchar(20),
    post_code varchar(20)
)
SERVER fs_local_files
OPTIONS (
```

```
    format 'csv',
    header 'true',
    filename '/usr/data/london/stations.csv',
    delimiter ',',
    null '',
    encoding 'latin1'
);
```

Use the OPTIONS parameter to specify the location and character-istics of the file.

In our example our file is located on a Linux file system. If you're on Windows, substitute the Linux path with a Windows path, such as C:/pgr/data/london/stations.csv.

Should you ever need to change the location of the file, or amend other attributes, you don't need to recreate the foreign table.

Use ALTER FOREIGN TABLE instead, as in:

Listing 7.2: Change path and encoding of foreign table

```
ALTER FOREIGN TABLE fdwt.ft_london_stations
OPTIONS (
    SET filename 'C:/pgr/data/stations.csv',
    SET encoding 'win1252'
);
```

Note how you must prefix each option with the word SET.

With the foreign table readied, you query it the same as a local table, as in the following:

Listing 7.3: Query stations foreign table

```
SELECT * FROM fdwt.ft_london_stations WHERE station LIKE 'Abbey%';
```

Another handy practice we follow is to wrap foreign tables in a view. This lets us add derived columns that may not be part of the original foreign table. Because a foreign table is no different than a local table as far as querying is concerned, you can create views that draw from multiple foreign tables or even use a combination of foreign and non-foreign tables.

In the next listing we create a view against a foreign table, adding a computed column in the process:

Listing 7.4: Wrap stations foreign table in a view

```
CREATE OR REPLACE VIEW fdwt.vw_london_stations AS
    SELECT
        *,
        ST_Point(longitude,latitude)::geography(POINT,4326) As geog
    FROM fdwt.ft_london_stations;
```

You'll see the new view we created listed in the `geography_columns` table because it has a geography column, and we can query the view (which in turn is querying the file) with PostGIS functions to find what stations are within 800 meters of a point:

```
SELECT station
    FROM fdwt.vw_london_stations
    WHERE ST_DWithin(geog, ST_Point(-0.28,51.503)::geography, 800);
```

The result of our query is:

```
    station
-------------
  Acton Town
  South Acton
```

As we've already mentioned, querying foreign tables tends to be much slower than local tables. Furthermore, `file_fdw` cannot support indexes, so every query necessitates a table scan. That being said, the convenience of `file_fdw` cannot be understated, especially for handling continual data feeds. Once you have prepared the foreign table, all you have to do is replace the old file with the new file.

7.2   Importing with ogr Foreign Data Wrappers: ogr_fdw

Our favorite FDW, particularly for pgRouting and PostGIS work, is the *ogr_fdw*. Sadly this is not available in binary form for all binary distributions of PostgreSQL. The PostGIS bundle for Windows version 2.2 and above includes it. The yum.postgresql.org also includes ogr_fdw as an install option. For Linux/Unix/MacOSX, the compile process shouldn't be too difficult if you already have gdal-dev and PostgreSQL headers installed (generally a quick install or already installed if you installed PostGIS).

GDAL/OGR is a suite of open source libraries and command line tools designed to provide uniform access across disparate spatial data. Think of it as ODBC or JDBC for the spatial world. GDAL/OGR is an invaluable tool for converting from one data format to another. GDAL drivers handle raster formats whereas OGR drivers handle vector formats.

Refer to http://loc8.cc/pgr/ogr_fdw_compile_co for instructions on how to compile on CentOS. Instructions for most Linux distributions should be similar.

The ogr_fdw extension is a foreign data wrapper for querying data formats supported by OGR, currently close to a hundred vector formats and growing. Popular formats include MapInfo, GML, ODBC, ESRI, SQLite, and of course PostGIS.

GDAL stands for Geospatial Data Abstraction Layer; OGR stands for nothing. See https://trac.osgeo.org/gdal/wiki/FAQGeneral

ogr_fdw is available in source form from:

http://loc8.cc/pgr/srcogrfdw.

The formats supported by OGR depend on the version of OGR. Generally, all versions will support the most popular formats.

> Be sure to have the GDAL library installed with the GDAL development library on your server first before compiling ogr_fdw. GDAL is generally installed already if you installed PostGIS from precompiled sources.

Refer to Appendix B, on page 269 for links providing installation help. We've also authored several articles delving into the more specifics when using on Windows systems and installing on Linux systems. See http://loc8.cc/pgr/poogrfdw.

After installing the ogr_fdw binaries, connect to your database and use the following command to enable the extension,

Although GDAL/OGR were designed for spatial data formats, it does support plenty of non-spatial formats, such as delimited text files, spreadsheets, and databases with merely textual and numeric data.

```
CREATE EXTENSION ogr_fdw;
```

> ogr_fdw only works with databases with UTF-8 encoding (generally the default). If you have another encoding, the extension will fail to install with a non UTF-8 warning.

When it comes to ogr_fdw, the concept of a foreign server becomes even more amorphous. The foreign server could be a file, a directory of files, a connection to a relational database, or even a URL to a web service.

ogr_fdw_info

Installing of ogr_fdw includes a command-line tool called ogr_fdw_info. This time-saving tool generates the SQL for creating foreign tables by interrogating the data source. This could save you quite a bit of typing if you have hundreds of tables.

For file based data sources, ogr_fdw_info can take a single file name or an entire directory.

For relational databases, ogr_fdw_info takes the database connection information.

Using ogr_fdw with ESRI Shapefiles

For ESRI shapefiles, we'll create a foreign server at the directory level.

We use the term "shapefile" to mean a set of physical files that minimally includes files with extensions of .shp, .shx, and .dbf.

Each shapefile within the directory would then be a foreign table.

You don't need to create foreign tables for all the shapefiles in the directory, just ones that you need.

Start by creating a folder called /usr/data/shp. Then copy into this folder at least two shapes files. When you copy, be sure to drag along all the helper files, not just the .shp files.

We chose London subway lines and world airports.

Let's use ogr_fdw_info to relieve ourselves from having to type all the column names.

Run ogr_fdw_info with -s and pass in the directory name:

```
ogr_fdw_info -s "/usr/data/shp"
```

The output lists list all the shape files within the folder as shown below:

```
Layers:
  london_tube_lines
  ne_10m_airports
```

Next we'll ask `ogr_fdw_info` to generate the SQL scripts we need to create the foreign server and the foreign table. `ogr_fdw_info` can only generate one foreign table script per command, so you must indicate the shapefile. In our case, we chose the airports layer.

```
ogr_fdw_info -s "/usr/data/shp" -l ne_10m_airports
```

This generates the following:

```sql
CREATE SERVER myserver FOREIGN DATA WRAPPER ogr_fdw
    OPTIONS (
        datasource '/usr/data/shp',
        format 'ESRI Shapefile'
);

CREATE FOREIGN TABLE ne_10m_airports (
  fid integer,
  geom geometry,
  scalerank integer,
  featurecla varchar,
  type varchar,
  name varchar,
  abbrev varchar,
  location varchar,
  gps_code varchar,
  iata_code varchar,
  wikipedia varchar,
  natlscale real
)
SERVER myserver
OPTIONS (layer 'ne_10m_airports');
```

You can then copy, paste, and execute the generated SQL in `psql`, pgAdmin, or your preferred PostgreSQL management tool. If we want to create a foreign table from the subway data, we can continue to run the following:

```
ogr_fdw_info -s "/usr/data/shp" -l london_tube_lines
```

If you have PostgreSQL 9.5+ with `ogr_fdw` 1.0.1 or above, you can use the `IMPORT FOREIGN SCHEMA` construct. Refer to `http://www.postgresonline.com/article_pfriendly/359.html` for examples.

`IMPORT FOREIGN SCHEMA` provides a way to bulk link a bunch of tables without having to use ogr_fdw_info to determine table structure.

If you wanted to just link in `ne_10m_airports` and `london_tube_lines` in `/usr/data/shp` you would do:

```
IMPORT FOREIGN SCHEMA ogr_all
       LIMIT TO(ne_10m_airports, london_tube_lines)
       FROM SERVER myserver INTO public;
```

To link in all the shape files you have in that folder, you would leave out the `LIMIT TO(..)` clause.

Using ogr_fdw with OpenStreetMap

Many ogr_fdw foreign servers are file-based. Examples are MS Access, SQLite, and OpenStreetMap.

For a file-based data source, pass the file name to `ogr_fdw_info`. If you haven't already, download the Washington DC street data. Place the file into the directory `/usr/share/data/`, then run the following:

```
ogr_fdw_info -s "/usr/share/data/dc.osm.pbf"
```

The result is a listing of all the tables in the database:

```
Layers:
     points
     lines
     multilinestrings
     multipolygons
     other_relations
```

> This example will not work if you don't have GDAL compiled with SQLite and
> Expat support. Internally, OGR converts the OSM data into a temporary
> SQLite database. You will also need Expat support to use the .osm format,
> but you're better off using the superior .pbf format.

Next, to get the create server and create table statements, you would
add the -l (layer command):

```
ogr_fdw_info -s "/usr/share/data/dc.osm.pbf" -l lines
```

This gives us:

```
CREATE FOREIGN TABLE lines (
   fid integer,
   geom geometry,
   osm_id varchar,
   name varchar,
   highway varchar,
   waterway varchar,
   aerialway varchar,
   barrier varchar,
   man_made varchar,
   other_tags varchar )
   SERVER myserver
   OPTIONS ( layer 'lines' );
```

> The columns output by the OSM driver are controlled by a file called
> osmconf.ini, which resides in your gdal-data folder (GDAL_DATA environ-
> ment variable). As a result, you may get different columns than we listed here.
> IN GDAL 2.0+, the z_order value can be computed and is included by default.
> Refer to http://www.gdal.org/drv_osm.html for details.

When generating SQL, `ogr_fdw_info` resorts to the default server
name of "myserver". You should substitute a more meaningful
name by editing the generated SQL. While we're at it, we're going
to rename our table as well:

```
CREATE SERVER osm_dc...
```

```
CREATE FOREIGN TABLE fdwt.osm_dc_lines...
```

If you were to run the following:

```
SELECT ST_SRID(geom) FROM fdwt.osm_dc_lines LIMIT 1;
```

you would get back 0 for an answer using an older version of ogr_fdw.

Because of this, you should cast the geometry column and set the SRID after creating the foreign table:

```
ST_SetSRID(geom,4326)::geometry(LINESTRING ,4326)
```

In the above listing, replace 4326 with the SRID of your source data. For OSM data, the spatial reference system is almost always WGS84 Lon Lat with a SRID of 4326.

One of the pieces of information not brought in by latest versions of osm2pgrouting and osm2po are the road turn restrictions included in osm data. You can expect a future version of osm2pgrouting to provide this information as well. Luckily, the turn restrictions are available in the other_relations table of the ogr_fdw OSM foreign server. We'll use this information later in Routing with Turn Restriction Functions, on page 197 to extract the restrictions into a format that pgRouting can use.

In meantime, you can link the table using ogr_fdw_info, or for PostgreSQL 9.5+, using IMPORT FOREIGN SCHEMA as follows:

```
IMPORT FOREIGN SCHEMA ogr_all LIMIT TO(other_relations)
  FROM SERVER osm_dc INTO SCHEMA fdwt;

ALTER TABLE fdwt.other_relations
  RENAME TO osm_dc_other_relations;
```

OSM uses tags heavily. The other_tags column which ogr_fdw brought in as varchar, is really formatted like a PostgreSQL key-value hstore type. So to utilize the other_tags column as the key value store it is, we'd need to cast that field to hstore. But first, we must enable the hstore extension if we haven't already:

```
CREATE EXTENSION hstore;
```

Now we can write a query to get a sense of what keys are available:

Listing 7.5: Get list of keys in OSM data

```
SELECT
    DISTINCT unnest(akeys(other_tags::hstore)) As key
    FROM fdwt.osm_dc_lines
ORDER BY key;
```

We are using the akeys function which comes packaged with hstore and returns an array of all the keys in an hstore object. We then use the built-in PostgreSQL unnest function to explode the array of keys into rows, and finish off the dance with an SQL DISTINCT to give us a distinct set of values and an SQL ORDER BY to order the keys. This is a very intensive query because it has to scan every record in the lines table (17,207 rows) in addition to doing explosion and sorting to return the result.

The query took about 2 seconds with the DC dataset and looks something like below:

```
             key
----------------------------
 access
 :
 addr:housename
 addr:housenumber
 addr:name
 :
 bridge
 :
 maxspeed
 :
 oneway
 :
(302 rows)
```

We can now do an exploratory query utilizing some of these key value pairs as shown in Listing 7.6.

Listing 7.6: Explore OSM PBF data

```
1  WITH cte AS (
2      SELECT osm_id,
3          ST_SetSRID(geom,4326)::geometry(LINESTRING,4326) As geom,
4          name, highway, other_tags::hstore As tags
5      FROM fdwt.osm_dc_lines
6  WHERE highway > '' LIMIT 500)
```

```
 7  SELECT osm_id, name, highway,
 8      tags->'oneway' As oneway,
 9      tags->'lanes' As lanes, tags->'maxspeed' As maxspeed,
10      ((
11          ST_Length(geom::geography)/1609 ) /
12              replace(tags->'maxspeed', ' mph', '')::int*60
13          )::numeric(10,2) As cost
14  FROM cte
15  WHERE tags ? 'maxspeed' and name > '';
```

In listing 7.6, on the previous page, *lines 1-6* use an SQL common table expression to select a piece of data from the

district-of-columbia-latest.osm.pbf

lines layer. Note the casting of geom to geometry(LINESTRNG, 4326) in *line 3* and the other_tags to hstore in *line 4* so that we can eventually apply more useful operations specific to those data types. The final query is *lines 7-15* which selects out useful bits of information for building a road network. The -> operator used in *lines 8-9* and *line 12* is an operator which, when applied to an hstore object, returns the associated value of the given key. The ST_Length function used in *line 11* is the PostGIS geography method to return the length of a linestring in meters. There is one for geometry as well, which returns units in the spatial reference system units of the geometry.

By casting our geometry to geography, we are able to use the more useful, geography variant which always returns length in meters. The ? operator used in *line 15* is an operator which when applied to an hstore object, will return true or false if the hstore object has a value with that key. By using tags ? 'maxspeed', our query will only return roads with maxspeed attributes.

The output of the query would look like:

osm_id	name	highway	oneway	lanes	maxspeed	cost
5990429	Piney Branch Road	secondary		2	30 mph	2.78
6051295	South Capitol Street	motorway	yes	2	35 mph	0.22
6051620	Southeast Freeway	motorway	yes	3	40 mph	0.18
6051762	9th Street Tunnel	motorway	yes	3	35 mph	0.52
6051992	Butler Street Southwest	residential			10 mph	0.80

```
 6052271 | Maine Avenue Southwest  | primary     | yes   | 2     | 25 mph  | 0.03
 6052863 | T Street Northeast      | residential |       |       | 25 mph  | 0.50
(7 rows)
```

This will give us a sense of what is useful to pull in before we do
the final data load.

Part 3

Working with pgRouting Functions

8 *Writing pgRouting Wrapper Functions*

PostgreSQL supports many languages for composing user-defined functions with SQL and PL/pgSQL being most popular.

For GIS work, PL/R (leverages R statistical environment) and PL/Python are common favorites. If you are a web developer, you may also be attracted to PL/V8 (aka PL/JavaScript). In this chapter we'll cover the fundamentals of building PostgreSQL functions, with an eye for building functions that wrap pgRouting and PostGIS functionality. We will focus our attention on building functions with SQL and PL/pgSQL languages, since those are by far the most commonly used and accessible for wrapping pgRouting and PostGIS functionality.

8.1   *What are Wrapper Functions and Why Write Them?*

When we talk about wrapper functions in this book, we are talking about a PostgreSQL function like any other, that wraps the functionality of pgRouting and PostGIS in an easier to use and preferably terser form than what you would need when calling the pgRouting and PostGIS functions directly.

Native pgRouting functions were designed to be generic in order to accommodate a wide range of applications. While this provides flexibility, the downside is that you may have to temporarily reshape your own data structure before being able to apply pgRouting functions. This could make for a rather lengthy and busy-looking SQL. Writing a wrapper function tailored to your data structure mitigates the need to pass in bulky SQL each time.

Another general reason for wrapper functions is to circumvent SQL injection attacks. Erecting a functional barrier between your user input and native pgRouting functions lets you sanitize user inputs.

When it comes to wrapper functions, you're always faced with the trade-off between convenience and generality. The more you customize your functions to suit your specific structure the less you'll be able to reuse the function, but such is the balancing act that comes with the programming.

8.2   Writing Wrapper Functions with Just SQL

PostgreSQL lets you write functions with sophisticated flow control using many procedural languages, but many times, a function that wraps a piece of SQL will suffice. We demonstrate using our airports data.

Instead of calling pgr_dijkstra directly, we'll create a simple function that takes in two airport codes and returns the result as a table object:

Listing 8.1: Wrapper function: Dijkstra using dynamic costs

```
1   CREATE OR REPLACE FUNCTION air_dijkstra(param_from varchar, param_to varchar)
2   RETURNS TABLE (seq integer, route text,
3       cost double precision, agg_cost double precision)
4   AS
5   $$
6   SELECT X.seq,
7       N.city || COALESCE('-' || lead(N.city) OVER(ORDER By seq),'') As route,
8       X.cost, X.agg_cost
9   FROM pgr_dijkstra(
10      'SELECT id, source, target,
11          dist_km As cost
12          FROM routes',
13      (SELECT id FROM airports WHERE iata = $1),
14      (SELECT id FROM airports WHERE iata = $2),
15      FALSE
16  ) X   INNER JOIN airports AS N ON X.node = N.id
17  ORDER BY seq;
18  $$
19  language 'sql';
```

Using our function, our earlier query to find the shortest path between JFK and Mumbai simplifies to:

```
SELECT *
```

```
FROM air_dijkstra('JFK', 'BOM');
```

The wrapper handles three pieces of functionality for us. First, it automatically looked up the airport identifier for us. Second, it generated a neat hyphenated sequence of the optimal route using IATA identifiers. Third, it retrieved the city name to be a part of the final output.

Other than adding a function declaration before and after and using numbered parameters, we did virtually nothing to the original SQL. You don't need to teach yourself any new procedural languages to accomplish what we just did!

Although using the function results in much more concise code, it is also much less flexible. We made some uncompromising decisions regarding our data: all the tables must be named to our convention and the measure of cost is distance.

Before you start down the path of packaging your SQL into sweet morsels of SQL functions, we need to issue some advisories:

> Prior to PostgreSQL 9.2, SQL functions could not reference input arguments by name. SQL arguments had to be used with alias $1, $2, etc, based on order of input. In PostgreSQL 9.2+ you have the option of using the old $1 syntax or referencing the arguments by name. This allows you to replace $1 and $2 with the more meaningful param_from and param_to in your wrapper function(s).

SQL Functions can't Execute Dynamic SQL

Dynamic SQL is SQL built step-by-step within a function. The input parameter dictates the constituents of the SQL.

Below is a quick pseudo-code of a function that generates dynamic SQL:

function foo (x)

if x = 'TRUNCATE'
   execute 'TRUNCATE table1'
else
   execute 'SELECT * FROM table1'

SQL functions cannot execute dynamic SQL.

The saving grace when it comes to pgRouting is that native functions often accept SQL as a parameter. So even though you can't vary the core SQL of the function, you can vary the snippet passed into the native pgr_dijkstra function.

Here is a redefinition of the air_dijkstra function that parameterizes the variable used for cost:

Listing 8.2: Wrapper function: Dijkstra using user input dynamic costs

```
1    DROP FUNCTION IF EXISTS air_dijkstra(varchar, varchar);
2    CREATE OR REPLACE FUNCTION air_dijkstra(param_from varchar, param_to varchar,
3        param_cost_formula text
4            DEFAULT 'dist_km' )
5    RETURNS TABLE (seq integer, route text,
6        cost double precision, agg_cost double precision)
7    AS
8    $$
9    SELECT X.seq,
10       N.city || COALESCE('-' || lead(N.city) OVER(ORDER By seq),'') As route,
11       X.cost, X.agg_cost
12   FROM pgr_dijkstra(
13       'SELECT id, source, target,
14          ' || $3 || ' As cost
15          FROM routes',
16       (SELECT id FROM airports WHERE iata = $1),
17       (SELECT id FROM airports WHERE iata = $2),
18       FALSE
19   ) X   INNER JOIN airports AS N ON X.node = N.id
20   ORDER BY seq;
21   $$
22   language 'sql';
```

This new air_dijkstra function demonstrates that even though we can't alter the structure of the outer SQL, we're able to manipulate the SQL that goes into the pgr_dijkstra function.

Now we can call our new function like this:

```
SELECT *
FROM air_dijkstra('JFK', 'BOM');
```

or even override the default cost formula like this:

```
SELECT *
FROM air_dijkstra('JFK', 'BOM',
    'CASE WHEN dist_km > 7500 THEN ln(dist_km)*dist_km ELSE 2*dist_km END');
```

SQL Functions can't have Flow Logic

SQL is a declarative language with no support for conditionals and loops.

You can't even declare a new variable inside the function.

To compensate for the lack of looping, you can use SQL functions with built-in looping logic such as `generate_series`. To compensate for the lack of variables, you can use common table expressions (CTEs).

However, if you're at a point where you need conditionals, loops, and variables, we advise that you graduate to a full-blown procedural language such as PL/pgSQL procedural language variant.

SQL Functions are Often Transparent to PostgreSQL

The PostgreSQL query engine does not always treat SQL functions as black boxes. This could lead to undesirable side effects. The query engine peeks inside the SQL function and tries to inline the function with the rest of the query. This has its benefits: Namely, that the query engine will attempt to optimize what's inside your function. You can control the extent to which the query engine intrudes into the SQL function with the strictness setting. Marking your function as "non-strict" invites inspection.

Another plus of transparency is that the query engine will validate your function when you first define it. Besides checking that you have legal syntax, it'll check that all embedded functions are present and accessible via your database search path.

This does mean that when you create a function you have to make sure that the search path includes the schemas of the dependent functions or you have to schema qualify your function calls. By schema qualify, we mean using `postgis.pgr_dijkstra` instead of just `pgr_dijkstra`. One way to ensure the right search_path is always available, is to do so as part of the function definition. Something like

```
ALTER FUNCTION air_dijkstra(varchar, varchar)
    SET search_path=postgis,public;
```

Furthermore, if you're restoring across different versions of pgRouting, you need to make sure that all embedded functions have a corresponding signature in the version you're restoring to. For example, if you created a function using the pgRouting 1.0 `shortest_path` function and later try to restore to a server with pgRouting 2.1 where `shortest_path` no longer exists, your restore will fail.

8.3   Writing Wrapper Functions with PL/pgSQL

PL/pgSQL is a full-fledged procedural language supporting conditionals, loops, and declaration of variables. It also has an `EXECUTE` function that will run dynamic SQL assembled on the fly, however complex.

Wrapping Commonly Used Routines

One of the main reasons for writing wrapper functions is to reuse functionality you find yourself repeating over and over again. A common repetitive pattern in pgRouting is to be able to pass in a point, rather than a node identifier. To obtain the node closest to the point, we need to perform a distance check. In the chapter covering OSM, we wrote code that applied the built-in `pgr_pointToEdgeNode` function to find the edge closest to a point. Now, we're going to create a function that finds the nearest node from a function to showcase PL/pgSQL.

Listing 8.3: upgr_nodeNearestPoint - Find closest node to a geometric point

```
1   CREATE OR REPLACE FUNCTION upgr_nodeNearestPoint(node_table text, pt geometry,
2           tol_dist double precision DEFAULT -1) RETURNS bigint AS
3   $$
4   DECLARE var_result_pt geometry;
5           var_result_node_id int8;
6   BEGIN
7           EXECUTE 'SELECT n.the_geom, n.id FROM ' || _pgr_quote_ident(node_table) ||
8                   ' AS n ORDER BY n.the_geom <-> $1 LIMIT 1'
9                       INTO var_result_pt, var_result_node_id USING pt;
10          IF var_result_node_id IS NOT NULL AND (tol_dist = -1 OR
11              ST_DWithin(pt, var_result_pt, tol_dist) ) THEN
12              RETURN var_result_node_id;
13          ELSE
14              RAISE NOTICE 'No node within tolerance found';
15              RETURN NULL;
16          END IF;
17  END
18  $$
19  LANGUAGE 'plpgsql'
20    STRICT COST 200;
```

We prefixed our function with the letter "u" to distinguish it from a built in function. We intentionally did not include a schema which means our function will reside in the default schema. (In most cases, this is the public schema.)

Our example uses _pgr_quote_ident to literalize and quote table names. Because we're already passing a single quoted string into the EXECUTE function, adding quotes around a variable table name poses a challenge—and no, you can't just add more single quotes. We count on _pgr_quote_ident to take off the quoting for us. You'll notice an underscore in front of the function. This signals the function to be a function meant to supplement pgRouting, and not one meant to perform routing. PostgreSQL does have a quote_ident function of its own, but the pgRouting variant can properly handle dotted identifier such as table with a schema name prepended. For instance, ospr.edges will come out as "ospr"."edges" instead of "ospr.edges".

Reusing Wrappers to Write Other Wrappers

The default behavior of the native `pgr_pointToEdgeNode` function accepts a point geometry and finds the closest edge. Once the edge is found, the function returns the node closest to the point passed in.

In the previous section, we augmented this with our own `upgr_nodeNearestPoi` Our new function finds the closest node without checking for the closest edge.

With both functions now at our disposal, we can craft a Dijkstra routing function where the user has the choice to use either closest edge or closest node when points are passed in.

We create our own `pgr_dijkstra` function calling `upgr_dijkstra`. The code follows:

Listing 8.4: Wrapper function: Dijkstra using geometric points instead of nodes

```
1   CREATE OR REPLACE FUNCTION upgr_dijkstra(
2       sql text, start_pt geometry, end_pt geometry,
3       directed boolean,
4       tol_dist double precision DEFAULT 0.1,
5       node_table text DEFAULT '')
6   RETURNS TABLE ( seq integer, node bigint,
7       edge bigint,
8       cost double precision,
9       agg_cost double precision) AS
10  $$
11    DECLARE
12      var_source_id bigint; var_target_id bigint;
13    BEGIN
14      -- this function unlike the pgr_dijkstra
15      -- assumes that the_geom field is passed into the query
16      IF node_table = '' THEN -- go by start, end node edge distance
17            EXECUTE 'CREATE TEMP VIEW vw_upgr_dijkstra_edge AS ' || sql || ';
18          var_source_id := pgr_pointToEdgeNode('vw_upgr_dijkstra_edge',
19            start_pt, tol_dist);
20            var_target_id := pgr_pointToEdgeNode('vw_upgr_dijkstra_edge',
21              end_pt, tol_dist);
22            DROP VIEW vw_upgr_dijkstra_edge;
23        ELSE -- find by closest by node
24            var_source_id := upgr_nodeNearestPoint(node_table,
25              start_pt, tol_dist);
```

```
26                    var_target_id := upgr_nodeNearestPoint(node_table,
27                       end_pt, tol_dist);
28        END IF;
29        RETURN QUERY SELECT d.seq, d.node, d.edge, d.cost, d.agg_cost
30           FROM pgr_dijkstra(sql, var_source_id,
31              var_target_id, directed) AS d;
32     END
33  $$
34    LANGUAGE plpgsql VOLATILE
35    COST 1000
36    ROWS 100;
```

The last parameter of upgr_dijkstra to pass in the name of the nodes table is optional. If you omit it, the default is an empty string. The function's main conditional checks to see if you named a nodes table. If you did, then the function uses upgr_nodeNearestPoint to find the closest nodes to the start and end points. Otherwise, the function uses pgr_pointToEdgeNode to find the closest nodes. From there on, the function calls pgr_dijkstra to finish the job.

The native pgr_dijkstra that Listing 8.4, on the facing page tries to mimic, takes as its first parameter, an SQL query that defines the network. The edges in the result rows of the query will be the only ones that Dijkstra takes into consideration as a possible path. pgr_pointToEdgeNode expects a named table of edges and cannot accept SQL. If our edges table has a million rows and we only need to route based on ten rows, passing the entire edges table to pgr_pointToEdgeNode adds much superfluous computation.

Our work around is to take advantage of temporary views. We create a named temporary view of edges using the same SQL as the one for Dijkstra. We can then pass this SQL to pgr_pointToEdgeNode in lieu of the entire edges table.

Temporary views, similar to temporary tables, persist through the life of a database session. You can also explicitly drop them. A temporary view has the advantage over a temporary table in that indexes from the underlying table carry over to the view, whereas a temporary table starts with no indexes.

All functions have a volatility setting. Any function that alters data structure or data should be tagged as VOLATILE. Functions that may return different outputs with the same input or no input, such as functions using random() OR CURRENT_DATE, should also be marked as VOLATILE. Contrast a volatile function with an immutable or stable function. An immutable function does not alter data or data structure and will always return the same answer given the same input across all queries. A stable function will not alter data or data structure and will always return the same answer within a specific query run. However if you run the same query again and the underlying data the function relies on has changed between runs, the stable function could give a different answer in the second run. A frivolous example is a function that sums the first hundred prime numbers. Marking a function as IMMUTABLE lets PostgreSQL optimizer cache the function results which could greatly speed up repeated calls to the same function. Once the optimizer has figured out the sum of the first hundred, 24133, it has the flexibility of reading the answer from a cache rather than repeating the calculation the next time you call the function.

VOLATILE is the default setting, but for clarity, we recommend explicitly setting this.

With our new function, we can rewrite our osm2pgrouting loaded data query as:

Listing 8.5: Use upgr_dijkstra to find path by node distance

```
1   SELECT r.seq, r.node, w.name As street,  r.cost,
2     SUM(w.length_m) OVER(ORDER BY r.seq) As dist_m
3   FROM upgr_dijkstra('SELECT gid AS id,
4                            source,
5                            target,
6                            cost, reverse_cost, the_geom
7                       FROM ospr.ways',
8        ST_SetSRID(ST_Point(-77.03649,38.89754), 4326) ,
9        ST_SetSRID(ST_Point(-77.022733,38.8878), 4326) , true) AS r
10       LEFT JOIN ospr.ways AS w ON r.edge = w.gid;
```

In our example, we did not pass in a node table. Accordingly, our function will find the closest edge to our input points and then pick out the node.

We added a maximum distance parameter to our function for locating nodes (tol_dist). If a node cannot be located within this maximum distance from the point, our function will not continue to Dijkstra and will just return NULL.

When using edges to locate the closest node, our maximum distance measures the perpendicular from our point to the edge.

Listing 8.6: Use upgr_dijkstra to find travel from New York to New Dehli

```
1   SELECT r.seq, r.node, w.city,  r.cost,
2     r.agg_cost
3   FROM upgr_dijkstra('SELECT id,
4       source,
5       target,
6       dist_km/1000 + (dist_km - 1000)/2000 * 4 + (dist_km - 2000)/4000 * 10 As cost,
7       geom AS the_geom
8     FROM routes',
9         ST_SetSRID(ST_Point(-73.93524,40.730610), 4326) ,
10        ST_SetSRID(ST_Point(77.2245,28.635), 4326) , false,
11            15,'routes_vertices_pgr') AS r
12        INNER JOIN airports AS w ON r.node = w.id;
```

In the above example we set our tolerance distance to 15 degrees, which means that we must find an edge within 15 degrees for both source and target.

8.4 Accounting for Large Networks

The *pgr_dijkstra* function lets you pass in an SQL. By judicious use of a WHERE clause in the SQL, you can eliminate edges from consideration.

For example, if you have an edges table of all roadways in a large city and you're trying to route a one-hundred ton semi, you probably should remove roads that cannot support the tonnage or the over head clearance. In the United States, especially in the Northeast, the government built many scenic parkways in the early part of the 1900s for the exclusive use of small passenger cars. Often one hears a story or see pictures of trucks with their tops sheared off in a low underpass on one of these parkways.

Another example, if you're a general manager of a city's bus line: after a heavy snow storm, you may need to re-route your buses by eliminating narrower streets. Even after plowing, the traversable width of a street could be halved. Often one hears stories of a bus stuck on a tiny street; local news stations besiege the angry passengers. Everyone pointing fingers at the general manager—you.

Filtering edges by an attribute is easy with a WHERE clause. We want to demonstrate another technique that uses spatial queries.

Let's say we're tasked with routing for the Kansas Highway Patrol, but all we have is a map of interstate highways for the entire United States. Policies in place do not permit patrol cars to egress Kansas so including edges outside the state is nothing but a waste of computation.

If our edges have an attribute marking which state it is in, our work would be simple. If not, we must resort to a spatial intersection query.

In all the examples we've seen thus far, we've had pretty small edges tables. Our biggest only has about 32,000 edges which is tiny for a road network. As you get into networks that are larger, you don't want to have pgRouting inspect edges that can never be candidates for a solution. A way to account for that and not burden all your queries is create a wrapper that is smart enough to filter the edges list for you.

Revisiting the upgr_dijkstra we defined in Listing 8.4, on page 90, we are going to modify it to be able to filter the network passed in before it pushes the query to pgr_dijkstra. Note since this new version replaces the old, you'll want to drop the old function with:

Listing 8.7: upgr_dijkstra - Dijkstra that takes points and bounds

```
DROP FUNCTION IF EXISTS
    upgr_dijkstra(text, geometry, geometry, boolean, float8,text);
```

The first step is to take in a percent of distance argument that can be used, so *lines 1-5* of Listing 8.4, on page 90 get replaced with:

Listing 8.8: upgr_dijkstra - Dijkstra that takes points and bounds

```
CREATE OR REPLACE FUNCTION upgr_dijkstra(
```

```
sql text, start_pt geometry, end_pt geometry,
directed boolean,
tol_dist float8 DEFAULT 0.1,
node_table text DEFAULT '', expand_percent_dist float4 DEFAULT 0.5)
```

Then next, we add an extra line of code shown in Listing 8.9 to the DECLARE section of Listing 8.4, on page 90 right after *line 12*.

Listing 8.9: upgr_dijkstra - Dijkstra that takes points and bounds: add additional variables

```
var_new_sql text; var_expand_geom geometry;
```

The var_new_sql variable will hold the revised sql that includes a bounding box filter we will pass to pgr_dijkstra. The var_expand_geom will hold the computed bounding box filter which is a function of the expand_percent_dist passed in the function, and the distance between the start and end input points.

Finally we add logic to compute all these and a final new SQL to pass to pgr_dijkstra as shown in Listing 8.10.

Listing 8.10: upgr_dijkstra - Dijkstra that takes points and bounds: compute bounds and new sql statement

```
var_new_sql := sql;
IF expand_percent_dist IS NOT NULL THEN
    -- create an expand box that is expanded x percent
    -- around the bounding box of start and end
    var_expand_geom := ST_Expand(ST_MakeLine(start_pt, end_pt),
        ST_Distance(start_pt, end_pt) * expand_percent_dist );
    -- only include edges that overlap the expand bounding box
    var_new_sql := 'SELECT * FROM (' || sql || ') AS e
        WHERE e.the_geom &&  '
        || quote_literal(var_expand_geom::text) || '::geometry';
END IF;
RETURN QUERY SELECT d.seq, d.node, d.edge, d.cost, d.agg_cost
    FROM pgr_dijkstra(var_new_sql, var_source_id,
        var_target_id, directed) AS d;
```

The query in Listing 6.3, on page 61 is more or less equivalent to the query in Listing 8.11, on the next page except Listing 8.11, on the following page only utilizes a subset of the network; that portion of network that overlaps the bounding box you get by expanding the source point and target point bounding box by 20%.

Listing 8.11: upgr_dijkstra - Dijkstra that takes points and bounds: compute bounds and new sql statement

```
SELECT r.seq, r.node, w.name As street,  r.cost,
  SUM(w.length_m) OVER(ORDER BY r.seq) As dist_m
 FROM upgr_dijkstra('SELECT gid AS id,
                  source,
                  target,
                  cost, reverse_cost, the_geom
                FROM ospr.ways',
  ST_SetSRID(ST_Point(-77.03649,38.89754), 4326)  ,
  ST_SetSRID(ST_Point(-77.022733,38.8878), 4326) , true,
  tol_dist:=0.01,
  expand_percent_dist := 0.2) AS r
        LEFT JOIN ospr.ways AS w ON r.edge = w.gid;
```

Even with this relatively small data set the upgr_dijkstra is about four times faster than the pgr_dijkstra one, returning the same answer in 43 ms compared to 191 ms.

8.5   SQL Injection Attacks

Because many pgRouting functions take SQL statements as input, they are prone to SQL injection attacks. Before we go any further, what's an SQL injection?

An SQL Injection Attack in the Making

Let's suppose you wanted users to be able to define their own costs for travel, so you proffered them the function air_dijkstra. Simple enough.

A user comes along to help with testing the function by running the following:

```
SELECT *
FROM air_dijkstra('JFK', 'BOM', 'pg_sleep(300) As test, 1');
```

The function call injected an pg_sleep function call which causes each row in the query to take 300 seconds. If you allowed your application to run under a super user account, a user could do even more damage such as using `pg_terminate_backend` to kill all database connections.

Most serious SQL Injection attacks cause harm by injecting action statements like DELETE, UPDATE as additional statements or instead of the intended statement. They do so with tricks such as using the - - code comment. They also do so by adding on extra variables as we did. For the `air_dijkstra` function as it is currently written, it's hard to come up with an injection that would cause more damage aside from say killing connections, reading system values, or performing certain system actions.

How much effort you should put into protecting your system, really depends on how well you know the people that will be using the system. If it's just you and a small trusted group of people, you shouldn't worry so much—locking things down may inflict more damage by causing other things not to work.

Here are some general safeguards to protect against SQL injection.

Use Read-only Access or Account with Low Privileges

Secure-minded IT folks often recite the following mantra: Never grant a user more access than necessary to accomplish what needs to be done.

For applications open to many, abide by this principle by running your applications under accounts with only read-access if they do not need to update data. Grant write-access judiciously.

```
1  CREATE ROLE app_user_read LOGIN PASSWORD 'whatever';
2
3  GRANT ALL ON SCHEMA public TO app_user_read;
4
5  ALTER DEFAULT PRIVILEGES IN SCHEMA public
6   GRANT SELECT, REFERENCES ON TABLES TO app_user_read;
7
8  GRANT SELECT, REFERENCES
9   ON ALL TABLES IN SCHEMA public TO app_user_read;
```

Set Security Levels of Functions

By default, functions execute within the context of the user who invoked the function.

On occasion, if you need just for the period of the function the executing user to be able to run under a higher account, use SECU-RITY DEFINER, but use that with caution and make the owner of that function be an account with enough permissions to do what it needs to do, but no more.

Validate Input Parameters

Immediately reject anything that contains SQL keywords such as DELETE, TRUNCATE, DROP, etc. If necessary and doable go one step further and restrict parameters against a reference table.

The validation requires more work and could limit the versatility of the function.

For instance, the oft-used `pgr_dijkstra` accepts SQL as input.

You can wrap this function as follows:

At the first sign that the user might be doing something fishy, we halt execution.

In case you're wondering... the internal implementation pgr_dijkstra does not guard against SQL injection.

For the next example, we'll alter our `air_dijkstra` function to only allow choices from a reference table for the cost parameter.

To start, we create a reference table called `lu_air_costs`:

```
CREATE TABLE lu_air_costs(type varchar(50) primary key, formula text);
INSERT INTO lu_air_costs(type, formula)
VALUES (  'cost default',
    'dist_km/1000 + (dist_km - 1000)/2000 * 4 + (dist_km - 2000)/4000 * 10' ),
    ('cost linear', 'dist_km*10');
```

Then we write our function to only allow predefined formulas from `lu_air_costs`.

Listing 8.12: air_dijkstra: Rewritten to prevent SQL injection

```
1   CREATE OR REPLACE FUNCTION air_dijkstra(param_from varchar, param_to varchar,
2       param_cost_formula text
3           DEFAULT 'cost default' )
4   RETURNS TABLE (seq integer, route text,
5       cost double precision, agg_cost double precision)
6   AS
7   $$
8   SELECT X.seq,
9       N.city || COALESCE('-' || lead(N.city) OVER(ORDER By seq),'') As route,
10      X.cost, X.agg_cost
11  FROM pgr_dijkstra(
12      'SELECT id, source, target,
13          ' || (SELECT formula FROM lu_air_costs WHERE type = $3) || ' As cost
14          FROM routes',
15      (SELECT id FROM airports WHERE iata = $1),
16      (SELECT id FROM airports WHERE iata = $2),
17      FALSE
18  ) X   INNER JOIN airports AS N ON X.node = N.id
19  ORDER BY seq;
20  $$
21  language 'sql';
```

The key change in the function is that we now compare the input cost against type in the lu_air_costs table.

So an evil attack fashioned as follows would fail:

```
SELECT *
  FROM air_dijkstra('JFK', 'BOM',
    $$CASE WHEN
        EXISTS (SELECT 1 FROM geometry_columns
          WHERE f_table_schema = 'of'
          AND f_table_name = 'routes_vertices_pgr')
      THEN (SELECT 1 FROM
        DropGeometryTable('of','routes_vertices_pgr') )
        ELSE 0 END$$);
```

Whereas a well-formed invocation of the function as in the following would be rewarded with an answer:

```
SELECT *
  FROM air_dijkstra('JFK', 'BOM', 'cost linear');
```

The obvious downside to using a reference table is that we greatly limit the choices available as cost formulas, but unfortunately such

trade-offs between freedom and security are inescapable in the world
that we live in today.

9 *Data Fixing and Applying Costs*

In this chapter, we'll explore functions for fixing less than perfect data. We'll also cover how to compute costs of edges based on data elements.

9.1   Costs and Good Data

There are two key elements to any good routing machine. You need good edge and node data and you need to apply costs to these edges in some meaningful way.

Good edge data connects at node junctions. So wherever it is possible to have a stopping point, that point is either the start or end of an edge. The directionality of the data is not mixed. You never have one edge that connects to another and the vector of each is opposing.

There are other factors about good edge/node data that are hard to troubleshoot. Things like, does your data have all useful and accurately stated attributes. For example is the road speed limit really 30 kph. Is there a train station at the end of this track, etc?

Routing is about the economics of minimizing costs in your objective to get from A to B. What cost means in that context changes based on what you are trying to minimize. Here is a sampling of costs you can think of:

- Minimizing time in walking—consider length and if the path allows pedestrians.
- Minimize effort in walking—consider length, if the path allows pedestrians, and slope of path.
- Minimize monotony of travel—give low cost to scenic paths and high cost to boring paths like highways with a lot of congestion and those with stretches of repetitive grass fields.
- Minimize driving time—consider only edges that allow vehicles

(might be dependent on vehicle), max speed limit, directionality, and traffic congestion.

- Maximize calorie consumption—same as saying walkable and minimize inverse of effort in walking.
- Minimize time using public transportation / walking—only consider routes that are walkable or serviced by bus or train.
- Minimize monetary cost of driving—consider gas consumption and toll prices.

Keep in mind that pgRouting, like many routing engines assumes, you are trying to minimize costs—so don't define a cost where the desired effect is to increase cost. Restate your costs to be always decreasing to achieve the desired effect. The only exception to this rule is negative costs like -1. Negative cost values have special meaning in pgRouting, and signify infinity to denote an edge route that is not allowed.

9.2   Fixing Edge Data

There are many kinds of problems you will find in your data. In this chapter we'll cover issues you will find with commonly available edge data.

- Noding data—ensuring that intersections in the network are represented as start or end of an edge.
- Gaps—ensuring that edges are connected and you don't have small gaps that result in dead ends where there should not be dead ends
- Self-intersections—a node that self-intersects causing an infinite spiral
- Directionality—ensuring you don't have nodes where flow can come in but not escape
- Ring geometries—where the start of the edge and the end of the edge are the same. This is not a valid edge for pgRouting.

Finding Noding Issues with pgr_analyzeGraph

The first step in fixing edge data is to use the `pgr_analyzeGraph` function to help detect these kinds of issues. We'll analyze the data we loaded with osm2pgrouting with this command:

```
SELECT pgr_analyzeGraph('ospr.ways', 0.00001, 'the_geom', 'gid');
```

One key argument to the `pgr_analyzeGraph` function is the tolerance, in this case `0.00001`, which is in units of the spatial reference
system of your data. Our data is in WGS 84 long/lat therefore the
units are degrees. This indicates we expect edges and nodes to be
within `0.00001` degrees to be considered connected.

Our query output looks like this:

```
NOTICE:  PROCESSING:
NOTICE:  pgr_analyzeGraph('ospr.ways',1e-005,'the_geom','gid','source','target','true')
NOTICE:  Performing checks, please wait ...
NOTICE:  Analyzing for dead ends. Please wait...
NOTICE:  Analyzing for gaps. Please wait...
NOTICE:  Analyzing for isolated edges. Please wait...
NOTICE:  Analyzing for ring geometries. Please wait...
NOTICE:  Analyzing for intersections. Please wait...
NOTICE:              ANALYSIS RESULTS FOR SELECTED EDGES:
NOTICE:                    Isolated segments: 14
NOTICE:                            Dead ends: 1774
NOTICE:  Potential gaps found near dead ends: 19
NOTICE:              Intersections detected: 775
NOTICE:                      Ring geometries: 14

Total query runtime: 3.5 secs
1 row retrieved.
```

The other arguments to the function are optional, but must be stated
if your columns are not named `the_geom` (for geometry column), `id`
for unique identifier, and `source` and `target` for source and target
node columns.

Fixing Gaps and Intersections with pgr_nodeNetwork

pgRouting comes packaged with a function called `pgr_nodeNetwork`
which is designed to fix the lack of noded intersections. Though it's
purpose is to add nodes at intersections, by introducing these new
nodes, it ends up fixing other issues such as dead-ends or gaps near
ends. What it will do is create a new table from an input edge table.

It won't help you fix ring geometries though. The basic fix for ring
geometries is to add a node in the middle of the ring and break into
two edges at the new node.

The default table name will be the original with noded appended to the end. You can override the suffix if you prefer. To use it with the osm2pgrouting ways table we do this:

```
SELECT pgr_nodeNetwork('ospr.ways', 0.00001, 'gid', 'the_geom');
```

which outputs:

```
NOTICE:  PROCESSING:
NOTICE:  pgr_nodeNetwork('ospr.ways',1e-005,'gid','the_geom','noded','')
NOTICE:  Performing checks, please wait .....
NOTICE:  Processing, please wait .....
NOTICE:    Splitted Edges: 700
NOTICE:  Untouched Edges: 31693
NOTICE:      Total original Edges: 32393
NOTICE:  Edges generated: 2038
NOTICE:  Untouched Edges: 31693
NOTICE:       Total New segments: 33731
NOTICE:  New Table: ospr.ways_noded
NOTICE:  ---------------------------------

Total query runtime: 3.3 secs
1 row retrieved.
```

The new table it creates, ospr.ways_noded, has standard named columns of id, the_geom, source, and target. In addition it has an old_id to denote the gid of the ospr.ways table the edge was created from. In addition it has a sub_id to denote the node segment. For example, you'll notice that gid=265 was broken into several edge subsegments.

> pgr_nodeNetwork does not handle things like overpasses and underpasses. In many cases, for performance reasons, you may also wish to node only a portion of your network. In case of overpasses/underpasses you would ideally create a temp table that excludes these before you pass to pgr_nodeNetwork or exclude them by some other means. In pgRouting 2.2.0, the function was enhanced to take an optional rows_where argument that allows you to only node a portion of your network. This defaults to true, meaning all rows in a table are used by default.

The ospr.ways_noded table does not have a companion vertices table and does not have source and target columns filled in. We need to update the source and target and create a vertices table by running `pgr_createTopology` before we can rerun `pgr_analyzeGraph`.

```
SELECT pgr_createTopology('ospr.ways_noded', 0.00001);
```

which will output:

```
NOTICE:  PROCESSING:
NOTICE:  pgr_createTopology('ospr.ways_noded',1e-005,'the_geom','id','source','target','true')
NOTICE:  Performing checks, please wait .....
NOTICE:  Creating Topology, Please wait...
NOTICE:  1000 edges processed
NOTICE:  2000 edges processed
:
NOTICE:  33000 edges processed
NOTICE:  ------------> TOPOLOGY CREATED FOR  33731 edges
NOTICE:  Rows with NULL geometry or NULL id: 0
NOTICE:  Vertices table for table ospr.ways_noded is: ospr.ways_noded_vertices_pgr
NOTICE:  --------------------------------------------

Total query runtime: 25084 ms.
1 row retrieved.
```

Now analyze new table with:

```
SELECT pgr_analyzeGraph('ospr.ways_noded', 0.00001, 'the_geom', 'id');
```

which yields:

```
NOTICE:  PROCESSING:
NOTICE:  pgr_analyzeGraph('ospr.ways_noded',1e-005,...'source','target','true')
NOTICE:  Performing checks, please wait ...
NOTICE:  Analyzing for dead ends. Please wait...
NOTICE:  Analyzing for gaps. Please wait...
NOTICE:  Analyzing for isolated edges. Please wait...
NOTICE:  Analyzing for ring geometries. Please wait...
NOTICE:  Analyzing for intersections. Please wait...
NOTICE:             ANALYSIS RESULTS FOR SELECTED EDGES:
NOTICE:                  Isolated segments: 10
NOTICE:                         Dead ends: 1765
NOTICE:  Potential gaps found near dead ends: 10
NOTICE:             Intersections detected: 0
NOTICE:                    Ring geometries: 14

Total query runtime: 2924 ms.
1 row retrieved.
```

Though `pgr_nodeNetwork` fixed some issues, we still have a lot of
the same left. The `pgr_nodeNetwork` function also does not pre-

serve the additional columns we had in our original table—columns
like cost, reverse_cost, osm_id, one_way, maxspeed_forward, and
maxspeed_backward, if we need them need to be re-added.

> PostgreSQL updates of existing tables is more costly than plain inserts be-
> cause they are really deletes followed by inserts. If you need to update all
> records in a table such as needs to be done to add back in all the missing info
> in the generated noded table, it is generally easier to just create a new table
> joined with the noded table. Also, you may want to only node a part of your
> network so your generated noded network may not comprise your full network.

There are a couple of approaches we can use to merge the new
noded data with our original data. We can:

1. Work with our original table and delete old edges and replace
   with new edges
2. Create a whole new table from scratch joining our old table with
   our new table
3. Work with our new table and add back columns and update from
   the old table

Updating fields tends to be slow, so for performance reasons we
avoid the last option. For large datasets where there are relatively
few splits (relative to data set size) introduced by pgr_nodeNetwork,
option 1 tends to be the best.

Listing 9.1: Add split edges back to the original table

```
1   ALTER TABLE ospr.ways ADD COLUMN old_id bigint;
2
3   INSERT INTO ospr.ways(old_id,class_id, length, length_m, name,
4       x1, y1, x2, y2,
5       cost, reverse_cost, cost_s, reverse_cost_s,
6       rule, one_way, maxspeed_forward, maxspeed_backward,
7       osm_id, source_osm, target_osm, priority, the_geom)
8   SELECT o.gid, o.class_id, n.length, n.length_m, o.name,
9       ST_X(n.sp) As x1, ST_Y(n.sp) AS y1, ST_X(n.ep) As x2, ST_Y(n.ep) AS y2,
10     o.cost*n.length_m/o.length_m, o.reverse_cost*n.length_m/o.length_m,
11         o.cost_s*n.length_m/o.length_m, o.reverse_cost_s*n.length_m/o.length_m,
12         o.rule, o.one_way, o.maxspeed_forward, o.maxspeed_backward,
13         o.osm_id, o.source_osm, o.target_osm, o.priority, n.geom
14     FROM (SELECT * FROM ospr.ways WHERE length_m > 0) AS o
15         INNER JOIN (
16       SELECT old_id, sub_id, COUNT(sub_id) OVER (PARTITION BY old_id) as num_segs,
```

```
17        the_geom As geom, ST_StartPoint(the_geom) As sp, ST_EndPoint(the_geom) As ep,
18           ST_Length(the_geom) As length,  ST_Length(the_geom::geography) As length_m
19        FROM ospr.ways_noded
20        ) As n On ( o.gid = n.old_id and n.num_segs > 1 );
```

Line 1 creates a new column in the original table called `old_id`. This new column will only be filled in for the new split edges we are appending from ospr.ways_noded. *Line 14* creates a subquery called *o* used to pick attributes from the original edge before it was split. We are filtering out edges that have no length since they are single point junctures and would cause division by zero if we left them in. If you wanted to exclude overpasses and underpasses, you could do so in this subquery. *Lines 16-19* creates a subquery we call *n* which represents the edges that are split. Note the use of window aggregation in *line 16* for the `num_segs`. For each edge that is a subset of a larger original edge, this value will be > 1 and will be the same count for all edges that belong to the same original edge. In *line 20* we use this to only join with those original edges that are split. In many cases the split edges share the same attributes as the original edge, but in cases such as cost, the costs should be distributed across the segments. We make the assumption that any segment cost is just a percentage of the original cost where the percentage is that the percent of the segment length / original length as follows `segment_cost = original_cost*segment_length/original_length`. In *lines 10-11* you see this logic in effect.

After this exercise, we will have the original set of edges plus the new set of edges formed by splitting the edges. We need to get rid of those original unsplit edges. Since those we inserted are the only ones that have old_ids and that old_id matches the original gid, we can delete the original edges with this step.

Listing 9.2: Delete original edges that have been split

```
DELETE FROM ospr.ways
WHERE old_id IS NULL
    AND gid IN(SELECT o.old_id
        FROM ospr.ways AS o
        WHERE o.old_id IS NOT NULL);
```

Now that the duplicate edges have been removed, next we'll need to regenerate new node ids and re-update the source and target fields with the new node ids. To do so, we rerun `pgr_createTopology` as shown in listing 9.3. Note the use of the `clean` argument to force re-generation and update of all nodes. By default `pgr_createTopology` will only populate the the vertices table and edge table for records with no assigned nodes. Since we deleted some edges, we've got orphans that may be connected to existing edges that we want to purge. So its safest to just rebuild it.

Listing 9.3: Recompute topology

```
SELECT pgr_createTopology('ospr.ways',  0.00001, 'the_geom', 'gid', clean:= true
```

The output will look like:

```
NOTICE:  PROCESSING:
NOTICE:  pgr_createTopology('ospr.ways',... 'gid',... rows_where := 'true', clean
NOTICE:  Performing checks, please wait .....
NOTICE:  Creating Topology, Please wait...
NOTICE:  1000 edges processed
NOTICE:  2000 edges processed
:
NOTICE:  33000 edges processed
NOTICE:  ------------> TOPOLOGY CREATED FOR  33731 edges
NOTICE:  Rows with NULL geometry or NULL id: 0
NOTICE:  Vertices table for table ospr.ways is: ospr.ways_vertices_pgr
NOTICE:  ---------------------------------------------

Total query runtime: 27.0 secs
```

To spot check the revised graph, we rerun the analyze graph checker:

Listing 9.4: Reanalyze graph

The output, as expected, looks like the same as what we got running on `ospr.ways_noded`.

```
NOTICE:  PROCESSING:
NOTICE:  pgr_analyzeGraph('ospr.ways',1e-005,'the_geom','gid',...)
NOTICE:  Performing checks, please wait ...
NOTICE:  Analyzing for dead ends. Please wait...
NOTICE:  Analyzing for gaps. Please wait...
NOTICE:  Analyzing for isolated edges. Please wait...
```

```
NOTICE:   Analyzing for ring geometries. Please wait...
NOTICE:   Analyzing for intersections. Please wait...
NOTICE:             ANALYSIS RESULTS FOR SELECTED EDGES:
NOTICE:                    Isolated segments: 10
NOTICE:                            Dead ends: 1765
NOTICE:   Potential gaps found near dead ends: 10
NOTICE:                Intersections detected: 0
NOTICE:                       Ring geometries: 14

Total query runtime: 3.2 secs
1 row retrieved.
```

Our next step is to deal with the directionality of edges and making
sure one-way street directions make sense.

Fixing Directionality Issues

pgRouting comes with a function called pgr_analyzeOneway which
is useful for finding directionality issues. It will analyze streets in
a graph based on directionality rules stated and will flag any edges
that violate the rules.

The table created by osm2pgrouting had one column called *one_way*
to denote if a road is bidirectional, one-way, or sometimes one-way
and sometimes bidirectional. The values for the DC dataset have
the following values:

-1 one-way in opposite direction of how edge is drawn

0 unknown

1 one-way in direction edge is drawn

2 two way

3 reversible (one-way depending on factor such as time of day)

> If you are working with raw OSM data, the one-way designations are a little dif-
> ferent and sometimes text. osm2pgrouting converts them to numbers for ease
> of use. Refer to http://wiki.openstreetmap.org/wiki/Key:oneway if you need to
> work directly with the original raw OSM data.

If it is one-way, the edges should be drawn such that the direction of the one-way is from source node to target node. Traffic would come from source and into target.

During analysis, pgr_analyzeOneway will update the columns ein, eout, and cnt of the companion vertices_pgr table. pgr_analyzeOneway takes as input four text arrays in addition to the standard table name, source and target. The four text arrays denote the rules for directionality. The rules for directionality are values that can be found in the oneway designated column. By default any values not in the stated set of rules will be treated as bidirectional. This next listing checks for directionality issues in ospr.ways.

Listing 9.5: Check for one-way issues

```
1   SELECT pgr_analyzeOneway('ospr.ways',
2       s_in_rules:= ARRAY['0', '-1', '2','3'],
3       s_out_rules:= ARRAY['0', '1','2','3'],
4       t_in_rules:= ARRAY['0', '1','2','3'],
5       t_out_rules:= ARRAY['0', '-1','2','3'],
6       oneway:= 'one_way');
```

We are using named arguments for this exercise except for the first argument (the table name). Named argument syntax is a PostgreSQL feature supported for functions with named input arguments. The inputs to the functions, if named, do not need to be in the order of the arguments of the function. Named argument calling syntax is especially useful for functions that take a lot of optional arguments, where some of the optional arguments you want to specify are not at the end of the function list and can't be simply left out. It's also useful if the function takes a lot of arguments of the same type and you don't want to worry about specifying them in the wrong order. The names used must be those that are part of the function definition. You can find these listed in the pgRouting help manual or by inspecting the function definition via pgAdmin, or in psql using \df:

```
\connect pgr
\df pgr_analyzeOneway
```

The output of the above `psql` call is:

```
Schema |        Name      | Result data ..|     Argument data types     | Type
-------+------------------+---------------+-----------------------------------------------
public | pgr_analyzeoneway| text          | edge_table text,            | normal
                                          | s_in_rules text[],
                                          | s_out_rules text[],
                                          | t_in_rules text[],
                                          | t_out_rules text[],
                                          | two_way_if_null boolean DEFAULT true,
                                          | oneway text DEFAULT 'oneway'::text,
                                          | source text DEFAULT ..
                                          | target text DEFAULT ..
(1 row)
```

Some functions don't have named arguments, and thus can't be called with named argument syntax.

> In PostgreSQL 9.5+, named arguments can be called with just =>. So instead of doing `arg_name:= val`, you may see `arg_name => val`. This new syntax is not backward-compatible with older versions, so use `arg_name:= val` if you need your code to be backward-compatible.

Line 7 denotes the column name for the oneway designation column which will be used as input to the directionality rules. We excluded the option `source` and `target` arguments which denote the name of `source` and `target` columns—since those default to `'source'` and `'target'` if not specified.

Line 2 is the `s_in_rules` argument and denotes the array of values in the one_way column that are valid for traffic coming into the source node of the edge. Note for the case we have where 1 denotes a one-way where traffic comes out of source and into target, source in is not allowed.

Line 3 is the `s_out_rules` argument and denotes the array of values allowed in the one_way that are valid for traffic coming out of the source node of the edge. In this case both bidirectional one_way=0 and one_way=1 one-way roads can have traffic coming out of their source nodes.

Lines 4-5 follow the same pattern except designating rules for traffic coming into and out of the `target` nodes of the edge.

For simplicity we are treating 3 as bidirectional meaning traffic can come in or out of source / target since in theory it depends on other factors. So all our rules have 0,2,3 denoting that they are bidirectional (traffic can come in or out of either source or target nodes).

The output is as follows:

```
NOTICE:  PROCESSING:
NOTICE:  pgr_analyzeOneway('ospr.ways','{0,-1,2,3}',..,'one_way','source','target
NOTICE:  Analyzing graph for one way street errors.
NOTICE:  Analysis 25% complete ...
NOTICE:  Analysis 50% complete ...
NOTICE:  Analysis 75% complete ...
NOTICE:  Analysis 100% complete ...
NOTICE:  Found 108 potential problems in directionality


Total query runtime: 1.9 secs
1 row retrieved.
```

`pgr_analyzeOneway` populates the `cnt`, `chk`, `ein`, and `eout` fields of the corresponding vertices table for the edge, `ospr.ways_vertices_pgr`.

In a stable system, (think fluid flow) if you don't want flow to be stuck at a node, any flow coming thru a pipe (edge) from source has to be able to come out of target node and vice versa. Since `pgr_analyzeOneway` uses the vertices table for bookkeeping, we can itemize all the nodes where there is a directionality problem with:

Listing 9.6: Itemize one-way node issues
```
SELECT id, ein, eout, the_geom
  FROM ospr.ways_vertices_pgr
  WHERE ( ein = 0 and eout > 0 ) or ( eout = 0 and ein > 0);
```

As expected, the number of rows is equal to the number of potential problems noted by `pgr_analyzeOneway`.

To get the list of the related edges, we'd use this query:

Listing 9.7: Itemize one-way edge issues

```
WITH pn As (SELECT id, ein, eout
    FROM ospr.ways_vertices_pgr
    WHERE ( ein = 0 and eout > 0 ) or ( eout = 0 and ein > 0) )
SELECT e.*
FROM (SELECT gid, the_geom, source, target, rule, cost, reverse_cost
    FROM ospr.ways ) As e
    WHERE EXISTS(SELECT 1 FROM pn
        WHERE pn.id = e.source or pn.id = e.target);
```

To graphically see where the issues are, we can plot both these queries on QGIS, and use Marker Set labeling to draw an arrow in direction of the edge. The output should look something like Figure 9.1, on the following page.

The green circles in Figure 9.1, on the next page are the location of nodes where we have directionality issues. The red arrows are the direction of the edge draw. The numbers 1 or -1 denote what should be one-ways in the direction or opposite direction of edge.

At a quick glance, quite a few of the problem nodes look like nodes that should have been merged. This might have been solved by increasing tolerance when running pgr_createTopology or pgr_nodeNetwork at the risk of merging things that should not be merged. Alternatively we can do it after the fact by just dealing with these problem nodes and updating the source and target accordingly where nodes are sufficiently close enough to be considered the same node.

Listing 9.8: Merge problem nodes within tolerance of each other

```
WITH pn As (SELECT id, the_geom As geom
    FROM ospr.ways_vertices_pgr
    WHERE ( ein = 0 and eout > 0 ) or ( eout = 0 and ein > 0) ),
pmerge AS ( SELECT o.id As old_id, MIN(n.id) AS new_id
    FROM pn AS o INNER JOIN pn AS n ON ST_DWithin(o.geom, n.geom, 0.0001)
    GROUP BY o.id)
UPDATE ospr.ways AS w
SET source = CASE WHEN n.old_id = source THEN n.new_id ELSE source END,
    target = CASE WHEN n.old_id = target THEN n.new_id ELSE target END,
    the_geom = ST_SetPoint(ST_SetPoint(w.the_geom, 0,
        CASE WHEN n.old_id = source
            THEN n.the_geom ELSE ST_StartPoint(w.the_geom) END ),
        ST_NPoints(w.the_geom) - 1,
            CASE WHEN n.old_id = target
```

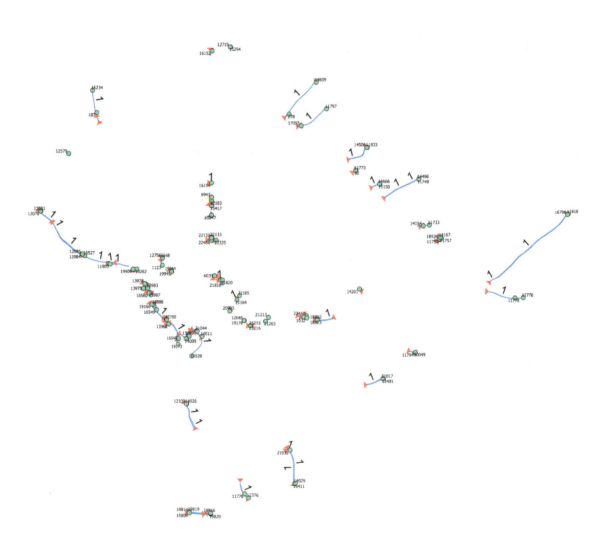

Figure 9.1: QGIS view of directional
issues

```
              THEN n.the_geom ELSE ST_EndPoint(w.the_geom) END)
FROM (
SELECT pmerge.*, n.the_geom
FROM pmerge INNER JOIN ospr.ways_vertices_pgr As n On (pmerge.new_id = n.id)
WHERE old_id <> new_id ) AS n
WHERE w.source = n.old_id or w.target = n.old_id;
```

We can then delete orphaned nodes with:

Listing 9.9: Delete orphan nodes

```
DELETE FROM ospr.ways_vertices_pgr AS v
WHERE NOT EXISTS (SELECT 1
    FROM ospr.ways AS w WHERE w.source = v.id or w.target = v.id);
```

After running this update, if we then rerun our analyze graph and one-way, we've alleviated a couple of dead end and directionality issues.

```
NOTICE:  PROCESSING:
NOTICE:  pgr_analyzeGraph('ospr.ways',1e-005,'the_geom'...
NOTICE:  Performing checks, please wait ...
NOTICE:  Analyzing for dead ends. Please wait...
NOTICE:  Analyzing for gaps. Please wait...
NOTICE:  Analyzing for isolated edges. Please wait...
NOTICE:  Analyzing for ring geometries. Please wait...
NOTICE:  Analyzing for intersections. Please wait...
NOTICE:            ANALYSIS RESULTS FOR SELECTED EDGES:
NOTICE:                  Isolated segments: 10
NOTICE:                          Dead ends: 1755
NOTICE:  Potential gaps found near dead ends: 10
NOTICE:              Intersections detected: 0
NOTICE:                     Ring geometries: 15


NOTICE:  PROCESSING:
NOTICE:  pgr_analyzeOneway('ospr.ways','{0,-1,2,3}...)
NOTICE:  Analyzing graph for one way street errors.
NOTICE:  Analysis 25% complete ...
NOTICE:  Analysis 50% complete ...
NOTICE:  Analysis 75% complete ...
NOTICE:  Analysis 100% complete ...
NOTICE:  Found 97 potential problems in directionality
```

9.3   Defining Costs

There are two types of costs in pgRouting. There is the regular cost, generally referred to as cost which denotes the cost of travel from source node to target node and, in cases where directionality doesn't matter, would also be used for travel from target to source. Then there is the reverse_cost which denotes the travel in the reverse direction of how the edge is drawn. Our directionality rules check in the prior section, did not double-check to make sure the cost and reverse_cost values are set in accordance of our directionality rules. In the case of this OSM data, we would expect reverse_cost to be negative in cases where one_way is 1 to denote traffic only flows in direction of how the edge is drawn. Ultimately all the functions in pgRouting only care about the columns you denote as cost and reverse_cost. In cases such as the one_way=3, you could dynamically replace such costs with a formula that depends on time of day, for example, if you have that additional information.

> Versions of pgRouting prior to 2.1 required all costs columns to be positive, meaning that your edge geometries always had to be drawn such that the direction of the edge matched the direction of the one-way. In cases where it wasn't, you'd have to use something like the PostGIS ST_Reverse function to flip the direction of the edge.

The data loaded by osm2pgrouting has a couple of columns we can choose from for costing. We can go by time in seconds which is a function of the max speed limit or assumed max speed limit and directionality is based on rules only relevant when you are driving. If you are walking or biking, your costs would be vastly different. To have costs based on some other travel strategy such as walking, we could do one of the following:

1. Add a new cost column and reverse_cost (if direction is relevant) to the existing table
2. Create a side-line table with new costs but same edge ids, only having edge ids where our choice of travel is valid.
3. Have some sort of function that outputs the cost given some set

of parameters.

Using Functional Costs

We'll go with option three for our first example. Keep in mind using option three is probably not the most efficient, so you may want to experiment with it to see how slow it is. At any rate, it is still useful for what-if type analysis that you can then use to statically define costs. We'll create a walking function that gives us cost in time (minutes).

For walking, let's make the following assumptions:

1. Directionality does not matter. If you had data such as a DEM, you could conceivably compute the z-slope of a street (by intersection of raster DEM) and then use that to compute a reverse_cost that is different from cost. Since we don't have such data for DC, we'll dismiss that option.
2. Assume that a person is not allowed to walk on motorways, motorway_junctions, or motorway links. Looking at ospr.osm_way_classes, we'd return negative costs for class_ids (101,102, 103)
3. Assume an average walker can walk one mile per hour.

The resulting function would look something like:

Listing 9.10: Walking function

```
CREATE OR REPLACE FUNCTION walking_cost(param_class_id integer,
    param_length_m float8) RETURNS float8 AS
$$
  SELECT CASE WHEN $1 IN(101,102, 103) THEN -1
    ELSE $2/1609.34*60 END
$$
language 'sql';
```

and we would use it as follows:

Listing 9.11: Walking function usage in pgr_dijkstra

```
SELECT r.seq, r.node, w.name As street,  r.cost,
  ( SUM(r.cost) OVER(ORDER BY r.seq) )::numeric(10,2) As time_minutes
 FROM pgr_dijkstra('SELECT gid AS id,
         source,
```

```
        target,
        walking_cost(class_id, length_m) As cost
        FROM ospr.ways',
    pgr_pointToEdgeNode('ospr.ways',
      ST_SetSRID( ST_Point(-77.009003, 38.889931)
      , 4326)
      , 0.01)  ,
    pgr_pointToEdgeNode('ospr.ways',
      ST_SetSRID( ST_Point(-77.036545, 38.897096), 4326)
      , 0.01) , false) AS r
        LEFT JOIN ospr.ways AS w ON r.edge = w.gid;



-- add cost columns to routes
```

Defining Costs Based on Attributes and Consideration for Long Distance

For this next example, we'll use data from `http://openflights.org` that we have installed in schema `of`. This is a revisit of our airport/route examples, but with real data and a larger set of airports. You can build the `of` schema yourself from the source data, or restore the of.backup file included in the book download.

The OpenFlight data includes a routes dataset consisting of commercial airlines and their standard commuter routes. It however is devoid of pricing information and length/time of travel. It also doesn't include the time(s) of the day each travel option is available. Given the lack of information, we can still make educated guesses about some things based on attributes provided.

1. Number of stops—we can make a guess that each stop delays you by 1.5 hours from your destination vs. going straight.

2, Kind of airplane used—each kind has a cruising speed we can lookup and infer time

3. Geographic distance between source and target airports
4. Each route represented is a one-way directed route, so we can ignore reverse_cost in all cases and assume all our queries will be directed.

Given these inputs we can make assumptions about time of flight. The cost of an airline ticket is a bit trickier. Ticket fares are a function of operating cost per mile or kilometer which varies widely based on routes and is cheaper on more popular routes. We'll make the wide generalization that each kilometer flown costs the airline 8 cents, of which they markup by 20% and always tack on a $50 surcharge.

Non-stop flights are also generally pricier than flights with many stops and the price increases with length of flight. We must emphasize that these are vast generalizations. We are also not taking into consideration here exchange rate effects which can significantly reduce the cost in airfare. The Canadian/US exchange rate and proximity of Canada to US for example often makes US Citizens drive across the border to fly a Canadian airline. Also note that since we are dealing with world data where there could be issues like over the date-line and where the shorted Cartesian distance does not always mean shortest spheroidal distance, we cast our geometries to geography so we get a spheroidal distance calculation in meters.

Listing 9.12: Assigning costs to flight routes

```
ALTER TABLE of.routes ADD COLUMN time_minutes float8;
ALTER TABLE of.routes ADD COLUMN price_us float8;

UPDATE of.routes AS r
    SET time_minutes = 60 + 1.5*60*stops + ST_Length(geom::geography)
        /1000/ar.speed_kph*60,
    price_us = (50 +
        ST_Length(geom::geography)
            /1000*(0.06)*(1.1 - 0.03*r.stops))::numeric(10,2)
FROM  (SELECT COALESCE(MIN(a.speed_kph),500) As speed_kph, r.id
FROM of.routes As   r
    LEFT JOIN of.equipment AS a ON a.equipment_id = ANY(r.equipment)
GROUP BY r.id) As ar
WHERE ar.id = r.id;
```

We must stress that our assumptions are very simplistic. For example we assume all connections are available all the time and that the reputation of the airline and services they offer on the plane (which greatly changes pricing) have no bearing on cost.

10 Multiple Routes to Single Destination (KSP)

10.1 Getting Multiple Solutions to a Travel Using pgr_ksp

In many routing problems, you may wish to see more than the optimal solution; you may wish to view the top five or ten solutions. The pgr_ksp function is well-suited for this task.

For these exercises, we use airport and airlines data from http://openflights.org/. The data is included in the data download for this book.

Code for this section is in `code/finding_multiple_routes.sql` of this book's download file.

pgr_ksp is another function that changed in pgRouting 2.0. Although you can use the old deprecated call syntax (where last argument is `has_reverse_cost`) the newer syntax determines if reverse cost calculation is needed based on whether the `SELECT` statement argument defining edge network has a column named `reverse_cost`. The newer calling syntax has the more descriptive output columns `seq`, `path_id`, `path_seq`, `node`, `edge`, `cost`, and `agg_cost` instead of the older less meaningful `seq`, `id1`, `id2`, and `id3`. In examples that follow, we'll be using the newer syntax. For a similar query using the old syntax, see pgr_ksp pgRouting 2.0 syntax, on page 267.

Let's say you're in the market for an airline ticket from Newark, NJ to Mumbai, India. You want the cheapest ticket, but you may not want to fly on the cheapest. Perhaps, you may have a grudge against the airline or balk at the strange routing (flying over the Pacific rather than the Atlantic, for example). You want to scan through a range of cheap airfares.

Listing 10.1 will provide you with the top three cheapest flights.

Listing 10.1: pgr_ksp 2.1+ to find multiple solutions

```
SELECT
```

```
        k.path_id AS sol,
        k.path_seq AS lgn,
        COALESCE(a.name || ': ' || s.city || ' - ' || t.city, 'Total Trip') AS leg,
        CASE WHEN k.edge = -1 THEN k.agg_cost ELSE NULL END AS total_cost
FROM
    pgr_ksp(
        'SELECT id, source, target, price_us AS cost FROM of.routes ',
        (SELECT id FROM of.airports WHERE icao = 'KEWR'),
        (SELECT id FROM of.airports WHERE icao = 'VABB'),
        3,
        directed := TRUE
    ) AS k LEFT JOIN
    of.routes AS r ON k.edge = r.id LEFT JOIN
    of.airports AS s ON r.source = s.id LEFT JOIN
    of.airports AS t ON r.target = t.id LEFT JOIN
    of.airlines AS a ON r.airline_id = a.airline_id
ORDER BY k.path_id, k.path_seq;
```

Listing 10.1, on the preceding page gives us:

```
 sol | lgn |                      leg                       | total_cost
-----+-----+------------------------------------------------+-----------
   1 |   1 | United Airlines: Newark - Mumbai               |
   1 |   2 | Total Trip                                     |    879.26
   2 |   1 | Delta Air Lines: Newark - Amsterdam            |
   2 |   2 | KLM Royal Dutch Airlines: Amsterdam - Mumbai   |
   2 |   3 | Total Trip                                     |    941.54
   3 |   1 | Etihad Airways: Newark - Brussels              |
   3 |   2 | Jet Airways: Brussels - Mumbai                 |
   3 |   3 | Total Trip                                     |    944.55
(8 rows)
```

```
Time: 247.882 ms
```

Similar to pgr_dijkstra, pgr_ksp solves the problem of: given a
source and destination node, what edges need to be traversed to
accomplish the task. Unlike *pgr_dijkstra*, it returns multiple answers
to the question, and as a result, needs to output path_id column to
denote which segments belong to which path answer. The path_id
is just a sequential numbering from 1 to i<= n where n is the number of answers requested.

Note that path_seq is also used by pgr_ksp similar to the pgr_dijkstra
variant that takes an array of destinations to denote the order within

the answer of the segment. Instead of asking multiple questions and expecting one solution per question, with `pgr_ksp` we are asking one question and expecting multiple solutions to the question.

The inputs of `pgr_ksp` are very similar to `pgr_dijkstra`, except `pgr_ksp` by default assumes a directed graph (you can change this with `directed:=false`).

In the directed case, it only computes the path in the direction of the edges unless you also provide a `reverse_cost` column in your query. We also need to tell the function how many answers we want back as denoted by the number 3, the last unnamed argument in the `pgr_ksp` function call. Since we asked for three solutions we got solutions numbered from 1-3 where each set denotes an answer to the question and the lowest numbered solution is the best answer.

What if we wanted to restrict travel to only legs originating in Newark or Brussels. Our revised query would look like:

Listing 10.2: pgr_ksp 2.1+ only allow originating from Brussels or Newark

```
SELECT
    k.path_id AS sol,
    k.path_seq AS lgn,
    COALESCE(al.name || ': ' || s.city || ' - ' || t.city, 'Total Trip') AS leg,
    CASE WHEN k.edge = -1 THEN k.agg_cost ELSE NULL END AS total_cost
FROM
    pgr_ksp(
        'SELECT id, source, target, price_us AS cost
        FROM of.routes
        WHERE source = ANY (' ||
        quote_literal(
            ARRAY(
                SELECT id FROM of.airports WHERE city IN ('Newark','Brussels')
            )
        ) ||
        '::integer[])',
        (SELECT id FROM of.airports WHERE icao = 'KEWR'),
        (SELECT id FROM of.airports WHERE icao = 'VABB'),
        3,
        directed := TRUE
    ) AS k LEFT JOIN
    of.routes AS r ON k.edge = r.id LEFT JOIN
    of.airports AS s ON r.source = s.id LEFT JOIN
```

```
        of.airports AS t ON r.target = t.id LEFT JOIN
        of.airlines AS al ON r.airline_id = al.airline_id
    ORDER BY k.path_id, k.path_seq;
```

Our solution with a leg originating from Amsterdam would be removed

```
sol | lgn |              leg                | total_cost
----+-----+---------------------------------+-----------
  1 |   1 | United Airlines: Newark - Mumbai |
  1 |   2 | Total Trip                       |     879.26
  2 |   1 | Etihad Airways: Newark - Brussels |
  2 |   2 | Jet Airways: Brussels - Mumbai   |
  2 |   3 | Total Trip                       |     944.55
(5 rows)
```

```
Time: 75.110 ms
```

As expected, our solutions only include flights that stop in Brussels
or are direct flights. You can perform similar restrictions, for example on airlines if you have frequent flyer miles on only one or two
airlines and want to restrict your travel to those, or hate a particular airline for some reason. Although we only demonstrated this
filtering in pgr_ksp, the same kind of filtering can be done with any
routing functions that take a query for input.

10.2 Getting Only One Row per Path Solution with Total Cost

In many cases, you don't want a bunch of rows per solution, you
just want one row and also have that row include aggregate cost.
Just as in the case of pgr_dijkstra there is a special edge that has
an edge_id = -1. This denotes the end of the trip. Since it's the
end, the agg_cost denotes the total cost of that trip path. In prior
examples, we marked these as 'Total Trip' since they would be the
only segments that have no matching edge. Here is how you would
write such a query if you just want the cost.

Listing 10.3: pgr_ksp 2.1+ Single row per solution with total cost

```
1  SELECT
```

```
2        k.path_id AS sol,
3        string_agg(n.city, ' - ' ORDER BY path_seq) AS route,
4        MAX(CASE WHEN k.edge = -1 THEN k.agg_cost ELSE NULL END) AS total
5    FROM
6        pgr_ksp(
7            'SELECT id, source, target, price_us AS cost FROM of.routes',
8            (SELECT id FROM of.airports WHERE icao = 'KEWR'),
9            (SELECT id FROM of.airports WHERE icao = 'VABB'),
10           3,
11           directed := TRUE
12       ) AS k INNER JOIN of.airports AS n
13       ON k.node = n.id
14   GROUP BY k.path_id;
```

This query is very similar to our earlier ones, except for three key differences. We aren't outputting the edges since our resulting answer will just list nodes hopped; our prior answer left out the -1 edge since it was filtered out by the INNER JOIN with airport_routes. We are using the PostgreSQL string_agg function which, like all PostgreSQL aggregate functions (since PostgreSQL 9.0), includes an optional ORDER BY clause to control the order of aggregation. The node names will be glued together based on order of travel denoted by path_seq. Finally, to get the total cost, we use a CASE statement in *line 4* that will only return a value for the -1 edge and exclude the NULLs using the aggregate MAX function. Grouping by solution number in *line 14* ensures we get only one row per path solution.

The resulting output is:

```
 sol |            route            |  total
-----+-----------------------------+--------
   1 | Newark - Mumbai             | 879.26
   2 | Newark - Amsterdam - Mumbai | 941.54
   3 | Newark - Brussels - Mumbai  | 944.55
(3 rows)


Time: 157.711 ms
```

10.3 *Handling Parallel Routes with pgr_ksp*

The approach that pgr_ksp uses has a problem when you have edges that have the same source and target nodes. If you look closely at the of.routes, there are two nonstop flights between Newark and Mumbai.

Listing 10.4: Direct flights from Newark to Mumbai

```
SELECT * FROM of.routes WHERE source = 3494 and target = 2997;
```

They also have the same cost. So both should have come up as solutions in the queries, but one was arbitrarily chosen. Even if they did have different costs, one would be left out. The issue and work-around for this situation is detailed in the pgRouting docs "Handling parallels after getting a path" (http://loc8.cc//pgr/parallell_handling).

The basic workaround for the issue is to join back the KSP solution with your edges table to pick out the edges that were excluded. If they happen to have same costs as in our case, our solution is simple, we just aggregate and show to the user that they have several airline options for flying a particular leg of a trip.

Listing 10.5: Handling Parallel Routes

```
WITH ksp AS (
    SELECT path_id AS sol, path_seq AS leg, node, edge
    FROM
    pgr_ksp(
        'SELECT id, source, target, price_us AS cost FROM of.routes',
        (SELECT id FROM of.airports WHERE icao = 'KEWR'),
        (SELECT id FROM of.airports WHERE icao = 'VABB'),
        3,
        directed := TRUE
    )
)
SELECT
    sol, leg,
    string_agg(al.name, E'\r') AS airlines,
    r.source_airport_iata_faa AS sap,
    r.destination_airport_iata_faa AS tap,
    array_agg(DISTINCT r.price_us) AS prices
FROM
    ksp INNER JOIN
    of.routes AS r1 ON ksp.edge = r1.id INNER JOIN
    of.routes AS r ON r1.source = r.source AND r1.target = r.target LEFT JOIN
    of.airlines AS al ON r.airline_id = al.airline_id
GROUP BY sol,leg, r.source_airport_iata_faa, r.destination_airport_iata_faa
ORDER BY sol,leg;
```

The output of Listing 10.5, on the preceding page is:

```
 sol | leg |         airlines          | sap | tap |   prices
-----+-----+---------------------------+-----+-----+----------
   1 |   1 | United Airlines           | EWR | BOM | {879.26}
     |     | Air India Limited         |     |     |
   2 |   1 | Lufthansa                 | EWR | AMS | {438.37}
     |     | United Airlines           |     |     |
     |     | Delta Air Lines           |     |     |
     |     | KLM Royal Dutch Airlines  |     |     |
   2 |   2 | KLM Royal Dutch Airlines  | AMS | BOM | {503.17}
     |     | Delta Air Lines           |     |     |
   3 |   1 | United Airlines           | EWR | BRU | {440.93}
     |     | Jet Airways               |     |     |
     |     | Brussels Airlines         |     |     |
     |     | Lufthansa                 |     |     |
     |     | Etihad Airways            |     |     |
   3 |   2 | Brussels Airlines         | BRU | BOM | {503.62}
     |     | Jet Airways               |     |     |
(5 rows)


 Time: 216.993 ms
```

11 *Dijkstra In-depth*

The Dijkstra family of pgRouting functions is the most extensively used and tested of the pgRouting functions. We saw some examples of these earlier in the book. In this section we'll get into more detail on how to use Dijkstra functions.

Code for this section is in `code/dijkstra.sql` of this book's download file.

11.1 Routing Between Two Points that are Not Nodes in Network

Most pgRouting routing functions are designed to route between nodes in a network. What happens when your desired start and end points are not always nodes in your network or sufficiently close enough to nodes in your network?

There are two common ways of dealing with this case.

In pgRouting 2.1 and below, you would have to find the edges your start and end points fall on and then for the first edge returned in your solution, take the closest node on each edge for your start and end node. Then after the route segments are returned, take only that portion of the first edge from the start node to where your start point falls, and for the last edge, return only that portion of the edge up through your end point.

pgRouting 2.2+ provides a second option, and that option is to inject your points into the network as virtual nodes using the `pgr_withPoints` Dijkstra based function. The virtual nodes are passed in as an argument to the function and only exist for that particular call of the function. `pgr_withPoints` works exactly like `pgr_dijkstra` except it takes an additional argument which is an SQL statement denoting the virtual nodes you want to be part of the network.

In this section we'll demonstrate both approaches.

> pgr_withPoints in 2.2 and 2.3 is marked as a proposed stable function. This means it could change signature in pgRouting 3.0.

Using Linear Interpolation to Approximate Node Location

Both approaches require some linear interpolation to compute where your points fall on the closest edge. The common approach is to use PostGIS linear interpolation functions ST_LineLocatePoint and also as needed, ST_LineSubString.

To aid us in this endeavor, we'll create a helper function that will take an SQL statement defining our network as well as an array of points and return a table consisting of closest edge, node, side of street, and a virtual node id number. We'll be using this function with both approaches.

In order to contend with determining the side of street a point is on, we'll create another utility function called upgr_sideOfStreet. This function is shown in Listing 11.1.

Listing 11.1: upgr_sideOfStreet function to determine side of street

```
1   CREATE OR REPLACE FUNCTION upgr_sideOfStreet(param_line_geom geometry,
2       param_pt_geom geometry) RETURNS text AS
3   $$
4   DECLARE geom_l geometry; geom_r geometry; dist float;
5   BEGIN
6       dist := ST_Distance(param_line_geom, param_pt_geom) ;
7       geom_l := ST_OffsetCurve(param_line_geom, dist ); -- left side
8       geom_r := ST_OffsetCurve(param_line_geom, -dist); -- right side
9   -- Figure out which side the point is closest too
10      RETURN CASE WHEN ST_Distance(geom_l, param_pt_geom)
11              < least(dist, ST_Distance(geom_r, param_pt_geom)) THEN 'l'
12          WHEN ST_Distance(geom_r, param_pt_geom) < dist THEN 'r'
13          ELSE 'b' END;
14  END;
15  $$
16  language 'plpgsql';
```

> The side of street is an optional column in many functions. It's relevant when
> driving and you can only drive on one side of the street. We won't be using
> side of street for the first set of examples.

The upgr_sideOfStreet function uses the PostGIS ST_OffsetCurve
function to create two parallel lines to the right and left of an edge.
It then determines which side of the street a point is on, by looking
at which of the three linestrings (left, center line (the edge), or right)
the point is closest to.

We can now incorporate upgr_sideOfStreet function in our virtual
node generation function upgr_vnodes as shown in Listing 11.2.

Listing 11.2: Function definition virtual nodes

```
1   CREATE OR REPLACE FUNCTION
2       upgr_vnodes(param_network_sql text,
3       param_pts geometry[], param_tolerance float DEFAULT 0.01)
4   RETURNS TABLE (id bigint, pid bigint, edge_id bigint,
5       fraction float, side text, closest_node bigint) AS
6   $$
7   -- network sql must contain edge_id, geom, source, target
8   DECLARE var_sql text;
9   BEGIN
10    var_sql := ' WITH p AS (
11    SELECT id::bigint AS id, f.geom
12      FROM unnest($1) WITH ORDINALITY AS f(geom, id)
13      )
14    SELECT p.id, CASE WHEN e.fraction < 0.01 THEN e.source
15          WHEN e.fraction > 0.99 THEN e.target ELSE -p.id END::bigint AS pid,
16          e.edge_id::bigint, e.fraction,
17            upgr_sideOfStreet(e.geom, p.geom) As side,
18          CASE WHEN e.fraction <= 0.5 THEN e.source
19          ELSE e.target END As closest_node
20    FROM p,
21      LATERAL (
22      SELECT w.id As edge_id, w.source, w.target, cost,
23       ST_LineLocatePoint(w.geom, p.geom) AS fraction, w.geom
24       FROM (' || param_network_sql || ') As w
25         WHERE ST_DWithin(p.geom, w.geom, $2)
26       ORDER BY ST_Distance(p.geom, w.geom) LIMIT 1 ) AS e ';
27    RETURN QUERY EXECUTE var_sql USING param_pts, param_tolerance;
28  END;
29  $$ language 'plpgsql';
```

> WITH ORDINALITY is an ANSI SQL construct introduced in PostgreSQL 9.4.
> For lower versions this function will not install. In many cases, you will want to
> use your own generated nodes from a serial key so can take out the return of
> pid from the function.

To use the function in Listing 11.2, on the preceding page we would
do the following:

Listing 11.3: Convert array of points to row of nodes

```
SELECT id, pid, side, edge_id, fraction::numeric(10,4) As frac, side
    FROM upgr_vnodes(
    $$SELECT gid As id, source, target, the_geom As geom,
            cost
    FROM ospr.ways$$,
    ARRAY[ ST_SetSRID( ST_Point(-77.009003, 38.889931), 4326),
        ST_SetSRID( ST_Point(-77.036545, 38.897096), 4326)  ] );
```

> For this query and many others we are using dollar-quoting PostgreSQL syn-
> tax. Dollar-quoting is useful if you have single quotes in your SQL. You don't
> need to escape the quotes if you are using dollar-quoting for the string.

The output of which returns:

```
id |  pid  | side | edge_id |  frac  | side
---+-------+------+---------+--------+------
 1 | 11280 | b    |   29793 | 1.0000 | b
 2 |    -2 | r    |   30413 | 0.0424 | r
(2 rows)
```

For this set of exercises, we are going to assume walking as the
mode of travel, so the only thing relevant is the length of the streets;
directionality of roads is not important.

Computing Partial Edge Costs

The first approach is to use the regular Dijkstra function and revise
the final results to account for the fact that our start and end points
may not fall on an existing node. So we need to compute the cost to
get to the closest start point (which would be the partial cost of edge
our virtual node is on) and compute the cost to get to the closest end
point. Note that if we are already at a node in the network as in the

case in end point of listing 11.2, on page 131, the additional cost is
zero.

Similarly if our location is already on the edge, then we have par-
tially traversed the edge. For this exercise we are assuming walking
so we don't consider direction or side of the street.

Listing 11.4: Routing between points using linear referencing

```
1   WITH
2   vn AS ( SELECT *
3       FROM upgr_vnodes(
4       $$SELECT gid As id, source, target, the_geom As geom,
5               length_m As cost
6         FROM ospr.ways$$,
7         ARRAY[ ST_SetSRID( ST_Point(-77.009003, 38.889931), 4326),
8           ST_SetSRID( ST_Point(-77.036545, 38.897096), 4326)  ] )
9   )
10  SELECT r.edge, r.seq, r.node, w.name As street,
11      ( COALESCE(r.cost,0) +
12          COALESCE( least(vn.fraction, 1-vn.fraction) * wp.length_m ,0) )::numeric(12,4) As cost,
13      SUM( (COALESCE(r.cost,0) +
14          COALESCE( least(vn.fraction, 1-vn.fraction) * wp.length_m ,0) ) )
15              OVER(ORDER BY r.seq)::numeric(10,2) As dist_m
16    FROM pgr_dijkstra($$SELECT gid AS id,
17                        source,
18                        target,
19                        length_m As cost
20                      FROM ospr.ways$$,
21  (SELECT closest_node FROM vn WHERE id = 1) ,
22  (SELECT closest_node FROM vn WHERE id = 2) , false) AS r
23          LEFT JOIN ospr.ways AS w ON r.edge = w.gid
24          LEFT JOIN vn ON ( vn.closest_node = r.node )
25          LEFT JOIN ospr.ways AS wp ON vn.edge_id = wp.gid;
```

```
 edge  | seq | node  |            street            |  cost   | dist_m
-------+-----+-------+------------------------------+---------+--------
 29794 |  1  | 11280 | Capitol Circle Northeast     | 41.9201 |  41.92
  2662 |  2  | 14678 | Northwest Capitol Circle     |  6.9553 |  48.88
  2663 |  3  | 20941 | Northwest Capitol Circle     | 44.8304 |  93.71
  2664 |  4  |  1534 | Northwest Capitol Circle     | 84.1488 | 177.85
 29874 |  5  | 19651 | New Jersey Avenue Northwest  |  6.7183 | 184.57
 :
  8006 |  7  | 18117 | New Jersey Avenue Northwest  | 18.3420 | 208.51
  1652 |  8  |  6839 | Constitution Avenue Northwest| 11.0706 | 219.58
 :
 14199 | 19  |  5614 | Constitution Avenue Northwest| 13.5471 | 749.04
 29926 | 20  |   731 | Pennsylvania Avenue Northwest| 16.1294 | 765.17
 :
```

```
15221 |   56 | 14743 | Pennsylvania Avenue Northwest    |    5.7088 | 2330.91
13597 |   57 |  7864 | E Street Northwest               |   12.4788 | 2343.38
   :
13591 |   63 | 12104 | E Street Northwest               |   26.9853 | 2708.12
   :
 4982 |   67 | 10998 | State Place Northwest            |   69.5127 | 2813.34
25215 |   68 | 18913 | West Executive Avenue Northwest  |    7.6518 | 2820.99
   :
   -1 |   75 | 14141 | NULL                             |    2.3075 | 3005.23
(75 rows)
```

Using pgr_withPoints for Point to Point

pgr_withPoints is a function introduced in pgRouting 2.2 which allows you to route including points that are not vertices in your network.

The simplest form of the function looks like:

```
pgr_withPoints(edges_sql, points_sql, start_vid, end_vid)
```

The edges_sql denotes the SQL of your existing network and is the same as what we saw for pgr_dijkstra. The points_sql consists of the virtual nodes you want to create in your network. At a minimum it must have columns named pid, edge_id, and fraction. The edge_id corresponds to an edge in your network. The fraction is the percent along the edge the point falls on (from 0 to 1).

There is an optional column side, which denotes the side of the road the point falls on. When present this column should have values: b, r, l, or NULL for both, right, left, or unknown.

We repeat the exercise in Listing 11.4, on the preceding page, but using pgr_withPoints in listing 11.5. We are also reusing the upgr_vnodes helper function we created in Listing 11.2, on page 131 which conveniently provides us with the set of columns we need for points_sql.

Listing 11.5: Routing between points

```
1   WITH vn AS (
2       SELECT *
3       FROM upgr_vnodes($$SELECT gid As id, source, target,
4           the_geom As geom, length_m As cost
5           FROM ospr.ways$$, ARRAY[ ST_SetSRID( ST_Point(-77.009003, 38.889931), 4326)
```

```
6            ST_SetSRID( ST_Point(-77.036545, 38.897096), 4326)  ] )
7    )
8    SELECT r.edge, r.seq, r.node,  w.name As street,
9        r.cost::numeric(10,2), r.agg_cost::numeric(10,2)
10   FROM pgr_withPoints($$SELECT gid AS id,
11                              source,
12                              target,
13                              length_m AS cost
14                           FROM ospr.ways$$,
15   -- these need to be expressed as positive and only include nodes not on network
16                      (
17   SELECT string_agg('SELECT ' || vn.pid*-1 || '::bigint AS pid, '
18       || vn.edge_id || '::bigint AS edge_id, '
19       || vn.fraction || '::float AS fraction ',
20          'UNION ALL') As points_sql
21            FROM vn
22       WHERE vn.pid < 0 ) ,
23       -- these need to be negative
24       (SELECT pid FROM vn WHERE id = 1),
25       (SELECT pid FROM vn WHERE id = 2),
26          false, details:=false) AS r
27       LEFT JOIN ospr.ways AS w ON r.edge = w.gid;
```

The only difference between the two solutions is that by using pgr_withPoints
we don't need to add partial costs because our virtual nodes are
part of the network while the function is running and the resulting
answer includes our virtual node as the final.

edge	seq	node	street	cost	agg_cost
29794	1	11280	Capitol Circle Northeast	41.92	0.00
2662	2	14678	Northwest Capitol Circle	6.96	41.92
:					
2664	4	1534	Northwest Capitol Circle	84.15	93.71
29874	5	19651	New Jersey Avenue Northwest	6.72	177.85
:					
8006	7	18117	New Jersey Avenue Northwest	18.34	190.17
1652	8	6839	Constitution Avenue Northwest	11.07	208.51
:					
14199	19	5614	Constitution Avenue Northwest	13.55	735.49
29926	20	731	Pennsylvania Avenue Northwest	16.13	749.04
:					
15221	56	14743	Pennsylvania Avenue Northwest	5.71	2325.20
13597	57	7864	E Street Northwest	12.48	2330.91
:					
13591	63	12104	E Street Northwest	26.99	2681.13
:					
4982	67	10998	State Place Northwest	69.51	2743.83

```
25215 |  68 | 18913 | West Executive Avenue Northwest |   7.65 |  2813.34
   :
   -1 |  76 |    -2 | NULL                            |   0.00 |  3005.23
(76 rows)
```

If we have more than two virtual nodes to contend with, the first approach that doesn't use pgr_withPoints becomes very difficult.

11.2   *Routing Between Multiple Points*

Besides the point to point case, pgr_withPoints also supports one point to several points, several points to one point, and several points to several points.

Let's suppose you are a DC tourist and you want to plan your weeks travel for each day. You'll always start off at your hotel and then each day go to a different place. You want to figure out the total itinerary.

Updating Points Of Interest With Virtual Node Ids and edge_ids

In this case we have several points of interest to inject as virtual nodes. When you have more than a few virtual nodes, it's best to create a table to store them.

Listing 11.6: Create visit_pois

```
CREATE TABLE visit_pois(id serial PRIMARY KEY, name text,
    geom geometry(POINT, 4326), pid bigint,  edge_id bigint,
    fraction float, side varchar(1), closest_node bigint );

INSERT INTO visit_pois(name, geom)
VALUES ('American Guest House BB', ST_SetSRID(ST_Point(-77.04586, 38.91766),4326)
    ('Capitol Building', ST_SetSRID(ST_Point(-77.009003, 38.889931),4326) ),
    ('Newseum', ST_SetSRID(ST_Point(-77.01924,38.893219), 4326) ),
    ('Holocaust Museum', ST_SetSRID(ST_Point(-77.033021, 38.886992), 4326) );

CREATE INDEX idx_visit_pois ON visit_pois USING gist(geom);
```

In Listing 11.6 we created a table of points of interest, first being the hotel we'll be staying at. We created place holder fields for fraction and edge_id needed by pgr_withPoints which we'll fill in using the function upgr_vnodes which we created in Listing 11.2, on page 131.

Now to update those place holder fields, execute the code in Listing 11.7.

Listing 11.7: Update fraction edge_id and side of visit_pois

```
UPDATE visit_pois AS vp
    SET (pid, edge_id, fraction, side, closest_node) =
        (SELECT CASE WHEN n.fraction > 0 AND n.fraction < 1
                THEN -vp.id ELSE n.pid END  AS pid,
                n.edge_id, n.fraction, n.side, n.closest_node
    FROM
        upgr_vnodes($$SELECT gid As id, source, target,
        the_geom As geom, length_m As cost
    FROM ospr.ways$$, ARRAY[geom] ) As n );
```

In Listing 11.7 we are making a call to upgr_vnodes for each point in our table. Each call only consists of one point. Since it's just one point the pid returned from upgr_vnodes is not meaningful because it will always be equal to 1. Instead we replace our Point ID using the generated -id from our table, only in the case where we get back a virtual node since non-virtual nodes will have returned real node ids from the network.

Using pgr_withPoints for Point to Several Points

Now that we have our set of possible points of interest with the associated fractional edges, we can use this to build our itinerary.

For our first itinerary, we want to to build a result set that consists of travel from our hotel (which has id=1 in visit_pois) to all other locations.

This can be done using the variant

```
pgr_withPoints(edges_sql, points_sql, start_vid, end_vids[])
```

which returns output columns: seq, path_seq, end_pid, node, edge, cost, and agg_cost.

This variant has additional columns path_seq and end_pid since it returns a set of paths corresponding to each visited node. The end_pid is the node id of the final node in the path.

The variant of `pgr_withPoints` is shown in Listing 11.8.

Listing 11.8: Path from hotel to other points of interest

```
SELECT r.*
FROM pgr_withPoints($$SELECT gid AS id,
                            source,
                            target,
                            length_m AS cost
                     FROM ospr.ways$$,
              $$SELECT pid*-1 As  pid, edge_id, fraction
                   FROM visit_pois WHERE pid < 0$$,
         (SELECT pid FROM visit_pois WHERE id = 1),
         ARRAY(SELECT pid FROM visit_pois WHERE id > 1),
              false, details:=false) AS r;
```

The output of 11.8 is:

```
 seq | path_seq | end_pid | node  | edge  |        cost        |      agg_cost
-----+----------+---------+-------+-------+--------------------+-------------------
   1 |        1 |      -4 |    -1 | 20336 | 60.8105766963955   |                 0
   2 |        2 |      -4 |  6934 | 19665 | 57.732137183652    | 60.8105766963955
   :
   :
  70 |       70 |      -4 | 17338 | 31715 | 67.861556095923    | 3944.89504045404
  71 |       71 |      -4 |    -4 |    -1 |                  0 | 4012.75659654996
  72 |        1 |      -3 |    -1 | 20336 | 60.8105766963955   |                 0
  73 |        2 |      -3 |  6934 | 19665 | 57.732137183652    | 60.8105766963955
   :
 179 |      108 |      -3 |    -3 |    -1 |                  0 | 4185.68181768844
 180 |        1 |   11280 |    -1 | 20336 | 60.8105766963955   |                 0
   :
 303 |      124 |   11280 | 14678 | 29794 | 41.920076131042    | 4913.19436797851
 304 |      125 |   11280 | 11280 |    -1 |                  0 | 4955.11444410955
(304 rows)
```

Note that the `path_seq` restarts numbering for each trip (path), but seq is continuous throughout. Also the ending node of each path is returned as `end_pid`.

What if we only cared about the cost for each path? Then we can implore the sister function `pgr_withPointsCost` as shown in Listing 11.9.

Listing 11.9: Cost from hotel to other points of interest

```
SELECT p.name, r.*
FROM pgr_withPointsCost($$SELECT gid AS id,
```

```
                source,
                target,
                length_m AS cost
            FROM ospr.ways$$,
    $$SELECT pid*-1 As  pid, edge_id, fraction
        FROM visit_pois WHERE pid < 0$$,
(SELECT pid FROM visit_pois WHERE id = 1),
ARRAY(SELECT pid FROM visit_pois WHERE id > 1),
    false) AS r INNER JOIN visit_pois AS p ON
        r.end_pid = p.pid;
```

As with any function that returns a table, we are able to join back the result with a reference table. Listing 11.9, on the facing page joins with `visit_pois` to get meaningful names for our destinations.

The output of Listing 11.9, on the preceding page is:

```
      name       | start_pid | end_pid |     agg_cost
-----------------+-----------+---------+------------------
 Holocaust Museum |       -1 |      -4 | 4012.75659654996
 Newseum          |       -1 |      -3 | 4185.68181768844
 Capitol Building |       -1 |   11280 | 4955.11444410955
(3 rows)
```

11.3   *Visiting Points of Interest in Specific Order*

The last example assumes you are always coming from your hotel to the site of interest. In most cases when site-seeing, you'll want to travel from the last site of interest to the next site, and then in your final hop go back to your hotel.

Luckily, pgRouting 2.2+ has a function for that. It's called `pgr_dijkstraVia`.

Unfortunately, `pgr_dijkstraVia` can only work with nodes in your network and not virtual nodes like `pgr_withPoints`. To work with virtual nodes in your network, you can use `pgr_trspViaEdges` which we'll cover in a later chapter.

For this next example we'll use the closest physical network node to each point of interest as our stop points and assume we want to travel to our points of interest in a specific order. The order of nodes in the array dictates the order in which the `visit_pois` will be visited.

Listing 11.10: dijkstra via points of interest

```
SELECT r.*
FROM pgr_dijkstraVia(
$$SELECT gid AS id, source, target, length_m AS cost
      FROM ospr.ways$$,
ARRAY(SELECT closest_node
      FROM visit_pois
      ORDER BY id)
) AS r;
```

seq	path_id	path_seq	start_vid	end_vid	node	edge	cost	agg_cost	route_agg_cost
1	2	1	11280	18816	11280	29794	41.920076	0	0
...									
50	3	23	18816	6626	1286	30200	11.468956	864.86715	2141.51428588
51	3	24	18816	6626	5105	30201	150.35132	876.33611	2152.98324265
52	3	25	18816	6626	11765	30202	138.06882	1026.6874	2303.33456434
53	3	26	18816	6626	16731	30203	18.89604	1164.7562	2441.40339272
54	3	27	18816	6626	14438	30204	16.574748	1183.6523	2460.29943909
55	3	28	18816	6626	5362	30205	154.40333	1200.2270	2476.87418794
56	3	29	18816	6626	2829	30206	8.7156568	1354.6304	2631.27752758
57	3	30	18816	6626	1059	29274	5.5526716	1363.3460	2639.99318444
58	3	31	18816	6626	18128	29275	152.87560	1368.8987	2645.54585614
59	3	32	18816	6626	2505	29276	152.10811	1521.7743	2798.42145859
60	3	33	18816	6626	17795	29277	16.477530	1673.8824	2950.52956935
61	3	34	18816	6626	8750	13024	13.446484	1690.3599	2967.00709953
62	3	35	18816	6626	2472	13025	71.396720	1703.8064	2980.45358399
63	3	36	18816	6626	7593	13026	13.620617	1775.2031	3051.85030482
64	3	37	18816	6626	1271	8120	6.7529601	1788.8237	3065.47092259
65	3	38	18816	6626	5593	8121	129.79649	1795.5767	3072.22388272
66	3	39	18816	6626	20954	8122	9.1097660	1925.3732	3202.02037437
67	3	40	18816	6626	3954	31088	9.496755	1934.4830	3211.13014044
68	3	41	18816	6626	3052	31089	106.75565	1943.9797	3220.62689580
69	3	42	18816	6626	21968	31090	11.486723	2050.7354	3327.38254966
70	3	43	18816	6626	7009	31711	17.584932	2062.2221	3338.86927302
71	3	44	18816	6626	16784	31713	8.2513752	2079.8070	3356.45420566
72	3	45	18816	6626	17338	31715	125.28544	2088.0584	3364.70558089
73	3	46	18816	6626	6626	-2	0	2213.3438	3489.99102184

(73 rows)

If you want to visit points of interest in the most efficient order, you can employ pgr_tsp to compute what order you should assign the records in your visit_pois.

pgr_tsp is covered in Traveling Salesperson Problems, on page 159.

12 *Catchment Areas and Isochrones*

You're chief of a local fire brigade. Your mandate is to be able to respond to all fires within five minutes. Question: Which houses fall under your protection? To solve this and other resource allocation problems, pgRouting offers `pgr_drivingDistance`. You can draw a polygon enclosing all reachable nodes—the catchment area—using the functions `pgr_alphaShape` and `pgr_pointsAsPolygon`.

12.1 Using pgr_drivingDistance

Let's see how we can use `pgr_drivingDistance` to compute a list of nodes within the reach of our fire engines.

To make our example more convincing, we'll use the OSM road data from Washington DC for our network.

The simplest signature use looks like:

```
pgr_drivingDistance(sql text, start_vid bigint, distance float8, directed boolean)
RETURNS SET OF (seq, node, edge, cost, agg_cost)
```

Engine Company 30 is situated at 50 48TH ST NE. We geocoded this address as -76.63 longitude and 38.89 latitude. This is the one we'll use first.

If we used our loaded DC OSM data to find the driving distance within five minutes from Engine 30 to any location, we'd use a query as shown in Listing 12.1.

Listing 12.1: Driving distance within five minutes from Engine 30

```
1  SELECT *
2      FROM pgr_drivingDistance(
3          'SELECT gid As id, source, target,
4              cost_s AS cost, reverse_cost_s AS reverse_cost
5              FROM ospr.ways',
6          (SELECT n.id
7              FROM ospr.ways_vertices_pgr AS n
8                  ORDER BY ST_SetSRID(
```

```
 9                      ST_Point(-76.933399,38.890703),4326) <-> n.the_geom LIMIT 1)
10            , 5*60, true
11         );
```

Lines 6-9 do a subquery that returns the closest road network node to Engine 30.

The output of the above query would look as follows:

```
seq | node  | edge  |         cost        |       agg_cost
----+-------+-------+---------------------+--------------------
  1 |  7801 |    -1 |                   0 |                  0
  2 |  2834 | 23513 |   1.5217398656579   |   1.5217398656579
  3 |  6158 | 23512 |   2.99736640904218  |   2.99736640904218
  4 |  4858 | 10294 |   3.60051846184696  |   3.60051846184696
  5 | 18137 | 10149 |   3.73533461743854  |   7.3358530792855
  6 | 15941 |  5121 |   5.25080607454009  |   8.24817248358227
  7 | 17942 |  5120 |   1.06791787946753  |   9.3160903630498
  8 | 20960 | 23514 |   7.90929212685492  |   9.43103199251281
  9 | 18619 |  4261 |   6.6067314908782   |   9.60409789992038
 10 |  9297 |  4262 |   6.90612589236125  |   9.90349230140343
  :
  :
(6255 rows)
```

Listing 12.1, on the preceding page assumes a directed graph (which is noted by last argument true). Just like other queries we've seen, the pgr_drivingDistance can handle networks where costs can be different. It will use a reverse_cost column if provided for reverse_cost, otherwise assume both directions have the same cost. Since time is provided in seconds in cost_s and reverse_cost_s our five minute limiting cost needs to be expressed in seconds: 5*60.

From this we get a list of edges and furthest nodes that are still within our five minute requirement.

> pgr_drivingDistance is another function that changed signature in pgRouting 2.1. If you pass in an additional boolean argument corresponding to has_rcost, you will get the old signature which returns a SETOF pgr_costresult type which has column names: seq, id1, id2, and cost.

Let's now consider the reverse route of the same problem. Which houses are within five minutes of the fire station—going from the house to the fire station? Practically speaking, people are not generally in a rush to visit their fire stations, but we present this example to demonstrate that reversing the route of travel may yield different nodes. Why? Think one-way streets. When rushing to a fire, an engine may not have to abide by the rules of the road. But after putting out the fire, we expect it to return to the station with sirens off and without racing down one-way streets.

Listing 12.2: Determine driving distance to Engine 30

```
SELECT *
    FROM pgr_drivingDistance(
        'SELECT gid As id, source As target, target As source,
            cost_s AS cost, reverse_cost_s AS reverse_cost
            FROM ospr.ways',
        (SELECT n.id
            FROM ospr.ways_vertices_pgr AS n
            ORDER BY ST_SetSRID(
                ST_Point(-76.933399,38.890703),4326) <-> n.the_geom LIMIT 1)
        , 5*60, true
    );
```

Which would give us a similar output in this case of:

seq	node	edge	cost	agg_cost
1	7801	-1	0	0
2	2834	23513	1.5217398656579	1.5217398656579
3	6158	23512	2.99736640904218	2.99736640904218
4	4858	10294	3.60051846184696	3.60051846184696
5	18137	10149	3.73533461743854	7.3358530792855
6	15941	5121	5.25080607454009	8.24817248358227
7	17942	5120	1.06791787946753	9.3160903630498
8	20960	23514	7.90929212685492	9.43103199251281
9	18619	4261	6.6067314908782	9.60409789992038
10	9297	4262	6.90612589236125	9.90349230140343
:				
:				

(6257 rows)

12.2 Catchment Area

We're able to generate a list of all the places that our fire engine can reach within five minutes. As a matter of presentation, we'd like to plot all the places on a map and encircle this catchment area with a tight-fitting polygon. Now there's an infinite number of polygons that will enclose all the points. We have to be more specific. We'll construct our catchment area using alpha shapes. Without getting too rigorous, alpha shapes is a methodical approach to creating enclosures around points by ascribing diameters to each point, giving each point an area. Now you're dealing with overlaid circles from which you can start to outline a polygonal shape. To control the "jaggedness" of the final polygon, you vary the diameter—the alpha value. To compute the alpha areas, take the nodes computed by pgr_drivingDistance and pass them to pgr_pointsAsPolygon. We could apply pgr_drivingDistance and pgr_pointsAsPolygon in tandem to avoid having to create a temporary table—see Listing 12.3.

Listing 12.3: Determine service area of the fire station

```
1   SELECT 1 As id, ST_SetSRID(pgr_pointsAsPolygon(
2     $$SELECT dd.seq AS id, ST_X(v.the_geom) AS x, ST_Y(v.the_geom) As y
3       FROM pgr_drivingDistance($sql$SELECT gid As id, source, target,
4           cost_s AS cost, reverse_cost_s AS reverse_cost
5         FROM ospr.ways$sql$,
6       (SELECT n.id
7         FROM ospr.ways_vertices_pgr AS n
8           ORDER BY ST_SetSRID(
9             ST_Point(-76.933399,38.890703),4326) <-> n.the_geom LIMIT 1)
10        , 5*60, true
11      ) AS dd INNER JOIN ospr.ways_vertices_pgr AS v ON dd.node = v.id$$
12    ), 4326) As geom;
```

The code in Listing 12.3 uses the double dollar sign delimiter ($$) in the body of the function to automatically escape single quotes. To allow escaping quotes within our query argument, we use named dollar quoting (sql). The value between the $$ can be anything you want as long as it isn't used elsewhere in your query. Should your function definition contain many single quotes, using $$ will make your code easier to read. Using a named dollar-quoting allows you to escape a string in an already dollar quoted string.

In pgRouting 2.4 and below, if you have quotes within your query, you need to enclose them in double quotes or use named dollar-quoting for the inner query as we do. This is a known bug and should be fixed in a later version. Using named dollar-quoting avoids the issue.

Listing 12.3, on the preceding page over-laid with the driving distance edges is shown in Figure 12.1

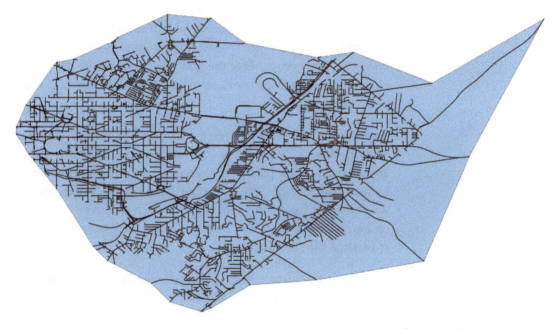

Figure 12.1: Engine 30 Service Area

pgr_alphaShape computes the alpha shape, but returns the points making up the polygon instead of the polygon itself. pgr_pointsAsPolygon internally runs alpha shape on the points provided and then forms a polygon from the points returned by pgr_alphaShape. Both pgr_pointsAsPolygon and pgr_alphaShape take an optional argument called alpha. If omitted, the functions will pick the alpha value that achieves the best balance between speed and accuracy.

12.3   Using pgr_drivingDistance with Multiple Starting Nodes

Let's suppose that you're now district fire chief of a small town with two fire stations. You need to figure out how to partition your stations into two catchment areas.

When calling `pgr_drivingDistance` with multiple starting nodes, you have two options. The naive approach considers each starting node separately. If you have two starting nodes, `pgr_drivingDistance` runs once for each node and outputs the result. The shortcoming to this approach is that you could end up with quite a number of overlaps, which could be undesirable. If a burning house falls in two catchment areas, fire engines from both stations would race to the scene. The occupants of the house may appreciate the extra engine, but if another fire breaks out, both fire stations would already be preoccupied.

The problem is even more pressing when it comes to allocating ride services. The proliferation of Uber and Lyft in major metropolitan areas means that a person is always within a few minutes from a roaming car service. If you're programming the dispatching software, the last thing you want is for a bunch of drivers to converge on a single passenger. The result is a waste of resources at best and at worst, a physical altercation.

Luckily, `pgr_drivingDistance` offers a secondary optimization stage to adjudicate overlapping catchment areas. To toggle it, all you have to do is set an additional parameter—equicost:=true—to true (the default is false). The function takes a bit longer to execute, but it'll be better than fist fights or burnt houses.

The function signature for this variant looks like:

```
pgr_drivingDistance(sql text, start_vids anyarray, distance float8,
    directed boolean default true,
    equicost boolean default false)
  RETURNS SET OF (seq, start_vid, node, edge, cost, agg_cost)
```

Aside from allowing multiple starting locations, it will output an additional start_vid to denote which starting location the solution represents.

The default behavior is equicost:=false which is the same as running the single start location pgr_drivingDistance for each location in your list, with the exception of the additional start_vid column to denote the starting location for each node/edge.

The more interesting case is when you set equicost:=true. The *equicost:=true* means that each edge node can only be represented once and goes with the starting location that gives the best cost.

To demonstrate pgr_drivingDistance with multiple starting nodes, we'll take a look at hospitals in the DC area. You'll find a file dc_hospitals.sql as part of the code download of this book. In the event of a medical emergency, you, or the ambulance with you in it, must rush to the nearest ER. We want to direct you or your ambulance drivers to exactly one ER, even if you fall within the catchment area of more than one. When you're hardly breathing, you don't want to be presented with choices and yelping each one.

We compiled a list of hospitals from DC and removed ones reserved for VIPs and military personnel. We wish to identify the closest hospital to each household in DC.

Listing 12.4: Driving distance to hospitals

```
SELECT dd.*, n.the_geom As geom
    INTO dd_dc_hospitals
    FROM pgr_drivingDistance(
        'SELECT gid As id, source As target, target As source,
            cost_s AS cost, reverse_cost_s AS reverse_cost
            FROM ospr.ways',
        ARRAY(SELECT v.id
    FROM dc_hospitals AS h
        ,LATERAL (SELECT id FROM ospr.ways_vertices_pgr AS n
            ORDER BY h.geom <-> n.the_geom LIMIT 1) AS v
            )
        , 5*60, true, equicost := true
    ) AS dd
        INNER JOIN ospr.ways_vertices_pgr As n ON dd.node = n.id;
```

Listing 12.4, on the previous page utilizes the multistart vertices variant of pgr_drivingDistance to compute all paths that will be optimally served by each hospital within a five minute driving time. It utilizes a LATERAL construct, a feature introduced in PostgreSQL 9.3, which allows for utilizing spatial indexes with KNN. In the subquery that returns node ids, each hospital location is treated as a constant. In order to utilize spatial indexes, one side of the KNN order by has to be a constant. It also dumps the results into a new table called dd_dc_hospitals which we will utilize for computing service areas. As earlier, we are switching the source and target columns since we want driving distance to the hospital rather than from the hospital.

The output of the pgr_drivingDistance part of query looks as follows:

```
 seq  | from_v | node  | edge  |        cost        |       agg_cost
------+--------+-------+-------+--------------------+-------------------
    1 |   3005 |  3005 |    -1 |                  0 |                 0
    2 |   3005 | 11396 | 16040 |  2.27501226553085  | 2.27501226553085
    3 |   3005 |  1756 | 16760 |  3.27310910783219  | 3.27310910783219
    4 |   3005 | 12533 | 16041 |  2.25622048262591  | 4.53123274815676
    5 |   3005 | 13124 | 16042 |  2.09737887022094  |  6.6286116183777
    :
    :
21953 |  21992 |  9719 | 27278 |   9.501887227683   | 296.310257758985
21954 |  21992 | 21181 |    20 |  3.74399190497501  | 296.925645987874
21955 |  21992 | 10626 | 15420 |  9.54676255118654  | 296.972552541318
21956 |  21992 |  5109 |  5663 |  2.83884182748688  | 297.801738731354
21957 |  21992 | 11153 |  4145 |  5.44739357126096  | 299.422803952938
21958 |  21992 | 18929 | 27232 |  4.07344535527725  | 299.745853967772
21959 |  21992 | 16940 |  4142 |  5.22346766499923  | 299.913815370897
(21959 rows)
```

If you run the same query for equicost:=false, you'll get more rows, but you will only have 21959 distinct nodes in the result

12.4   *Computing Service Areas Given Cost Constraint for Multiple Start Points Driving Distance*

Listing 12.5, on the facing page uses the dd_dc_hospitals table generated in Listing 12.4, on the previous page to compute the service area for all hospitals.

As in Listing 12.3, on page 144, Listing 12.5 employs pgr_pointsAsPolygon, but calls it for each hospital.

Listing 12.5: Determine service area for all hospitals

```
1  SELECT h.objectid, h.name, h.geom AS h_geom, v.the_geom As v_geom,
2         ST_SetSRID(pgr_pointsAsPolygon(
3         'SELECT seq As id, ST_X(geom) AS x, ST_Y(geom) As y
4           FROM dd_dc_hospitals
5         WHERE from_v = ' || v.id::text ) ,4326) As geom
6    FROM  dc_hospitals AS h
7          ,LATERAL (SELECT id, the_geom  FROM ospr.ways_vertices_pgr AS n
8              ORDER BY h.geom <-> n.the_geom LIMIT 1) AS v;
```

Output from Listing 12.5 is shown in Figure 12.2, on the next page.

The arrows in Figure 12.2, on the following page are the starting vertex nodes (closest edge vertex to a hospital) and the stars are the actual locations of the hospitals. At a glance our assumption that the closest edge vertex to the hospital is a good enough approximation for the hospital looks reasonable.

Oh, please don't use our program in the event of an actual medical emergency. Call 911.

12.5   Node Injection

Anyone who has driven through uninhabited deserts, be it in the American Southwest, Arabia, or the Australian Outback, would have encountered perfectly straight roads that stretch beyond the horizon.

When portrayed as a network, these lonely roads come across as a single edge, connecting two distant towns or oases.

Here's the problem. Suppose you got into an automobile accident while traversing between two towns; which town would dispatch emergency response?

Because the road segment is but a single edge, the default answer

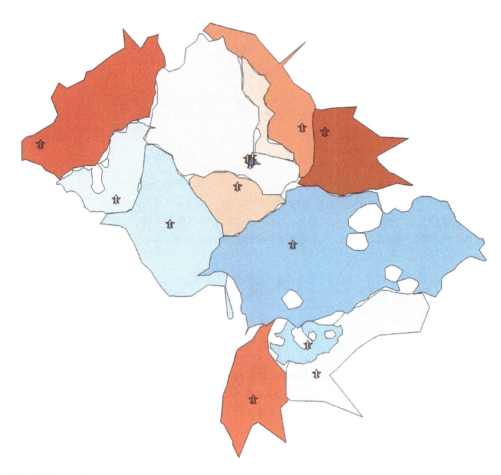

Figure 12.2: DC Hospital Service Areas

using techniques we've presented thus far would be that both towns respond or neither responds.

The first scenario is inefficient; the second scenario is deadly.

Ideally, the towns would come to an agreement on where one catchment area ends and another begins. But without additional nodes, pgRouting would not be able quantify, much less compute, any kind of arrangements.

Here's where injecting nodes play an important part.

If our edge stretches on for a hundred kilometers without any intervening nodes, we might consider adding nodes every kilometer.

For an example, let's consider the longest straight stretch of paved roadway in the world, a 146 kilometer span of the Eyre highway between Balladonia and Caiguna in western Australia.

Desert roads clearly demonstrate the need for node injection, but almost any limited access roadway must have identifiable nodes.

Caiguna WA 6443, Australia
   125.486674, -32.269597
Balladonia WA 6443, Australia
   123.860513, -32.465915

Versions of pgRouting 2.2 and greater are packaged with several functions that can take as input an additional query to supply virtual nodes. The structure of the table is the same in most all cases. To demonstrate, we'll create such a virtual nodes table with the two nodes we've provided. We'll assume our network has only one edge, with edge_id = 1 that goes from Caiguna to Balladonia. To create a table of virtual nodes injected into this edge, our virtual nodes must have node ids that are negative to distinguish them from fixed network nodes.

Listing 12.6: Virtual nodes from Caiguna to Balladonia

```
1   CREATE TABLE vnodes
```

```
2  AS
3  WITH vpoints AS (SELECT -dp.path[1] AS pid, dp.geom As geom,
4      ST_Distance(
5          ST_StartPoint(g.egeog::geometry)::geography,
6              dp.geom::geography) / ST_Length(g.egeog) AS fraction
7      FROM(SELECT ST_MakeLine(ST_Point(125.486674, -32.269597),
8          ST_Point(123.860513, -32.465915) )::geography ) AS g(egeog) ,
9          LATERAL  ST_DumpPoints(
10              ST_Segmentize( g.egeog, 1000))::geometry
11              ) AS dp)
12  SELECT 1 AS edge_id, pid, fraction
13  FROM vpoints
14  WHERE fraction > 0 and fraction < 1;
```

The output would look something like:

```
edge_id | pid |      fraction
--------+-----+--------------------
      1 |  -2 | 0.006450893102489
      1 |  -3 | 0.0129018116548323
      1 |  -4 | 0.0193527553415371
      1 |  -5 | 0.0258037238469813
      1 |  -6 | 0.0322547168556723
      :
      :
      1 | -152 | 0.974195493703715
      1 | -153 | 0.980646653937329
      1 | -154 | 0.987097791941676
      1 | -155 | 0.993548907401134
```

We can then inject these virtual nodes in any pgRouting withPoints family of functions such as pgr_withPoints, pgr_withPointsCost, and pgr_withPointsKSP, or the next function we will cover, pgr_withPointsDD that uses an edges table that includes our fictitious edge 1 going from Calguna to Balladonia.

There is an optional column we left out in this example which specifies the side of street the node is on.

When creating a virtual node table, you want to make sure that real nodes are not included, which is why we left off the start and end points since these represent true nodes (start and end of edge 1). We are also taking advantage of ST_Segmentize(geography) to get a more accurate breakup of nodes. The segmentize will add a point to the edge approximately every *1000* meters and using ST_DumpPoints(geometry) will dump out these points.

12.6   *Driving Distance with Virtual Nodes*

Our hospitals appear to be pretty close to start and end edge nodes. In fact, such an assumption might be fine since hospitals often take up an entire street block.

However, in the general case, your points of interest might be in the middle of a long road. A proposed function was introduced in pgRouting 2.2 called pgr_withPointsDD to handle this case.

pgr_withPointsDD first injects a set of virtual nodes into your edge network, corresponding to the location of a set of points provided by a point SQL statement.

You can use it if you are using pgRouting 2.2 or above with the caveat that the signature or output may change in pgRouting 3.0.

All the *withPoints* family of functions create virtual nodes using a point query. In order to create virtual nodes, they need, at the very minimum, an edge_id which corresponds to the edge the point is on and fraction which corresponds to the percent along the road the point is on.

If you need to reference these points as input, as is often the case, you need to know what node id is assigned to the point, which requires you give it a pid it will use as the point unique identifier.

Other things to be aware of:

1. The pid field in your point SQL needs to be a positive integer
2. To distinguish these from real nodes in the network, if you are using them as starting nodes, you need to specify them as negative integers for the start node.
3. Your point query should not include points where the closest point on an edge is the source or target of the edge. The reason

for this is these will coincide with real nodes so will not be able to be routed to if you assign them an additional identifier.

In order to take advantage of `pgr_withPointsDD` we need to prep the hospital points data as shown in Listing 12.7.

Listing 12.7: DC Hospitals prep for withPoints

```
1   ALTER TABLE dc_hospitals ADD edge_id bigint;
2   ALTER TABLE dc_hospitals ADD fraction float8;
3   ALTER TABLE dc_hospitals ADD pid bigint;
4
5   WITH pe AS ( SELECT DISTINCT ON(p.objectid) p.objectid,
6       e.gid As edge_id,
7        ST_LineLocatePoint(e.the_geom, p.geom) AS frac, e.source, e.target
8      FROM dc_hospitals As p INNER JOIN ospr.ways As e
9         ON ST_DWithin(e.the_geom, p.geom, 0.005)
10         ORDER BY p.objectid, ST_Distance(e.the_geom::geography, p.geom::geography) )
11  UPDATE dc_hospitals AS p
12    SET edge_id = pe.edge_id,
13         fraction = pe.frac,
14         pid = CASE WHEN pe.frac = 0
15             THEN pe.source WHEN pe.frac = 1 THEN pe.target ELSE -p.objectid END
16    FROM pe
17    WHERE pe.objectid = p.objectid;
```

Listing 12.7 does the following:

1. *Lines 1-3* create edge_id, fraction, and pid columns in `dc_hospitals`.
2. *Lines 5-10* defines a virtual table pe within a common table expression that computes data for the new columns.
3. *Lines 8-9* joins hospitals with the edges table to find all edges within 0.005 degrees to each hospital.
4. *Line 5* `DISTINCT ON` combined with the *line 10* `ORDER BY` will ensure only the closest edge to the hospital is returned for each hospital.
5. *Line 7* utilizes PostGIS linear referencing `ST_LineLocatePoint` to determine the fractional location of the point along the closest edge.
6. *Lines 11-17* of the CTE do the updating of the `dc_hospitals` table using the virtual pe table.
7. *Lines 14-15* will compute what node id to use when referencing the hospital as a start point. If the hospital is not a source or

target of an edge, use osm_id. Note we are multiplying by -1 since pids when passed in for starting need to be referenced as negatives if they are virtual nodes.

Listing 12.8: DC Hospitals withPoints

```
1   SELECT *
2       FROM pgr_withPointsDD(
3           'SELECT gid As id, source, target,
4               cost_s AS cost, reverse_cost_s AS reverse_cost
5               FROM ospr.ways',
6           'SELECT objectid AS pid, edge_id, fraction
7               FROM dc_hospitals
8               WHERE pid < 0',
9           ARRAY(SELECT pid FROM dc_hospitals), 5*60,
10          equicost := true);
```

Listing 12.8 is a rewrite of Listing 12.4, on page 147 using pgr_withPointsDD instead of pgr_drivingDistance.

Lines 6-8 of Listing 12.8 are the point query denoting the virtual points we need to create. It excludes points with pid >= 0 because these represent hospitals already in the graph since they fall on a source or target node of an edge. *line 9* returns an array of the point ids we computed.

12.7   *Making Isochrones*

Suppose you're an operator of a pizza franchise. Headquarters mandates that you come up with a map with color-coded regions by delivery time. Such regions are called isochrones.

(The Latin root 'iso' means same; 'chrone' means time.)

To construct an isochrone map:

- Enumerate all the points within the area under consideration.
- Use pgr_drivingDistance function to compute the travel time to each point.
- Partition the travel time into ranges of your choosing.
- Identify which points belong to which range.
- Generate separate alphashapes for each of the ranges.
- Render the alphashapes.

The steps combine all the techniques we've preached in this chapter and are the most intuitive approach to building isochrone maps.

But the shortcoming is, depending on your choice of alpha value, you'll end up with jagged regions, overlaps, and holes aplenty.

A cleaner approach would be to create cumulative alpha shapes by grouping points 'within' certain travel times.

For example, instead of finding all addresses reachable between 1-15, 15-30, 30-45 minutes. We group addresses that are less than 15 (0-15), less than 30 (0-30), and less than 45 (0-45) minutes. These regions naturally overlap and many of the holes at the boundaries between ranges would be filled by the greater range.

When rendering using these cumulative alpha shapes, you must lay down the most encompassing region first and the overlay ever smaller regions.

Before going to a code example, we should warn you that even with the layered approach, the choice of the alpha value could still greatly affect how smooth your ultimate map appears. Think high-speed beltways; sometimes called ring road, perimeter highways, or bypasses around a metropolitan area. If you're coming from outside the beltway, reaching a destination near an exit is generally much quicker than navigating into the city center, even though the exit could be much farther geographically. Your isochrone map will look far from a nice bullseye with well-defined regions. You could still have holes even if your points are spaced closely. Think cities with build ups around hills or littorals—Rio de Janeiro, Seoul, Madison, or Seattle.

Say you are interested in knowing how far you can go from Boston to any place by spending $0-$1000 one way. To help you in your endeavor, you might build an isochrone with breakouts of $0-$1000. We'll perform this in two steps.

Step 1, as shown in Listing 12.9, on the facing page, is to build a table consisting of the result of running driving distance through to our desired $1000 price.

Listing 12.9: Driving Distance for air cost $0-$1000

```
CREATE TABLE dd_air AS
SELECT dd.seq As id, dd.node, dd.edge,
    dd.agg_cost As ticket_price, v.id As airport_id,
    v.geog::geometry As geom
        FROM
        pgr_drivingDistance('SELECT id, source, target,
            price_us AS cost
            FROM of.routes',
        (SELECT n.id
            FROM of.airports AS n
             WHERE iata_faa = 'BOS')
        , 1000, false
    ) AS dd INNER JOIN of.airports AS v ON dd.node = v.id;
```

Step 2, shown in Listing 12.10, then uses the results of Step 1 to build our isochrone. Our resulting answer will have ten rows, for each price breakout going from 0-100 through 950-1000 in steps of 50. There is a subtlety here in that we know that each larger area includes smaller areas, so we order by i, the ticket price for that alpha in reverse order of size, so that the largest polygon is drawn first and doesn't overshadow the smaller.

Listing 12.10: Driving Distance for air cost $0-$1000

```
SELECT  i As ticket_price,
    ST_SetSRID(pgr_pointsAsPolygon(
    'SELECT id, ST_X(geom) AS x, ST_Y(geom) As y
      FROM dd_air
    WHERE ticket_price <= ' || i::text  ) ,4326) As geom
    FROM  generate_series(100,1000,50) As i
ORDER BY i DESC;
```

If we map this out, having our colors for price go from blue for low price to red for high price, we get the result shown in Figure 12.3, on the following page.

You can extend this model to work for multiple locations. For example, if you wanted to create an isochrone of all areas in the city broken out by how far they are from their nearest hospital, in chrone

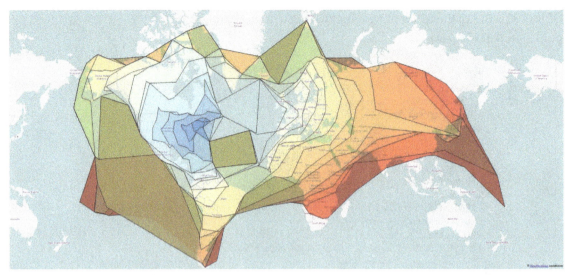

Figure 12.3: Isochrone 0-1000 price breaks

buckets of 1, 2, 3, 4, 5 minutes and so forth, you could reuse the dd_dc_hospitals table created earlier and draw a polygon based on time buckets rather than hospital as shown in Listing 12.11

Listing 12.11: Isochrone from DC Fire Stations in 1-5 minute

```
SELECT i As time_s,
    ST_SetSRID(pgr_pointsAsPolygon(
    'SELECT seq As id, ST_X(geom) AS x, ST_Y(geom) As y
        FROM dd_dc_hospitals
    WHERE agg_cost <= ' || i ) ,4326) As geom
FROM generate_series(1*60,5*60,60) As i
ORDER BY i DESC;
```

13 *Traveling Salesperson Problems*

13.1 *What is the Traveling Salesperson Problem?*

There is a famous problem in routing and operations research called *The traveling salesman problem (TSP)*.

The question goes like this excerpted from wikipedia (`https://en.wikipedia.org/wiki/Travelling_salesman_problem`):

Given a list of cities and the distances between each pair of cities, what is the shortest possible route that visits each city exactly once and returns to the origin city?

pgRouting has a function called `pgr_tsp` that solves this classic problem.

The core foundation of pgRouting's implementation of TSP, is the *distance matrix* which we briefly covered in the introduction to this book. The distance matrix is an nxn matrix consisting of nodes for rows and nodes for columns and in each cell of the matrix is the smallest cost required to go from node a to b, where a is the node in columns and b is the node in rows.

If you have no network constraints, and just care about pure distance, then since the shortest distance between two points is the line that connects them, your matrix would be a simple Cartesian product of : *ST_Distance(a,b)*.

If you do have network constraints, then you would use something like `pgr_dijkstra`, the multinode version to compute the cost from one node to every other node.

The `pgr_tsp` function has three overloaded functions:

```
pgr_tsp(sql text, start_id integer, optional end_id integer )
```

```
which returns set of pgr_costResult (this is deprecated in 2.3)

pgr_eucledianTSP(coordinates_sql text, start_id integer, optional end_id integer,
   lots of other optional arguments) :index:`pgr_eucledianTSP`
   which returns set of records with columns(seq, node, cost, agg_cost)

pgr_tsp(matrix float[][], startpt integer, optional endpt integer)
   which returns set of record with columns (seq, id)
```

In the case of the variants that take as input an sql column, where the expected SQL statement is of the form

```
SELECT id, x, y FROM sometable
```

The SQL variants returns a set of rows consisting of columns seq, id1, and id2. The id1 corresponds to the index in the distance matrix internally created, id2 corresponds to the id column you passed in the id of the sql statement. Keep in mind that the variants that take an SQL statement use euclidean distances to compute a distance matrix and then passes this along to the pgr_tsp variant that takes as input a matrix. This may change in future versions.

The start_id and end_id correspond to the ids in your SQL statement, and NOT the distance matrix row number.

As of pgRouting 2.2, the distance matrix created by the pgr_tsp variants that take an SQL statement, is done via the developer helper function _pgr_makeDistanceMatrix.

The second variants that take as input a distance matrix, are all-purpose, but require you already have a distance matrix or can easily create one. This second set of variants is different from the first in two key ways:

1. Input is a distance matrix and not an SQL statement of the nodes in your network
2. The start and end correspond to the row index in the distance matrix, and NOT the identifiers of your nodes.

Code for this section is in the code/traveling_sales.sql of this book's download file.

We'll start our exercises with the variant that takes an SQL statement.

13.2   Inspector Visiting Nuclear Power Plants (Using Euclidean Costs - SQL Variant)

Imagine yourself as a nuclear plant inspector working for the International Atomic Energy Agency (IAEA). Your mission is to visit all the nuclear power plants in the world in the most efficient order.

For costing, we are going to assume just distance with no network constraints and we'll use the variant of pgr_tsp that takes as input arguments sql and start_id. Since we aren't providing an end_id, end_id defaults to our start location.

We pulled the data from Wikipedia to create a table called nuclear_power_plants. You can create and load the table using the script data/nuclear_power_plants.sql included as part of the download for this book.

Instead of using longitude/latitude units WGS 84 (4326), we chose (3035) ETRS89 / LAEA Europe which is a meter based projection centered in Europe with a fairly wide area measurement preserving with measurements best in Europe. The reason we did this instead of falling on WGS 84 longitude/latitude is that TSP by default uses euclidean math and uses the edge distances for costs. Using longitude/latitude projected in euclidean space is very sub-optimal.

Listing 13.1: Traveling Nuclear Power Plants Basic

```
1   WITH
2       T AS (SELECT *
3           FROM pgr_tsp($$SELECT id, ST_X(geom) AS x, ST_Y(geom) AS y
4               FROM nuclear_power_plants$$, 19, 19)
5           )
6   SELECT seq, id2 AS id, N.geom , N.name, N.country
7           FROM T INNER JOIN nuclear_power_plants N ON T.id2 = N.id;
```

The output of Listing 13.1 will consist of 151 rows where each row corresponds to a visit to a nuclear power plant. Figure 13.1, on the next page shows Listing 13.1 with overlay of countries and nuclear power plants.

> If you are using pgRouting 2.3 or above, use pgr_eucledianTSP instead of pgr_tsp. pgr_eucledianTSP can be used like the older pgr_tsp, but in addition supports big integers for start and end_vids, and also has more meaningful column names and an additional agg_cost.

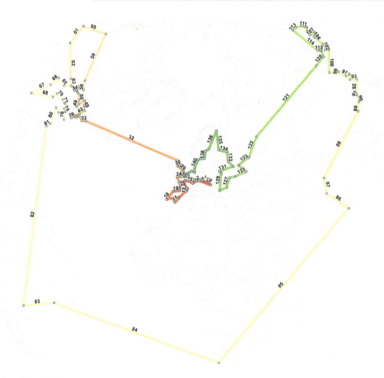

Figure 13.1: TSP Nuclear Power Plant

The numbers on the segments in Figure 13.1 denote the order of travel. The color of the segments start red and changes to green as trip progresses.

To draw the edges of the segment travel, we added another geometry column in the final SELECT statement of the form:

```
ST_MakeLine(N.geom,
        COALESCE(LEAD(N.geom) OVER(ORDER BY T.seq),
            (SELECT geom FROM N WHERE N.id = 19) ) ) As segment
```

This would create a two point line segment consisting of the current point and the point that follows based on T.seq order.

13.3 *Inspector Visiting Nuclear Power Plants (Spheroidal Distance Matrix Variant)*

Let's suppose we wanted to use spheroidal distance measurements instead of trying to find the best euclidean spatial reference system that covers our area of interest, or we had in mind a totally different kind of cost, like price of travel. We'd need to use a distance matrix as our input instead of allowing the function to create one based on euclidean distance.

In a distance matrix, the row index starts at zero and is sequentially numbered to uniquely identify each visit point. In our case our nuclear power plant ids are sequentially numbered, but in many cases, your primary key may not be a number or may have gaps. To speed up building our future matrices, we'll add a did column to the nuclear_power_plant table that will serve as the distance matrix row number as shown in Listing 13.2.

Listing 13.2: Add distance matrix row number to nuclear_power_plants

```
1   ALTER TABLE nuclear_power_plants ADD COLUMN did integer;
2   UPDATE nuclear_power_plants AS NO
3       SET did = N.did
4     FROM (SELECT id, row_number() OVER(ORDER BY id) - 1 As did, name,
5       ST_Point(lon,lat)::geography AS geog, geom
6           FROM nuclear_power_plants ) AS N
7   WHERE N.id = NO.id;
```

> Arrays as input to array_agg and ARRAY(..) was introduced in PostgreSQL 9.5. Prior versions will throw an error. As such our matrix examples utilizing array_agg only work in PostgreSQL 9.5+

The important piece in Listing 13.2 is the:

```
row_number() OVER(ORDER BY id) - 1
```

which creates a sequential number sorted by order of the id column and then subtracts 1 so that the numbering starts at 0.

Next we will use this to create the matrix.

Listing 13.3 is a repeat of Listing 13.1, on page 161, except it creates a distance matrix based on spheroidal distance and uses the variant of pgr_trsp that takes as input a distance matrix.

Listing 13.3: Traveling Nuclear Power Plants using Distance Matrix

```
1    WITH dmr AS (
2    SELECT  a.id, a.did,
3       array_agg(
4          ST_Distance(a.geog, b.geog)  ORDER BY b.did) As arow
5      FROM nuclear_power_plants As a, nuclear_power_plants As b
6      GROUP BY a.did, a.id ORDER BY a.did )
7      SELECT  t.seq, N.id, N.geom
8    INTO nuclear_visits_dmatrix_spheroid
9      FROM pgr_tsp( ( SELECT array_agg(arow ORDER BY did) FROM dmr  )
10        , (SELECT did FROM nuclear_power_plants AS N WHERE id = 19)::integer ) AS T
11        INNER JOIN nuclear_power_plants AS N ON T.id = N.did
12        ORDER BY t.seq;
```

In Listing 13.3, we are are doing the following:

1. *Lines 1-6* is our distance matrix rows, which we name dmr. There is a row for each nuclear power plant and a one-dimensional array called arow which holds the geodetic distance from each respective plant to the other. The ORDER BY within the array_agg ensures the distance values are in order of distance id.
2. In *line 9* we roll up our distance array of rows into a single matrix and feed that to pgr_tsp
3. In *line 10* we need to look up the distance row index based on the node id, since this variant of pgr_tsp requires the distance matrix row index. Alternatively we could just replace the whole sub-select with 18 for this case.

Note that using geography is about ten times slower than using geometry, so this particular variant takes about 10-20 times longer than the first. For this particular example, the general path of travel that both come up with is similar, except direction of travel is in the opposite direction.

Figure 13.2: TSP Nuclear Power Plant (Spheroid)

13.4 *Inspector Visiting Nuclear Power Plants (Dynamic Costs Distance Matrix Variant)*

As an inspector, you can't walk from place to place or swim across oceans. You also don't have access to a private jet. You are going to have to fly using some commercial airline. You have a couple of concerns when deciding what airline flights to take

1. The airport where commercial airlines fly should be closest to the plant.
2. You have frequent flyer mile cards for a couple of airlines, so you would prefer use those, all else being equal, to rack up miles.
3. You don't really care about cost, because IAEA is paying for it.
4. You do care about time, because you don't want to get stuck sitting in an airport.

Your concerns are a function of flight/wait time and airline. This calls for dynamic costing and by extension using the `pgr_tsp` matrix variant.

To take care of objective one, finding the closest airport, we'll add an airport_id to the `nuclear_power_plants` table.

Listing 13.4: Closest airport to plant

```
ALTER TABLE nuclear_power_plants ADD airport_id integer;
UPDATE nuclear_power_plants AS n
    SET airport_id = (SELECT id
        FROM of.airports AS A
            WHERE
                EXISTS(SELECT id  FROM of.routes AS r
                WHERE r.source = A.id OR r.target = A.id)
            ORDER BY A.geog <-> ST_Point(N.lon,N.lat)::geography LIMIT 1);
```

In Listing 13.4 we are using the geography KNN `<->` distance operator to find the closest airport, so it requires PostGIS 2.2. We also have an EXISTS clause to leave out airports that are only flown by private jets or non-airlines.

Next step is to build the distance matrix. To build the distance matrix, we can use `pgr_dijkstraCost`, the variant version that accepts many to many and returns the shortest cost from sources to targets.

There are a number of other distance matrix building functions, many of which are proposed. One in particular that does something similar is the proposed function, pgr_vidsToDMatrix, but this particular function as it stands is not flexible enough for our particular use-case, since our costs are dynamic based on airline.

> pgr_dijkstraCost is a new function in pgRouting 2.2. For older versions, you'd need to run pgr_kdijkstraCost for each plant

It is possible to produce a single query that solves this using CTEs. However we'll break it into steps using tables for a couple of reasons. For a large network, you don't want the whole thing in a CTE as performance would be bad and, the more primary reason, is the CTE still requires a whole page of code to show. If you were to do this particular example as a single query, it takes about 3-4 seconds of processing time.

The first step is to use Dijkstra to compute our airline costs as shown in Listing 13.5.

Listing 13.5: Nuclear Plant airline travel costs using Dijkstra

```
CREATE TABLE nuclear_wdijkstra AS
SELECT a.id AS a_id, a.did AS a_did,
    b.id As b_id, b.did As b_did, apc.agg_cost As cost
FROM pgr_dijkstraCost($$SELECT r.id, r.source, r.target,
    CASE WHEN al.name IN('JetBlue Airways', 'Air Japan', 'Air Canada')
        THEN 0.75 ELSE 1 END*time_minutes AS cost, al.name
FROM of.routes AS r
    INNER JOIN of.airlines As al ON r.airline_id = al.airline_id$$,
        ARRAY(SELECT DISTINCT airport_id FROM nuclear_power_plants),
        ARRAY(SELECT DISTINCT airport_id FROM nuclear_power_plants),
        directed := false) AS apc
            INNER JOIN nuclear_power_plants AS a On apc.start_vid = a.airport_id
            INNER JOIN nuclear_power_plants As b ON apc.end_vid = b.airport_id;
```

If you inspect the results of this table, you'd find that there are no entries for where target = source, which we'll need to have a balanced set of 151 x 151 matrix. Also some nuclear power plants have the same closest airport, which means presumably we'd want to drive from place to place for those plants. This means we need to augment our matrix rows to include these missing data points.

We'll do so by inserting records using Listing 13.6.

Since we have no road network data to do true costing, we'll assume that you can get from plant to plant by train or car or some other means by going at a speed of 50 km/hr and record our cost in minutes to match up with units of our flight time costing.

Listing 13.6: Nuclear Plant driving costs 50km/hr

```
INSERT INTO nuclear_wdijkstra(a_id, a_did, b_id, b_did, cost)
SELECT   a.id AS a_id, a.did As a_did,
         b.id As b_id, b.did As b_did,
         ST_Distance(a.geog, b.geog)/1000/50*60 AS cost
   FROM nuclear_power_plants As a
     INNER JOIN nuclear_power_plants As b ON ( a.airport_id = b.airport_id );
```

Listing 13.6 adds our sketchy drive time/commuter rail costs for those plants that are nearest the same airport. Note that in case of source = target, the cost will be 0 as we'd expect.

When you are done populating the table, you should have a total of 151*151 = 22801 corresponding to cells of a 151x151 matrix. Now we are ready to use this data with pgr_tsp as shown in Listing 13.7.

Listing 13.7: Nuclear Plant airline travel costs using Dijkstra and drive/commute

```
WITH dmr AS (
SELECT a_id As id, a_did AS did, array_agg( cost ORDER BY b_did) As arow
FROM nuclear_wdijkstra
GROUP BY a_did, a_id ORDER BY a_did)
 SELECT  t.seq, N.id, N.geom
 INTO nuclear_visits_dmatrix_dijkstra
 FROM pgr_tsp( ( SELECT array_agg(arow ORDER BY did) FROM dmr  )
   , 18 ) AS T
    INNER JOIN  nuclear_power_plants AS N ON T.id = N.did
  ORDER BY t.seq;
```

Listing 13.7 follows a similar pattern to prior pgr_trsp matrix examples. Except we are using an input table that contains the 151x151 distance matrix cells and we hardcoded the did value 18 which corresponds to the nuclear power plant record with id=19.

You should notice that the solutions can change drastically depending on your favoritism for certain airlines. You may even want to make your costing more harsh by refusing to travel to airports where your favorite airlines do not travel.

Please note that TSP is not a deterministic algorithm. It relies on heuristics, so even with the same inputs, you are not guaranteed to have the same outputs.

14 *Vehicle Routing Problems*

In Traveling Salesperson Problems, on page 159 you learned how to solve the classic problem of finding the least costly visit order using pgRouting TSP functions. The Traveling Salesperson Problem is a simple version of the more general problem called the Vehicle Routing Problem or VRP for short. With VRP, you no longer have a lone salesperson, but an entire sales team. And each salesperson must do more than calling on the customer; they must carry payload. The classical framing of VRP is to consider a fleet of vehicles and a set of stops. At each stop, the vehicle picks up payload, drops off payload, or does both. Each vehicle has a maximum capacity and a maximum rate of travel and the goods must be dropped off or picked up within given timeframes.

The optimization problem is generally one of computing route of travel that satisfies all the constraints while minimizing the number of vehicles and/or travel time.

In the canonical framing of VRP, you have a fleet of vehicles making pickups who need to visit a set of customers. You need to find a solution of assigning customers to salespeople and determining in what order each salesperson visits each customer.

In the case of TSP you have just one resource, the salesperson, and many customers to visit with no restrictions of when you can visit them, aside from the fact the salesperson can't be in two places at the same time. In the case of VRP you have several resources, your salespeople (or vehicles) and several customers. You generally don't want two salespeople visiting the same customer and you also don't want to overload a salesperson with too many customers in a given window of time.

The general class of VRP can get even more involved with resource constraints. For example if you are a shipping company, your trucks

can only carry so much weight and you might have different kinds
of trucks that can carry different amounts. You have warehouses
that house your products where your trucks pick up orders. The
depot has a given window of time it is open. In addition, the customers may only be available to receive packages at certain times
of day. This class of VRP is often referred to as depot pickup with
time windows.

Another variant of VRP which targets markets such as courier services is where you have a fleet of vehicles that are exactly the same
in terms of speed and capacity (weight or seats). Each vehicle must
pick up something from one location and deliver it to another location and continue on to next pickup/delivery from the last stop.

Unlike the pickup from a depot, in this case the pickups and deliveries are paired.

Code for this section is in the `code/vrp.sql` of this book's download
file. Data for this section can be found in `data/vrp_data.sql`.

The functions for supporting VRP are included starting with pgRouting 2.0. These functions are marked experimental proposed, which
means their inputs, outputs, and even the names are subject to
change. They are also not well tested so are prone to crash on some
inputs. Use with caution.

14.1   VRP Family of Functions

There are a couple of functions currently available in pgRouting for
supporting VRP. All these support the variant of VRP called *The
vehicle routing problem with time windows*. This means each delivery
and pickup location has a certain window of time the vehicle is
allowed to be at a certain location. All these functions use heuristics
to give an approximate best solution.

Function `pgr_vrpOneDepot` was introduced in pgRouting 2.0.

`pgr_gsoc_vrppdtw` was introduced in pgRouting 2.1.

A new function _pgr_pickDeliver was introduced in pgRouting 2.3. This method is currently considered a private function.

Private functions are foundations for other functions. The casual user of pgRouting should avoid calling private functions directly because the signature and usage of the functions could change from version to version, often unannounced. Private functions tend to be more generic in their inputs and de-emphasize user friendliness. pgRouting and PostGIS customarily precede the name of private functions with an underscore. Should you decide to use a private function in your projects, be aware that you may need to rewrite your dependent code with every new version.

14.2 *Vehicle Routing Single Depot with Time Windows*

We begin with a specialized version of VRP where all vehicles pick up from a single point of dispatch, or depot. Let's call this the Single Depot problem. At different stops, they make only deliveries. Think package delivery services like UPS, FedEx, DHL, and even your neighborhood letter carrier.

The current implementation in pgRouting lets us specify the following constraints:

- Maximum capacity of each vehicle.
- Your fleet can have a mixture of big trucks and small trucks.
- One speed for all vehicles, no slow or fast trucks.
- The window of time during which delivery must be made for each stop.
- The unloading time at each stop.

The sacrifices that we must make are the following:

Load must be quantified using one and only one metric. For example, for a package delivery service, you may specify the maximum weight that each truck could carry, but not the dimension. If you're an airport shuttle bus taking arriving passengers to their home or hotels, you can specify the total number of passengers, but not the total weight. A perfect fit for the problem would be a delivery service with uniform goods such as petrol delivery by land or by sea (volume), troop transport (soldiers of uniform size and shape), drug trafficking (weight), or feeding your collection of race horses (you can only carry so much hay though the appetite of the horses could vary). By taking the negative of our metric, the same problem could describe pick-up services: recycling or scrap metal services (weight), troop medivac, or larceny (value of stolen goods).

Speed of the vehicle must be the same for all vehicles—same truck, same driving habits. An empty truck won't be any faster than a fully loaded truck.

Even though we must construct a canonical cost matrix for the routes, only travel time between nodes matters in the end.

The pgRouting function to solve the Single Depot problem is `pgr_vrpOneDepot` (`http://loc8.cc/pgr/vrp1depot`), and has the following functional signature:

```
pgr_vrpOneDepot (
    order_sql text,
    vehicle_sql text,
    cost_sql text,
    depot_id integer
)
RETURNS SET OF (oid, opos, vid, tarrival, tdepart)
```

The `order_sql` argument should be an SQL SELECT outputting at least the following columns:

Column	Description
id	An integer that identifies the stop
x	x or longitude of stop
y	y or latitude of stop
order_unit	An integer indicating the number of units to be dropped off at the stop
open_time	A positive integer to indicate the beginning of the delivery window

... continued on next page

Column	Description
close_time	A positive integer to indicate the end of the delivery window.
service_time	A positive integer for the time needed to unload

The order_sql must include the depot location as well.

All the times in the function are "stop-watch" times, in that all deliveries begin at zero. The time can be any unit, you just have to make sure that units are consistent. For example, if you've chosen each unit of travel time in the cost matrix to mean minutes, then you should consider minutes as the duration of the delivery window. Let's say that our truck begins delivery at 9:00 AM; this would be the zeroith minute. If our truck delivers to restaurants that open between 10:00 AM and 10:00 PM, we would put down 60 as the open_time and 780 as the close_time.

The vehicle_sql argument should be an SQL statement consisting of at least the following columns:

Column	Description
vehicle_id	An integer that identifies the vehicle
capacity	Integer denoting how much the vehicle can hold (this can be weight, passengers, etc).

The cost_sql argument should be an SQL statement representing a distance matrix consisting of at least the following columns:

Column	Description
src_id	Integer denoting the source node location
dest_id	Integer denoting the destination node location.

... continued on next page

Column	Description
cost	Integer denoting cost of traveling from given source to given destination
distance	Distance from source to destination
traveltime	An integer denoting time to travel from source to destination

The src_id and dest_id, correspond to id from the order_sql.

The node id for depot must be included in the cost matrix.

The output of the function is a table consisting of the following columns:

Column	Description
oid	The order id
opos	Integer denoting the order in which the order will be delivered
vid	The vehicle identifier
tarrival	Time of arrival
tdepart	Time of departure

To work out a full example, let's say you own a brewery and you're charged with delivering kegs of beer to a restaurant chain. We picked the 99 restaurant chain, with locations in Connecticut only. (This is not an endorsement of any kind. They have the goldilock number of restaurants for our example.) Our table restaurants_99 lists the twelve locations along with their longitude and latitude. We sited our brewery at -72.51975, 41.98377 and we only have a pair of trucks christened Laurel and Hardy. Laurel can carry 400 kegs; Hardy, 800 kegs.

(A standard keg of average beer weighs in at 160 lbs.)

For simplicity, we assume that all the restaurants need the same number of kegs and keep identical operating hours. For variety, the location in Vernon is hosting an outdoor Oktoberfest celebration and will require an inordinate number of kegs.

We'll measure time in minutes with 9 AM being the zeroith minute. Restaurants open at 10 AM (60th minute) and closes at 10 PM (780th minute). At each restaurant the driver will spend 20 minutes unloading the beer and completing the paperwork.

With this information, we can create the table of delivery stops that we'll use for orders_sql.

Listing 14.1: Restaurants and Brewery

```
CREATE TABLE vrp1_orders AS
SELECT
    id, lon AS x, lat AS y,
    CASE WHEN id = 11 THEN 200 ELSE 50 END AS order_unit,
    60 AS open_time,
    780 AS close_time,
    20 AS service_time
FROM restaurants_99
UNION ALL
SELECT 13, -72.51975, 41.98377, 0 , 0, 800, 0; -- The brewery
```

Our table must include the origination point of our beer truck—the brewery, which we assigned the id of 13. For our order unit, we have 50 kegs for all restaurants except for restaurant 11 (corresponding to Vernon location) which will need 200 kegs for their celebration.

Before we can apply the VRP function we must set up a cost matrix.

The table we use for costs should include all restaurants and our brewery as nodes. Each row in the table is an edge between two nodes. You may exclude edges that are too "costly" to be considered. For example, two restaurants may be connected by tunnel with insufficient clearance. You don't want a beer truck, emblazoned with your logo to appear on the evening news with its top sheared off.

The cost matrix must have three weight columns: distance, cost, and travel time, although the current implementation of VRP will only consider travel time. And obviously, the travel time must be in the same units as the open, close, and service times of the stops.

These next steps utilize data we downloaded from http://loc8.cc/ pgr/ct_osm and processed with osm2pgrouting and prepped with osm2pgrouting. To save you the trouble of having to download and prep Connecticut data we've included vrp1_cost and vrp1_points tables in the vrp_data.sql file. We'll go thru the process of creating these tables, to demonstrate how you would do the same with your own data.

We begin by creating a table called vrp1_points to store all the nodes (our restaurant locations and depot location) using code in Listing 14.2.

Listing 14.2: Build vrp1_points Table

```
CREATE TABLE vrp1_points (
    id integer,
    pid integer,
    geom geometry(point,4326),
    edge_id integer,
    fraction float,
    closest_node integer
);
INSERT INTO vrp1_points (id, geom)
SELECT id, ST_SetSRID(ST_Point(lon,lat),4326) AS geom
FROM restaurants_99
UNION ALL
SELECT 13, ST_SetSRID(ST_Point(-72.51975,41.98377),4326) AS geom;


UPDATE vrp1_points AS vp
SET (pid, edge_id, fraction, closest_node) = (
    SELECT
        CASE
            WHEN n.fraction > 0 AND n.fraction < 1 THEN -vp.id
            ELSE n.pid
        END AS pid,
        n.edge_id, n.fraction, n.closest_node
    FROM
        upgr_vnodes(
            $$
                SELECT
                    gid AS id, source, target,
```

```
                    the_geom AS geom,
                    length_m AS cost
                FROM ct.ways
            $$,
            ARRAY[geom]
    ) AS n
);
```

We also take advantage of a function we created in an earlier chapter to compute the fraction edge location of each point using OSM Connecticut data.

To compute the cost matrix, we call the function pgr_withPointsCost to compute the pair-wise cost of nodes using the backdrop of Connecticut OSM data.

Listing 14.3: Build Costs Table

```
CREATE TABLE vrp1_cost AS
SELECT
    s.id AS src_id,
    e.id AS dest_id,
    r.agg_cost::integer AS cost,
    ST_Distance(s.geom::geography,e.geom::Geography)::integer AS distance,
    r.agg_cost/60.0 AS traveltime
FROM
    pgr_withPointsCost(
        $$
            SELECT
                gid AS id, source, target,
                cost_s AS cost, reverse_cost_s AS reverse_cost
            FROM ct.ways
        $$,
        $$
            SELECT pid * -1 AS pid, edge_id, fraction
            FROM vrp1_points
            WHERE pid < 0
        $$,
        ARRAY(SELECT pid FROM vrp1_points),
        ARRAY(SELECT pid FROM vrp1_points),
        true
    ) AS r
    INNER JOIN
    vrp1_points AS s ON r.start_pid = s.pid
    INNER JOIN
    vrp1_points AS e ON r.end_pid = e.pid;
```

If you have a simple network where as-the-crow-flies distance will suffice, you can skip OSM and create a simple distance-based cost matrix using the following:

Listing 14.4: Distance-based Cost Matrix

```
CREATE TABLE vrp1_gdist AS
SELECT s.id AS src_id, e.id AS  dest_id,
    ST_Distance(s.geom::geography,e.geom::geography)::integer  AS cost,
    ST_Distance(s.geom::geography,e.geom::geography)::integer AS distance,
    (
        ST_Distance(s.geom::geography,e.geom::geography) / 1000 / 70 * 60
    )::integer AS traveltime
FROM vrp1_points AS s, vrp1_points AS e
WHERE s.id != e.id;
```

Now that we have all the pieces in place, we "solve" our VPR depot problem with:

Listing 14.5: VRP One depot solution using Dijkstra matrix

```
SELECT
    d.*,
    SUM(o.order_unit) OVER (PARTITION BY vid ORDER BY d.opos) AS total
FROM
    pgr_vrpOneDepot(
        'SELECT * FROM vrp1_orders order by id',
        'SELECT id AS vehicle_id, capacity FROM trucks order by vehicle_id',
        'SELECT * FROM vrp1_cost order by src_id, dest_id', 13
    ) AS d
    INNER JOIN
    vrp1_orders AS o ON d.oid = o.id
ORDER BY vid, opos;
```

Which produces the result:

```
oid | opos | vid | tarrival | tdepart | total
----+------+-----+----------+---------+------
 13 |    0 |   1 |       -1 |       0 |     0
  3 |    1 |   1 |      108 |     128 |    25
  9 |    2 |   1 |      168 |     188 |    50
  6 |    3 |   1 |      254 |     274 |    75
  8 |    4 |   1 |      297 |     317 |   100
  7 |    5 |   1 |      372 |     392 |   125
 13 |    6 |   1 |      468 |      -1 |   125
 13 |    0 |   2 |       -1 |       0 |     0
  4 |    1 |   2 |       60 |      80 |    25
  1 |    2 |   2 |      126 |     146 |    50
```

```
10 |   3 |   2 |     176 |     196 |    75
12 |   4 |   2 |     243 |     263 |   100
 2 |   5 |   2 |     280 |     300 |   125
 5 |   6 |   2 |     313 |     333 |   150
11 |   7 |   2 |     356 |     376 |   400
13 |   8 |   2 |     400 |     -1 |   400
(16 rows)
```

Time: 7.211 ms

Using our simple distance matrix (replacing vrp1_cost with vrp1_gdist)
we end up with this solution:

```
oid | opos | vid | tarrival | tdepart | total
----+------+-----+----------+---------+------
13 |    0 |  1 |      -1 |      0 |     0
11 |    1 |  1 |      60 |     80 |   250
10 |    2 |  1 |      81 |    101 |   275
 1 |    3 |  1 |     101 |    121 |   300
 3 |    4 |  1 |     121 |    141 |   325
 9 |    5 |  1 |     141 |    161 |   350
12 |    6 |  1 |     161 |    181 |   375
 2 |    7 |  1 |     181 |    201 |   400
 6 |    8 |  1 |     201 |    221 |   425
 8 |    9 |  1 |     221 |    241 |   450
 7 |   10 |  1 |     241 |    261 |   475
 5 |   11 |  1 |     261 |    281 |   500
 4 |   12 |  1 |     281 |    301 |   525
13 |   13 |  1 |     301 |     -1 |   525
(14 rows)
```

Time: 5.592 ms

Note how the two solutions are very different. When considering
true road networks, where speed limits on some roads mean you
can't go as fast as your vehicle allows, the algorithm determines
you need two trucks to satisfy delivery constraints.

If you are just considering as the crow flies solution driving at a
constant speed, you may conclude you can achieve service level
requirements with just one truck.

What exactly constitutes a solution requires further clarification.
First and foremost, a solution must satisfy capacity and delivery
time constraints. This includes having all your vehicles return to

their starting point after making delivery. Having satisfied the two constraints, VRP will minimize your resources. In our beer example, it means having the fewest number of trucks that can do the job.

Even after minimizing resources, you could still have an infinite number of solutions. Think of the trivial case where you have one beer truck and one 24-hr restaurant. If the restaurant is close by, the driver can choose to leave whenever the brewery is open. Furthermore, he can choose to spend his time at the restaurant, taking in a long meal, before going back.

For the sake of speed, VRP won't consider every possible solution. It will output the first one that satisfies all the constraints and minimizes on vehicles. For most scenarios, this is good enough. Does it really matter if the driver spends his idle time at the restaurant or at the brewery? And generally speaking, meeting the delivery schedule is top priority anyway.

> In its current state, pgr_vrpOneDepot only supports one pickup per vehicle. As a result, if you have fewer vehicles than are required to fulfill service level requirements, you may get back no solution or a partial solution with stops missing. This is not an issue if you have more vehicles defined than needed. It should be noted that this function also is not well tested and has some stability issues. Though it works in pgRouting 2.2, it is broken in pgRouting 2.3 - 2.4. The future implementations of it will be wrappers around the _pgr_pickDeliver family of development functions.

We'll revisit the Single Depot problem later and demonstrate how to solve it using the newer and more stable _pgr_pickDeliver function.

14.3   Vehicle Routing with Pickup, Delivery, and Time Windows

At some point during the evolution of pgRouting, shared ride services overtook the world by storm. In the US, Uber and Lyft have become proprietary eponyms and threaten to topple the entrenched taxi industry. For those of you not familiar with shared ride services, they work like this:

- Enterprising drivers offer themselves, and their vehicles, up for paid rides.
- Anyone needing a ride summons a car by app working off a central database.
- A centralized system will dispatch the car closest to the the pickup point with enough seats to accommodate the traveling party.
- Rides could be shared by different parties to lower cost.

So how does the central database coordinate the innumerable drivers plying the roads, making sure that passengers are picked up and dropped with minimum delay, and cars don't arrive with insufficient seats to accommodate the entire party?

We don't know what the big players are using, but we proffer two functions in pgRouting.

In pgRouting 2.1, a function called `pgr_gsoc_vrppdtw` came to being. It solves the exact kind of problems raised by shared ride services—paired pickup and delivery problems with time windows. In pgRouting 2.3, a private function called `_pgr_pickDeliver` came under development and is expected to replace `pgr_gsoc_vrppdtw` by version 3.0.

As of 2.3, the signatures of the two functions are as as follows:

```
pgr_gsoc_vrppdtw(sql, vehicle_num, capacity)
  RETURNS SET OF pgr_costResult[]: Version 2.1, 2.2
  RETURNS SET OF rows (seq, rid, nid, cost): Version 2.3


_pgr_pickDeliver(customers_sql, max_vehicles,
  capacity, speed (optional), max_cycles(optional))

  RETURNS SET OF (
    seq,
    vehicle_id,
    vehicle_seq,
    stop_id,
    travel_time,
    arrival_time,
```

```
    wait_time,
    service_time,
    departure_time
)
```

Both `_pgr_pickDeliver` and `pgr_gsoc_vrppdtw` share the following constraints:

- All vehicles begin and end at the same stop. This should be identified with id = 0 in the input of `customers_sql` or `sql`.
- The `vehicle_num` and `max_vehicles` are required, but not actually used to limit the number of vehicles the result returns. You must pass in an integer greater than zero to pass input validation. Expect these arguments to be meaningful in future versions.
- The implementation optimizes for the fewest vehicles that can be used to satisfy the time window and capacity constraints.
- All vehicles are identical in terms of capacity and speed.
- Pick-ups and drop-offs must be paired. Pick-up has exactly one corresponding drop-off.
- Each record in the input SQL represents one traveling party. A party could have multiple passengers, but they must travel the same route and share the same time window.
- All passengers of a party must travel together. For instance, if the vehicle picks up a pair of love-birds as a single party, they must both be dropped off at the same location. No parting of ways. Two passengers who happen to be picked up together but traveling to different destinations are not to be considered a single party.
- The problem only assumes Euclidean space, no networks and no cost matrices. Plans are in place to add network input to `_pgr_pickDeliver` in future releases.
- For `pgr_gsoc_vrppdtw`, the speed is unity. This requires some normalization of the input coordinates. For example, if the speed of the vehicle is actually 50 mph and two destinations are 100 miles apart, the x and y positions of the two must be expanded or contracted so that the distance between them is two.
- Pooling is assumed and expected. If a car can hold five passengers but only picked up two, it could stop and pick up a party of three.

The `sql` column of `pgr_gsoc_vrppdtw` and the `customer_sql` column of `pgr_pickDeliver` arguments should be SQL statements outputting the following columns:

Column	Description
id	An integer that identifies the customer
x	x coordinate of location
y	y coordinate of location
demand	numeric denoting how much is picked up (+) or delivered (-) from
openTime (eTime in <=2.2)	a positive numeric denoting time customer opens (with 0 being beginning)
closeTime (lTime in <= 2.2)	a positive numeric denoting time customer closes (with 0 being beginning)
serviceTime (sTime in <= 2.2)	a positive numeric denoting duration of time needed for loading / unloading
pIndex	positive integer denoting the pickup location if customer is a delivery
dIndex	positive integer denoting the delivery identifier, if customer is a pickup

For our grand example, we've chosen a shared jet service that has a fleet of very light jets (VLJ). The operating principles are the same as that for vehicular travel without the need for a road network because, for the most part, planes fly in a straight line from take-off to landing.

We created some data using the airports we loaded earlier. The data is also available in the data/vrp_data.sql file. Our X and Y coordinates are in meters, obtained after transforming from our longitude and latitude to US National Atlas Equal Area (2163), a measure preserving spatial reference system suitable for the continental US.

Listing 14.6: Create jet_customers table

```
DROP TABLE IF EXISTS jet_customers;
-- create dummy customers for pick and deliver
CREATE TABLE jet_customers AS
```

```
WITH
    stops AS (
        SELECT id, iata_faa, ST_X(geom) AS x, ST_Y(geom) AS y
        FROM (
            SELECT id, ST_Transform(geog::geometry,2163) AS geom, iata_faa
            FROM of.airports
        ) AS a
        WHERE iata_faa IN ('TEB','ABE','BOS','BGR', 'MIA','MVY')
    ),
    pairs AS (
        SELECT
            ((row_number() OVER())::integer * 2 - 1) AS pid,
            ((row_number() OVER())::integer * 2) AS did,
            s1.iata_faa AS d_airport,
            s2.iata_faa AS a_airport,
            s1.x AS p_x, s1.y AS p_y, s2.x AS d_x, s2.y AS d_y,
            (1 + mod(s1.id,5))::integer AS num_passengers,
            mod(s1.id,7)*981*1000 AS openTime,
            (
                (mod(s1.id,7) + 2) *981*1000
            )::float AS closeTime,
            0 AS serviceTime
        FROM
            (SELECT * FROM stops) AS s1 ,
            (SELECT * FROM stops) AS s2
          WHERE s1.id <> s2.id
    )
SELECT
    d_airport AS airport,
    pid AS id, p_x AS x, p_y AS y, 0 AS pIndex, did AS dIndex,
    num_passengers AS demand,
    openTime, closeTime, serviceTime
FROM pairs AS pickups
UNION ALL
SELECT
    a_airport AS airport,
    did AS id, d_x AS x, d_y AS y, pid AS pIndex, 0 AS dIndex,
    -num_passengers AS demand,
    openTime, closeTime + 2*981*1000 AS closeTime, serviceTime
FROM pairs AS delivers
UNION ALL
SELECT
    'TEB' AS airport,
    0 AS id, x, y, 0 AS pIndex, 0 AS dIndex, 0 AS demand,
    0 AS openTime, 1000*981*12 AS closeTime, 0 AS serviceTime
FROM stops
WHERE iata_faa = 'TEB';
```

The important characteristics of this table creation, which all tables that are input to the pick and delivery functions should have, are:

1. For each pick-up record there must be a corresponding, but separate, drop-off record
2. The number of passengers (the demand) being dropped off should be expressed as a negative because the number being picked up is positive. Our VLJ can hold up to five passengers so we limit our pick-ups to no more than five. We measure demand in numbers of passengers and have it range from (+-) 1-5.
3. We always need to include a zeroith record representing the home-base of the jet—Teterboro in our example. The plane must start off and return to this airport. The first leg out of the home airport and the last leg into the home airport need not have passengers, in which case these legs would be called ferry legs in transport talk.

Our small jet cruises at 600 km/h. Given that speed is always the numeraire one, we need to rescale the grid of our airports so that 600 km represents one grid unit. For time measurement, we'll stick with hours.

We also assume that the duty time of our pilots will be twelve hours. They have a total of twelve contiguous hours to finish all their flying to avoid grounding by the FAA.

Though people may charter jets for sightseeing or surveying, we're not going to let this happen. The departure airport must be different from the arrival airport (s1.id <> s2.id).

To compute a good path of travel between the stops we'll start by using pgr_gsoc_vrppdtw.

Listing 14.7: Using pgr_gsoc_vrppdtw to compute itinerary

```
SELECT
    n.seq, n.id1 AS jet, n.id2 AS cust, pd.airport, pd.demand AS pas,
    (n.cost/1000/981.0)::numeric(10,2) AS c_hrs
FROM
    pgr_gsoc_vrppdtw(
        $$
            SELECT
                id, x, y, demand,
                opentime, closetime, servicetime,
                pindex, dindex
            FROM jet_customers
```

```
              ORDER BY id
      $$,
      2,
      5
   ) AS n LEFT JOIN
     jet_customers AS pd ON n.id2 = pd.id
ORDER BY n.seq;
```

We set the max capacity of each jet to 5. Our passengers generator,
num_passengers, ensures that no party will have more than five.

seq	jet	cust	airport	pas	c_hrs
1	1	0	TEB	0	0.00
2	1	55	ABE	1	1.00
3	1	45	MVY	1	2.00
4	1	56	MIA	-1	4.02
5	1	46	MIA	-1	4.02
6	1	37	TEB	5	5.84
7	1	38	MVY	-5	6.14
8	1	13	BGR	4	6.56
9	1	14	MIA	-4	9.00
10	1	0	TEB	0	10.82
11	2	0	TEB	0	0.00
12	2	47	MVY	1	2.00
13	2	48	TEB	-1	2.30
14	2	43	MVY	1	2.60
15	2	44	BGR	-1	3.02
16	2	9	BOS	4	4.00
17	2	10	ABE	-4	4.42
18	2	11	BGR	4	5.15
19	2	2	BGR	-4	5.15
20	2	1	BOS	4	5.49
21	2	12	BOS	-4	5.49
22	2	5	BOS	4	5.49
23	2	6	TEB	-4	5.80
24	2	33	TEB	5	5.80
25	2	20	ABE	-4	5.92
26	2	19	BGR	4	6.65
27	2	34	BGR	-5	6.65
28	2	15	BGR	4	6.65
29	2	16	TEB	-4	7.28
30	2	0	TEB	0	7.28
31	3	0	TEB	0	0.00
32	3	7	BOS	4	4.00
33	3	8	MVY	-4	4.12
34	3	17	BGR	4	5.00
35	3	18	MVY	-4	5.42
36	3	39	TEB	5	5.72

```
37 |   3 |   40 | ABE   |   -5 |   5.84
38 |   3 |   35 | TEB   |    5 |   5.96
39 |   3 |   30 | ABE   |   -2 |   6.08
40 |   3 |   29 | MIA   |    2 |   7.84
41 |   3 |   36 | MIA   |   -5 |   7.84
42 |   3 |   27 | MIA   |    2 |   7.84
43 |   3 |   25 | MIA   |    2 |   7.84
44 |   3 |   26 | TEB   |   -2 |   9.67
45 |   3 |   28 | MVY   |   -2 |   9.96
46 |   3 |    0 | TEB   |    0 |  10.26
47 |   4 |    0 | TEB   |    0 |   0.00
48 |   4 |   59 | ABE   |    1 |   1.00
49 |   4 |   57 | ABE   |    1 |   1.00
50 |   4 |   58 | TEB   |   -1 |   1.12
51 |   4 |   51 | ABE   |    1 |   1.24
52 |   4 |   53 | ABE   |    1 |   1.24
53 |   4 |   60 | MVY   |   -1 |   1.66
54 |   4 |   52 | BOS   |   -1 |   1.77
55 |   4 |   49 | MVY   |    1 |   2.00
56 |   4 |   42 | BOS   |   -1 |   2.12
57 |   4 |   41 | MVY   |    1 |   2.23
58 |   4 |   54 | BGR   |   -1 |   2.65
59 |   4 |   50 | ABE   |   -1 |   3.38
60 |   4 |   31 | TEB   |    5 |   5.00
61 |   4 |   32 | BOS   |   -5 |   5.31
62 |   4 |    3 | BOS   |    4 |   5.31
63 |   4 |    4 | MIA   |   -4 |   7.41
64 |   4 |   21 | MIA   |    2 |   7.41
65 |   4 |   23 | MIA   |    2 |   7.41
66 |   4 |   22 | BOS   |   -2 |   9.51
67 |   4 |   24 | BGR   |   -2 |   9.84
68 |   4 |    0 | TEB   |    0 |  10.47
(68 rows)

Time: 2224.260 ms
```

The result rightly shows that we can never accommodate more than five passengers; so a drop off is required when we have five onboard before we can pick up again. Also notice that the function ignored our input of the maximum number of jets. Although we stipulated we have a fleet of two, the solution came back calling for four jets.

If we have jets with higher capacity, we would be able to pick up more passengers before needing to drop off and, as a result, we could get by with a smaller fleet. For instance, in our previous example, if we upsize to large jets that can hold twenty passengers, we'd end up needing only two jets. See output below:

```
 seq | jet | cust | airport | pas | c_hrs
-----+-----+------+---------+-----+-------
   1 |   1 |    0 | TEB     |   0 | 0.00
   :
   8 |   1 |    1 | BOS     |   4 | 4.62
   9 |   1 |    3 | BOS     |   4 | 4.62
  10 |   1 |   15 | BGR     |   4 | 5.00
  11 |   1 |   11 | BGR     |   4 | 5.00
  12 |   1 |   34 | BGR     |  -5 | 5.00
  13 |   1 |    2 | BGR     |  -4 | 5.00
  14 |   1 |   19 | BGR     |   4 | 5.00
   :
  34 |   1 |    4 | MIA     |  -4 | 7.91
  35 |   1 |   14 | MIA     |  -4 | 7.91
  36 |   1 |    0 | TEB     |   0 | 9.74
  37 |   2 |    0 | TEB     |   0 | 0.00
   :
  51 |   2 |   45 | MVY     |   1 | 2.97
  52 |   2 |   56 | MIA     |  -1 | 4.98
  53 |   2 |   21 | MIA     |   2 | 6.00
  54 |   2 |   29 | MIA     |   2 | 6.00
  55 |   2 |   27 | MIA     |   2 | 6.00
  56 |   2 |   25 | MIA     |   2 | 6.00
  57 |   2 |   46 | MIA     |  -1 | 6.00
  58 |   2 |   23 | MIA     |   2 | 6.00
  59 |   2 |   30 | ABE     |  -2 | 7.76
   :
  64 |   2 |    0 | TEB     |   0 | 9.25
(64 rows)

Time: 1780.539 ms
```

Using _pgr_pickDeliver for Paired Pick/Deliver

The output of the pgr_gsoc_vrppdtw function contains the bare minimum for planning each jet's itinerary. Using the underlying _pgr_pickDeliver, we receive more details about each leg. Repeating the last exercise, using _pgr_pickDeliver:

Listing 14.8: Using _pgr_pickDeliver to compute itinerary

```
SELECT
    n.seq, n.vehicle_id AS jet, n.stop_id AS cust, pd.airport AS ap, pd.demand AS
    to_char(
        '8:00 AM'::time + (departure_time/1000/981*60 || ' minutes')::interval,
```

```
            'HH12:MM AM'
    ) AS dtime,
    (wait_time/1000/981)::numeric(10,2) AS w_hrs,
    (travel_time/1000/981)::numeric(10,2) AS tl_hrs,
    (n.departure_time/1000/981)::numeric(10,2) AS c_hrs
    FROM _pgr_pickDeliver(
        $$
            SELECT
                id, x, y, demand,
                opentime, closetime, servicetime,
                pindex, dindex
            FROM jet_customers
            ORDER BY id
        $$,
        max_vehicles:= 2,
        capacity := 20,
        speed := 1
    ) AS n  LEFT JOIN
    jet_customers AS pd ON n.stop_id = pd.id
ORDER BY n.seq;
```

```
 seq | jet | cust | ap  | pas | dtime    | w_hrs | tl_hrs | c_hrs
-----+-----+------+-----+-----+----------+-------+--------+-------
  1 |   1 |    0 | TEB |   0 | 08:00 AM | 0.00 |   0.00 |  0.00
  :
  8 |   1 |    1 | BOS |   4 | 12:00 PM | 0.00 |   0.31 |  4.62
  9 |   1 |    3 | BOS |   4 | 12:00 PM | 0.00 |   0.00 |  4.62
 10 |   1 |   15 | BGR |   4 | 01:00 PM | 0.04 |   0.33 |  5.00
 11 |   1 |   11 | BGR |   4 | 01:00 PM | 0.00 |   0.00 |  5.00
 12 |   1 |   34 | BGR |  -5 | 01:00 PM | 0.00 |   0.00 |  5.00
 13 |   1 |    2 | BGR |  -4 | 01:00 PM | 0.00 |   0.00 |  5.00
 14 |   1 |   19 | BGR |   4 | 01:00 PM | 0.00 |   0.00 |  5.00
  :
 34 |   1 |    4 | MIA |  -4 | 03:00 PM | 0.00 |   0.00 |  7.91
 35 |   1 |   14 | MIA |  -4 | 03:00 PM | 0.00 |   0.00 |  7.91
 36 |   1 |    0 | TEB |   0 | 05:00 PM | 0.00 |   1.83 |  9.74
 37 |   2 |    0 | TEB |   0 | 08:00 AM | 0.00 |   0.00 |  0.00
  :
 51 |   2 |   45 | MVY |   1 | 10:00 AM | 0.00 |   0.42 |  2.97
 52 |   2 |   56 | MIA |  -1 | 12:00 PM | 0.00 |   2.02 |  4.98
 53 |   2 |   21 | MIA |   2 | 02:00 PM | 1.02 |   0.00 |  6.00
 54 |   2 |   29 | MIA |   2 | 02:00 PM | 0.00 |   0.00 |  6.00
 55 |   2 |   27 | MIA |   2 | 02:00 PM | 0.00 |   0.00 |  6.00
 56 |   2 |   25 | MIA |   2 | 02:00 PM | 0.00 |   0.00 |  6.00
 57 |   2 |   46 | MIA |  -1 | 02:00 PM | 0.00 |   0.00 |  6.00
 58 |   2 |   23 | MIA |   2 | 02:00 PM | 0.00 |   0.00 |  6.00
 59 |   2 |   30 | ABE |  -2 | 03:00 PM | 0.00 |   1.76 |  7.76
  :
 64 |   2 |    0 | TEB |   0 | 05:00 PM | 0.00 |   0.00 |  9.25
 65 |  -1 |    0 | TEB |   0 | 02:00 AM | 4.02 |  14.97 | 18.99
```

```
(65 rows)

Time: 1870.948 ms
```

In addition to breaking down the time spent servicing versus flying, and providing clock times, the very last row (row corresponding to vehicle_id = -1) provides a summary.

In a future version of _pgr_pickDeliver, we'll be able to input a cost matrix as well as be able to have a mix of fleets with different speeds and capacities. By having a cost matrix we'll be able to adjust cost parameters by airport. For example, we expect a stop in Atlanta, the world's most congested airport, to take much longer than a stop in rustic Martha's Vineyard.

14.4   Using _pgr_pickDeliver for the One Depot Problem

The Vehicle Routing Single Depot with Time Windows, on page 173 solution to the one depot problem using pgr_vrpOneDepot masks a hidden shortcoming—trucks are not allowed to return to the depot to restock.

In our earlier beer delivery example, the trucks are filled to capacity at the beginning of the delivery run. Once they have exhausted their kegs, the trucks return to the brewery and call it a day. This leaves open the possibility that some restaurants could miss their delivery altogether if the trucks can't get to them within one fill-up. The more realistic scenario allows the trucks to return to the brewery for more. To arrive at this solution, we can repurpose the new _pgr_pickDeliver function by adding pick-up and drop-off pairs between the brewery and each of the restaurants. You will give up a few niceties when using _pgr_pickDeliver (at least until pgRouting 3.0) such as the ability to specify differing capacities for your vehicle, ability to feed in a cost matrix based on a network, and no ability to predefine the number of vehicles in your fleet. Still, for the sake of the patrons at the restaurant whose delivery would be canceled, _pgr_pickDeliver is infinitely more desirable than pgr_vrpOneDepot.

Let's restructure our input table for _pgr_pickDeliver:

Listing 14.9: Create vrpdtw_beer

```
1  CREATE TABLE vrpdtw_beer AS
2  WITH
3      depot AS (
4          SELECT id, ST_X(geom) As x, ST_Y(geom) AS y,
5                  open_time AS opentime, close_time AS closetime
6          FROM vrp1_orders,
7              LATERAL ST_Transform(
8                  ST_SetSRID(ST_Point(x,y),4326), 2163) AS geom
9          WHERE id = 13),
10     r AS (
11         SELECT  id,
12             ST_X(geom) AS x, ST_Y(geom) AS y,
13             order_unit As demand,
14             open_time AS opentime, close_time AS closetime,
15             service_time AS servicetime
16           FROM vrp1_orders,
17             LATERAL ST_Transform(
18                 ST_SetSRID(ST_Point(x,y),4326), 2163) AS geom
19         WHERE id <> 13
20     )
21  -- Our brewery
22  SELECT
23      id AS rid, 0 AS id,
24      x, y ,
25      opentime, closetime, 0 AS servicetime,
26      0 AS demand, 0 AS pIndex, 0 AS dIndex
27  FROM depot
28  UNION ALL
29  -- Our pickups, all from depot
30  SELECT
31      r.id AS rid, (r.id * 2 - 1) AS id,
32      r.x, r.y,
33      r.opentime, r.closetime, servicetime,
34      demand, 0 AS pIndex, r.id * 2 AS dIndex
35  FROM r CROSS JOIN depot d
36  UNION ALL
37  -- Our delivery to restaurants
38  SELECT
39      r.id As rid, id * 2 AS id,
40      x, y,
41      opentime, closetime, servicetime,
42      -demand, (id * 2 - 1) AS pIndex, 0 AS dIndex
43  FROM r;
```

In Listing 14.9, we create a table called vrpdtw_beer that consists
of orders in the format required by _pgr_pickDeliver. This is built

from the `vrp1_orders` we created for `pgr_vrpOneDepot`.

Note that for each delivery record, we must have a corresponding pickup from the depot spot and the depot must have an id of `0`.

We ensure that each pickup and delivery has a unique stop identifier by using a function of the restaurant identifier r.id

Pickups will have ids of (`r.id * 2 -1`) and deliveries will be `id *` 2.

We generate the pickup and delivery ids from the restaurant/depot identifiers to generate a predictable set of ids we can use to fill in the pickup stop ids and delivery stop ids.

In the case of the pickup rows generated by *lines 30-35*, the demand is a positive number denoting the number of kegs we are loading on our truck from depot `pIndex` (stop = `0`) for delivery stop denoted by `dIndex` which corresponds to the delivery `id` column defined in *line 39*.

Lines 37-43 generate the delivery stops. The `pIndex` in *line 42* denotes the id of the matching pickup stop defined in *line 31* and `0` in dIndex is where we got the delivery (the depot). Since we are dropping off load, our demand is negative of what we picked up.

We set our cost units to meters again using a measure preserving spatial reference system (2163) which is relatively accurate for our continental US. This will allow us to be able to use speed in meters/minute when we use the `_pgr_pickDeliver` function.

Now we apply our function using code in Listing 14.10.

Note that we set our mileage to be in units of meters, how many meters can we travel per minute, so our speed units line up with what we modelled for time.

Listing 14.10: VRP for 1 depot using pick deliver

SELECT

```
    n.seq, n.vehicle_id AS truck, n.stop_id AS stop,
    COALESCE(r.loc_name, 'Depot') AS name, demand,
    SUM(pd.demand) OVER(PARTITION BY n.vehicle_id ORDER BY seq) AS load,
    departure_time::integer AS tdepart, travel_time::integer AS ttravel
FROM
    _pgr_pickDeliver(
        $$
            SELECT
                id, x, y,
                demand, opentime, closetime, servicetime, pindex, dindex
            FROM vrpdtw_beer
            ORDER BY id
        $$,
        max_vehicles:= 1,
        capacity := 200,
        speed := 70 * 1000 / 60
    ) AS n LEFT JOIN
    vrpdtw_beer AS pd ON n.stop_id = pd.id LEFT JOIN
    restaurants_99 AS r ON pd.rid = r.id
ORDER BY n.seq;
```

In our revised beer truck example, we assume that our trucks can sustain a speed of 70 kph (70*1000/60 meters/minute) with a capacity of 200 kegs.

Though we lost the ability to have different kinds of trucks, we gained one ability. Because each pickup at the depot has a corresponding delivery record, our trucks don't have to pickup all the beer on their first trip, they can circle back to the depot if it's more convenient. Our solution tells us that we only need one truck which circles back to the brewery several times to restock.

The output is as follows

seq	truck	stop	name	demand	load	tdepart	ttravel
1	1	0	Depot	0	0	0	0
2	1	21	Depot	200	200	0	0
3	1	22	Vernon, CT	-200	0	15	15
4	1	9	Depot	50	50	31	15
5	1	3	Depot	50	100	31	0
6	1	23	Depot	50	150	31	0
7	1	17	Depot	50	200	31	0
8	1	8	Enfield, CT	-50	150	35	4
9	1	20	Torrington, CT	-50	100	77	43
10	1	4	Cromwell, CT	-50	50	114	36

```
 11 |    1 |  10 | Glastonbury, CT |  -50 |    0 |  126 |   13
 12 |    1 |   5 | Depot           |   50 |   50 |  152 |   26
 13 |    1 |   1 | Depot           |   50 |  100 |  152 |    0
 14 |    1 |  19 | Depot           |   50 |  150 |  152 |    0
 15 |    1 |  15 | Depot           |   50 |  200 |  152 |    0
 16 |    1 |  16 | Norwich, CT     |  -50 |  150 |  206 |   53
 17 |    1 |  12 | Groton, CT      |  -50 |  100 |  220 |   15
 18 |    1 |  14 | Dayville, CT    |  -50 |   50 |  269 |   48
 19 |    1 |  11 | Depot           |   50 |  100 |  315 |   46
 20 |    1 |   7 | Depot           |   50 |  150 |  315 |    0
 21 |    1 |  13 | Depot           |   50 |  200 |  315 |    0
 22 |    1 |  24 | Wallingford, CT |  -50 |  150 |  368 |   53
 23 |    1 |  18 | Stratford, CT   |  -50 |  100 |  404 |   36
 24 |    1 |   6 | Danbury, CT     |  -50 |   50 |  432 |   29
 25 |    1 |   2 | Bristol, CT     |  -50 |    0 |  477 |   45
 26 |    1 |   0 | Depot           |    0 |    0 |  518 |   40
 27 |   -1 |   0 | Depot           |    0 |    0 |  518 |  518
(27 rows)

Time: 99.079 ms
```

Our trucks can hold 200 kegs at a time. As such they begin delivery as soon as they are loaded up and must return to the brewery whenever stock falls below the demand of the next restaurant on the delivery schedule.

15 Routing with Turn Restriction Functions

In the real world, motorists face turn restrictions, such as no U-turns, no left turns, toll avoidance, or police avoidance.

15.1 Routing with turn restrictions

pgRouting has a family of functions, *Turn Restrictions Shortest-Path* (TRSP), which use an algorithm similar to `pgr_dijkstra` and `pgr_dijkstraVia`, but unlike these, they can incorporate additional tables to apply turn restrictions and path sequences.

In this chapter we'll focus on three elders of the family:

- `pgr_trsp`
- `pgr_trspViaVertices`
- `pgr_trspViaEdges`

The code and data for this chapter can be found in the book download file at `code/turn_restrictions.sql` and `data/ospr_data.psql` respectively. Make sure to load the data file with `psql`.

15.2 pgr_trsp

The bread winner of the TRSP family is `pgr_trsp`. This function has a number of signatures of which we'll only cover the most frequently used one.

The signature of the function as of pgRouting 2.2 is:

```
pgr_trsp(
    edges_sql text,
    start_vid integer,
    end_vid integer,
    directed boolean,
```

```
    has_rcost boolean,
    restrictions_sql text DEFAULT NULL::text)
RETURNS SETOF pgr_costresult
```

> The argument restrictions_sql has undergone name changes over the versions. In pgRouting 2.1.0 it was called turn_restrict_sql.

The signature of the parameters begins the same way as the old 2.0 Version pgr_dijkstra, but you have the option of tagging on an additional argument named restrictions_sql.

restrictions_sql must be able to return a set of rows with the following column names: target_id, to_cost, and via_path.

We recommend you create a separate table that will store turn restrictions and then select from this table for the restrictions_sql argument as in the following:

```
SELECT target_id, via_path, to_cost FROM restrictions;
```

Putting Together a Restrictions Table

In order to use the restriction feature, the easiest way is to create a restrictions table to hold the restrictions.

A restrictions table suitable for pgr_trsp would look something like:

```
CREATE TABLE restrictions (
    rid serial primary key,
    to_edge integer,

    via_path text,
    to_cost double precision,
);
```

Each restriction row can encompass multiple edges. All edges that are part of a single restriction must be adjacent. Specify the id of either the first or last edge of the restriction in to_edge. From there, enumerate connected edges until the other end of the restriction using via_path. Specify via_path as a comma separated list of edge ids excluding the id of to_edge. If a restriction spans no more than a single edge, leave `via_path` NULL. Strictly speaking, a single-edge restriction is not a turn restriction but we treat it as such anyway. `to_cost` lets you specify the cost surcharge for traversing the restriction in its entirety. This could be the expected value of the fine for an illegal left turn, a toll, or the extra driving time to navigate treacherous switchbacks.

Here's a diagram of a "double-ten" intersection (`https://en.wikipedia.org/wiki/National_Day_of_the_Republic_of_China`):

```
         1      2
         v      ^
         |      |
 ----5---+--6--+---7-----
         |      |
         v      ^
         3      4
```

A north-south divided highway intersecting an undivided, east-west road engenders the following restrictions.

No U-turns:

```
to_edge | via_path
2       | 6, 1
3       | 6, 4
```

No turns into oncoming traffic:

```
to_edge | via_path 1 | 6 1 | 5 4 | 6 4 | 7
```

Assuming that traffic signals are not in place, we should not allow left turns onto the divided highway.

```
to_edge | via_path 3 | 6 2 | 6
```

You're at liberty to choose the `to_cost` of violating the restriction. Make sure you abide by the general cost structure of your network. That is, if you're measuring dollars, impose cost as dollars; if measuring travel time, impose cost as travel times in the same unit. Cost could vary by restriction: a turn to oncoming traffic is infinitely costlier than an illegal U-turn. In fact, you probably should set the cost of all turn restrictions to some relatively huge number to prevent any algorithm from even considering their traversal.

Load Restrictions from OSM Data

If you're sourcing your network from OpenStreetMap, you're in luck. OSM data already includes turn restrictions. See http://wiki.openstreetmap.org/wiki/Relation:restriction for a full listing and descriptions. You'll get a taste of all the esoteric restrictions found around the world.

Despite their inclusion, you still must map the restrictions to pgRouting flavors. A more difficult task is to figure out the to_edge and the via_path. Remember that OSM does not come to us as a routable network. We have to impose a network onto the OSM data using PostGIS machinations. Before we show you how to do this, let's get hold of some OSM data.

Our practice is to treat OSM source as a foreign table to avoid having to lease space to OSM data in our database. Furthermore, why bother importing if we have the foreign data wrapper available. In Using ogr_fdw with OpenStreetMap, on page 74 we created a foreign table called fdwt.osm_dc_other_relations based on the other_relations layer found in the Washington, DC OSM file.

OSM stores restrictions as hstore tags named *restriction*. To access data stored as hstore use the ? operator as in the following:

Listing 15.1: Types of restrictions in OSM

```
SELECT DISTINCT other_tags::hstore->'restriction' AS val
FROM fdwt.osm_dc_other_relations
WHERE other_tags::hstore ? 'restriction'
ORDER BY val;
```

The following types should turn up. Your list could be different. Perhaps more than any other city, DC activates and deactivates restrictions at will to accommodate the latest political wind.

```
        val
-------------------
  no_left_turn
  no_right_turn
  no_straight_on
  no_u_turn
  only_right_turn
  only_straight_on
(6 rows)
```

We'll start by inserting all the restrictions from OSM into a new table `ospr.restrictions` as shown in Listing 15.2. We leave the to_edge and the via_path NULL for now and we assign a big number to cost to prevent traversal.

Listing 15.2: Create ospr.restrictions

```
WITH
    c AS (
        SELECT osm_id::bigint, other_tags::hstore, ST_SetSRID(geom,4326) AS geom
        FROM fdwt.osm_dc_other_relations
    )
SELECT
    c.osm_id, other_tags->'restriction' AS restriction_type,
    geom,
    100000::float8 AS to_cost,
    NULL::integer AS to_edge,
    NULL::text AS via_path
INTO ospr.restrictions
FROM c
```

OSM restrictions via ogrfdw are represented as geometry collections. OSM restrictions generally do not span more than two adjacent linestring segments. Should the restriction apply to more than two segments, OSM segregates them into different restrictions. This leaves us with the three common possibilities:

- A single linestring of two segments
- Two distinct one-segment linestrings that touch
- A one-segment linestring for en route restrictions

This is a good time to remind you that we already loaded the DC data using osm2pgrouting to create `ospr.ways`, the table of all edges, and `ospr.ways_vertices_pgr`, the table of all nodes.

As of this writing, osm2pgrouting does not load restrictions, however in a future version you can expect it to.

The foreign tables link to the same OSM data we used. We've included the `ospr.restrictions` table as part of `ospr_data.psql`, so you can skip these creation exercises if you want to.

In the most straight forward scenario, each linestring segment maps to an edge. Unfortunately, a linestring segment could map to more than one edge during noding. Typically this happens when an intersecting linestring bisects a continuous linestring forming an intersection.

To figure out `to_edge` of the restriction, we use the following query:

Listing 15.3: Update to_edge

```
UPDATE ospr.restrictions AS rn
SET to_edge = e.gid
FROM
    ospr.restrictions AS ro,
    LATERAL ST_GeometryN(ST_CollectionExtract(ro.geom,2),
        ST_NumGeometries(ST_CollectionExtract(ro.geom,2))) AS l_geom,
    LATERAL (
        SELECT gid, e.the_geom
        FROM ospr.ways AS e INNER JOIN ospr.ways_vertices_pgr AS n
            ON e.target = n.id
        WHERE
            ST_Covers(e.the_geom,l_geom) OR
            ST_Covers(l_geom, e.the_geom)
        ORDER BY ST_Distance(ST_EndPoint(l_geom), n.the_geom ) ASC
        LIMIT 1
    ) AS e
WHERE rn.osm_id = ro.osm_id;
```

We made use of PostGIS functions, `ST_Covers`, `ST_GeometryN`, and `ST_CollectionExtract` in Listing 15.3.

We use the `ST_CollectionExtract` function to extract just the linestrings (designated by type 2) in the geometry collection. It will return a MULTILINESTRING consisting of just the linestrings in the geometry collection.

We use ST_GeometryN and ST_NumGeometries to return just the last
linestring from the MULTILINESTRING collection. The ST_NumGeometries
function gives us the index to the last linestring. This is because the
restrictions in the OSM table are defined in order of traversal, but
we need the target (the last edge) as a separate element.

This linestring could conceivably be composed of more than one
edge, which is why we use ST_Covers in both directions, but only
want the first edge whose end point is closest to endpoint of our
first edge. This should correspond to the target edge (to_edge).

Next we'll compute the via_path using Listing 15.4 .

Listing 15.4: Update via_path

```
UPDATE ospr.restrictions AS rn
SET via_path = er.via
FROM (
    SELECT
        ro.osm_id,
        string_agg(
            CASE WHEN ro.to_edge <> e.gid THEN e.gid::text ELSE NULL END,
            ',' ORDER BY i DESC, e.rn DESC
        ) AS via
    FROM
        ospr.restrictions AS ro, LATERAL
        ST_CollectionExtract(ro.geom,2) AS ml_geom, LATERAL
        generate_series(1,ST_NumGeometries(ml_geom)) AS i, LATERAL
        ST_GeometryN(ml_geom,i) AS l_geom, LATERAL
        (
            SELECT
                ROW_NUMBER()
                OVER(
                    ORDER BY
                        ST_LineLocatePoint(l_geom, n.the_geom)
                ) AS rn,
                e.gid, e.source, e.target
            FROM ospr.ways AS e INNER JOIN ospr.ways_vertices_pgr AS n ON e.target = n.id
            WHERE  ST_Covers(l_geom,e.the_geom) OR ST_Covers(e.the_geom, l_geom)
        ) AS e
    GROUP BY ro.osm_id
) AS er
WHERE rn.osm_id = er.osm_id;

DELETE FROM ospr.restrictions WHERE to_edge IS NULL;
```

Since the subsequent linestrings can be composed of more than one edge, we use ST_Covers again to determine which edges are covered by each linestring. We use ST_LineLocatePoint to order the edges in the order they appear in the linestring. We delete the remaining restrictions that we couldn't match up either because they were invalid or didn't contain our relevant edges.

pgr_trsp Single Source and Target with Restrictions

With all the prep work done, we finally return to our pgr_trsp function.

We extract a snippet From our DC OSM data: connecting Georgetown to Virginia is the elegant Francis Scott Key bridge (not to be confused with the longer steel arch bridge of the same name in Baltimore harbor). We're in a car at the DC approach to the bridge and wish to end up on Whitehurst Fwy NW (US 29) eastbound, on our way into the heart of DC. An OSM restriction is in place to prevent us from getting on the bridge, making a U-turn on the bridge, and taking a right exit onto Whitehurst eastbound. A sensible restriction by all means! Let's take a look at this restriction using QGIS by pasting Listing 15.5 query into the QGIS DbManager SQL Window:

Listing 15.5: Display restrictions

```
SELECT r.osm_id, 0 AS rn, e.the_geom AS geom, e.gid AS edge_id
FROM
    ospr.restrictions AS r
    INNER JOIN
    ospr.ways AS e
    ON r.to_edge = e.gid
WHERE r.osm_id = 5299735
UNION ALL
SELECT r.osm_id, f.rn AS rn, e.the_geom AS geom, e.gid AS edge_id
FROM
    ospr.restrictions AS r,
    unnest( ('{' || r.via_path || '}')::bigint[]) WITH ORDINALITY AS f(eid,rn)
    INNER JOIN
    ospr.ways AS e ON f.eid = e.gid
WHERE r.osm_id = 5299735;
```

After we overlay the ospr.ways_vertices_pgr and ospr.ways with this query, we get image shown in Figure 15.1.

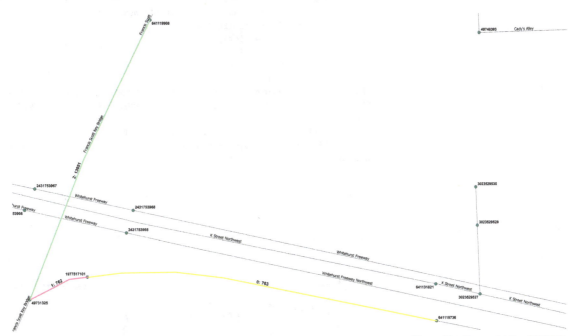

Figure 15.1: Turn restriction 5299735

This tells us that any solution that goes to edge 0 (corresponding to edge id: 763) from edge id: 13051 (2) via edge id: 762 (1) should not be allowed or should be given a high penalty.

In our restrictions table to_edge = 763 and via_path = '762, 13051'. The first via_path edge is the one that connects to the to_edge.

Our figure labels the OSM ID of the nodes, from which we can discern that a path from 641119908 to 641119736 must not include the U-turn on the bridge. We want to get to WhiteHurst eastbound junction (osm node: 641119744).

Let's first route without the restriction.

If we use without restriction, but considering with directed and reverse cost running query in Listing 15.6:

Listing 15.6: Not using turn restrictions

```
SELECT r.seq,  r.id1 AS node, n.osm_id AS node_osm, n.the_geom AS node_geom,
    r.id2 AS edge, e.name AS street, r.cost::numeric(10,4)
 FROM pgr_trsp('SELECT gid::int4 AS id,
                   source::int4,
                   target::int4,
                   cost, reverse_cost
                 FROM ospr.ways',
 (SELECT id::int4 FROM ospr.ways_vertices_pgr WHERE osm_id = 641119908),
 (SELECT id::int4 FROM ospr.ways_vertices_pgr WHERE osm_id = 641119744),
 true, true ) AS r
         INNER JOIN ospr.ways_vertices_pgr AS n ON r.id1 = n.id
         LEFT JOIN ospr.ways AS e ON r.id2 = e.gid
 ORDER BY r.seq;
```

it goes through the restricted path as shown in Figure 15.2.

Figure 15.2: Without restriction

```
seq | node  |  node_osm  | edge  |          street          | cost
----+-------+------------+-------+--------------------------+-------
  0 | 10834 |  641119908 | 13051 | Francis Scott Key Bridge | 0.0009
  1 | 16754 |   49731325 |   762 |                          | 0.0002
  2 |  4753 | 1977517101 |   763 |                          | 0.0011
  3 |  8039 |  641119736 | 13710 |                          | 0.0020
  4 |  9086 |  641119744 |    -1 | NULL                     | 0.0000
(5 rows)

Time: 155.559 ms
```

We repeat with the restriction activated, using Listing 15.7:

Listing 15.7: Using turn restrictions

```
SELECT r.seq,   r.id1 AS node, n.osm_id AS node_osm,
     n.the_geom As node_geom,
     r.id2 AS edge, e.name AS street, r.cost::numeric(10,4)
  FROM pgr_trsp('SELECT gid::int4 AS id,
                  source::int4,
                  target::int4,
                  cost, reverse_cost
              FROM ospr.ways',
 (SELECT id::int4 FROM ospr.ways_vertices_pgr WHERE osm_id = 641119908),
 (SELECT id::int4 FROM ospr.ways_vertices_pgr WHERE osm_id = 641119744),
 true, true,
      $$
          SELECT to_cost, to_edge AS target_id, via_path
          FROM ospr.restrictions$$ ) AS r
      INNER JOIN ospr.ways_vertices_pgr AS n ON r.id1 = n.id
      LEFT JOIN ospr.ways AS e ON r.id2 = e.gid
 ORDER BY r.seq;
```

seq	node	node_osm	edge	street	cost
0	10834	641119908	13723	Francis Scott Key Bridge	0.0001
1	20037	641119722	13709	Francis Scott Key Bridge	0.0003
2	21437	641119730	15034	M Street Northwest	0.0002
3	14157	459806081	15035	M Street Northwest	0.0002
4	3862	49845863	18300	M Street Northwest	0.0004
5	13656	1021653276	13052	M Street Northwest	0.0004
6	21976	641119877	13716	M Street Northwest	0.0003
7	5010	2431676888	13717	M Street Northwest	0.0001
8	2183	640965915	1300	Canal Road Northwest	0.0040
9	3274	647241842	1301	Canal Road Northwest	0.0014
10	168	883610478	1302	Canal Road Northwest	0.0027
11	12931	647241859	1303	Canal Road Northwest	0.0008
12	14135	800646501	1304	Canal Road Northwest	0.0001
13	19752	647241559	15028	Canal Road Northwest	0.0002
14	14926	647241451	15029	Canal Road Northwest	0.0082
15	14292	647241645	15030	Canal Road Northwest	0.0005
16	22016	49720215	13712	Whitehurst Freeway	0.0004
17	7403	641119757	13713	Whitehurst Freeway	0.0014
18	9553	2431753966	26532	Whitehurst Freeway	0.0003
19	12812	2431753965	26531	Whitehurst Freeway Northwest	0.0030
20	9086	641119744	-1	NULL	0.0000

(21 rows)

Time: 207.886 ms

As shown in Figure 15.3, on the next page, the routing asks you to head in the reverse direction, avoid the bridge entirely, and make your way onto Whitehurst using local streets.

Figure 15.3: With restrictions

We again remind you that if you don't have turn restrictions or know a priori that your restrictions aren't binding, choose `pgr_dijkstra` over `pgr_trsp`. If you're not sure if the restrictions bind, you can use `pgr_trsp` first to check. If the selected path is no where near your restrictions, you may wish to just stick to `pgr_dijkstra`. For example, if you're planning a cross country drive from Boston to San Francisco, highway closures in Oklahoma probably won't affect you. Best to check when in doubt.

15.3   *pgr_trspViaVertices and pgr_trspViaEdges*

Use `pgr_trspViaVertices` and `pgr_trspViaEdges` to place sequencing constraints.

`pgr_trspViaVertices` takes a set of vertex IDs with an argument named `vids`. The order of the IDs would be the order of prescribed travel sequence.

If you have no turn restrictions and are using pgRouting 2.2 or above, you should use `pgr_dijkstraVia` instead of `pgr_trspViaVertices`.

`pgr_trspViaEdges` takes a set of edges IDs with an argument named `eids` and fractional positions along the edges named `pcts`.

`pgr_trspViaEdges` is used when you have a set of stopping points that are not nodes in your network and you need to traverse them in a given order. As of pgRouting 2.4 there is no comparable `pgr_dijkstra` function for this, so even if you have no turn restrictions but need to use points instead of nodes, you need to use `pgr_trspViaEdges`.

`pgr_trspViaEdges` uses the edges and the fractional location of the point on the edge to represent the point as a node in the network. `pgr_trspViaEdges` takes as input an array of edge ids denoted by `eids` and an array of fractional positions (between 0-1) that tells what percent along each edge the point is located. This array is named `pcts`.

Note that you should have an equal number of edges and fractional positions and they must be aligned with each other. For example, you could have an edge with edge id 1, in position 3 and 5 of your edge array, and the corresponding fractional position of the points along the edge in the `pcts` array in position 3 and 5.

One reason to use `pgr_trspViaEdges` is when you have an order of stopping points. For the case where your stopping locations are nodes in the network and you have no turn restrictions, you should use `pgr_dijkstraVia` as we covered in Listing 11.10, on page 140.

In Listing 15.8 we repeat the same exercise as Listing 11.10, on page 140 but using the virtual nodes (actual points) instead of the closest node.

Listing 15.8: trsp via points of interest

```
SELECT r.seq, r.id1 AS route_id,
```

```
              r.id2 AS node, r.id3 AS edge,
              r.cost
     FROM pgr_trspViaEdges(
     $$SELECT gid::int4 AS id,
              source::int4, target::int4,
              length_m::float8 AS cost
              FROM ospr.ways$$,
     ARRAY(SELECT edge_id::int
            FROM visit_pois
            ORDER BY id),
     ARRAY(SELECT fraction
            FROM visit_pois
            ORDER BY id), false, false
     ) AS r;
```

```
 seq | route_id | node  | edge  |        cost
-----+----------+-------+-------+------------------
   1 |        1 |    -1 | 20336 | 60.8105766963955
   2 |        1 |  6934 | 19665 | 57.732137183652
   3 |        1 | 10324 | 19664 | 41.9212082098471
   :
 123 |        1 | 20941 |  2662 | 6.95532272497439
 124 |        1 | 14678 | 29794 | 41.9200761310422
 125 |        2 | 11280 | 29794 | 41.920076131042
 126 |        2 | 14678 |  2662 | 6.95532272497417
   :
 148 |        2 | 11258 |  1811 | 28.9690552532593
 149 |        2 | 22491 |  1812 | 176.889262893506
 150 |        3 | 18816 |  1813 | 8.60905790699112
 151 |        3 | 12320 | 29978 | 12.2980003788771
 152 |        3 | 18728 | 29977 | 59.6803506661826
   :
 191 |        3 | 16784 | 31713 | 8.25137522968043
 192 |        3 | 17338 | 31715 | 67.8615560959229
(192 rows)
```

Part 4

Using QGIS with pgRouting

In this part we explore QGIS and its related plugins that are commonly used with pgRouting. For these exercises we'll be using QGIS 2.16, but all these examples should work fine with QGIS > 2.8. If you do not have QGIS installed already, you can get binaries or instructions for installation from http://qgis.org.

Many of the figures you see in this book were generated using QGIS.

Setting up a PostGIS Connection using PostGIS Add Layer

The first step in using QGIS for any PostGIS work is setting up a connection to your database. Once the PostGIS connection is setup, it is saved for future QGIS work and can be used by many QGIS plugins.

To setup a PostGIS connection do the following:

1. Open up QGIS
2. *On Menu choose* Layer -> Add PostGIS Layer. *Click the* New *button* as shown in Figure 16.1

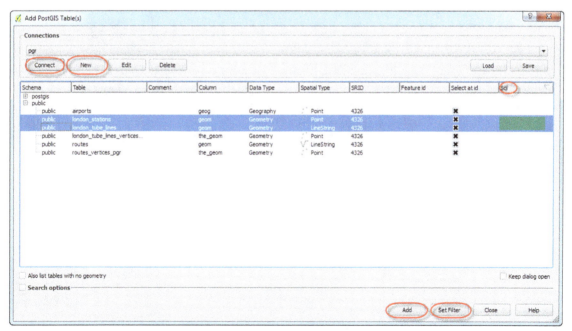

Figure 16.1: PostGIS Layer Add Screen

3. Fill in necessary credentials, database, and port information.
4. If you need to edit an existing connection, click the Edit button instead.
5. Click the *Connect* button to confirm your connection works and all your spatial tables show up.

Highlighted in Figure 16.1, on the preceding page are the following features you'll use often when working with the Add PostGIS Layer menu.

1. *New* allows you to define a new connection
2. *Connect* allows you to connect to the selected connection and lists the tables in that connection
3. *Set Filter* allows you to limit the records to view using an SQL where clause. When you set the filter for a table, the *Sql* column will show the filter.
4. *Add* will add selected tables to your map. We've selected two tables to add to our map.

Once you have a connection established in QGIS, you can use this connection for adding layers to the map overview or in other plug-ins. Once you click the *Add* button on the Add PostGIS Layer dialog your selected layers will be added to the Map View.

17 *Map View Panel*

The Map View is where all map data comes together.

In addition to spatial tables, you can also overlay spatial data files such as ESRI Shapefiles, MapInfo files, and raster files like GeoTiffs.

You can also overlay web services and also outputs of other plugins like the OpenLayers plugin which you'll see shortly.

In order to overlay all these disparate pieces of mappable data, the spatial projection of each should be encoded in the data sources and the data sources need to be reprojectable to a common spatial reference system. QGIS has capability to reproject some data sources so that all share the same common projection. If a data source doesn't specify a spatial reference system, QGIS will pop-up a dialog asking you to choose one.

Figure 17.1, shows the map view with the two layers added earlier. Since both layers are in the same projection they can be overlaid easily.

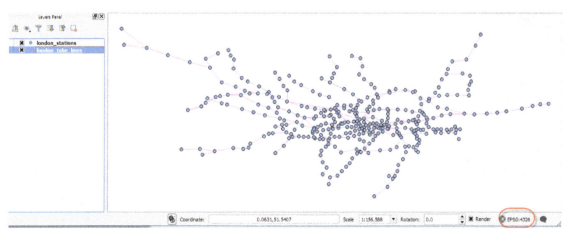

Figure 17.1: Map View

QGIS is very customizable, and is composed of various panels that can be moved around. In the default install state, you'll see the Layers Panel which shows the map layers listed beside the Map View Panel. The status bar of the Map View Panel displays the spatial reference system of the Map as highlighted in Figure 17.1, on the preceding page.

If you double-click on a layer in the Layers Panel, you'll be able to change the styling of it and also add labels using columns in your table for layering as shown in Figure 17.2.

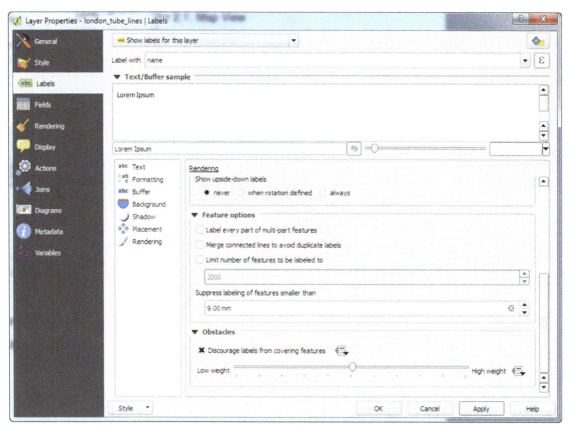

Figure 17.2: Layer | Label Properties

18 DB Manager Plugin

If you are using pgRouting or any kind of database work where ad-hoc queries are needed, the DB Manager is an indispensable tool for viewing your spatial queries.

DB Manager is a plugin that is usually installed as part of the basic QGIS installation. You should see it under the `Database` menu option. If per chance you don't have it installed already, you can install it from the `Plugins -> Manage and Install Plugins` menu, choosing `All`, and doing a search as shown in Figure 18.1

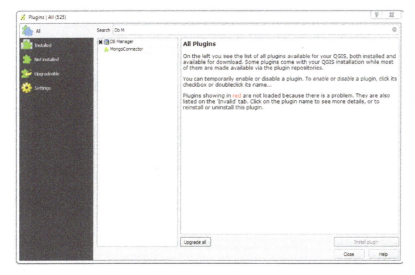

Figure 18.1: DB Manager Install

If it is already installed and active, it will be checked. If not, check it and click the *Install plugin* button. These are the same steps you would use to install any QGIS plugin.

DB Manager uses the same connections defined when you add a PostGIS Layer. You should find DB Manager accessible under `Database -> DB Manager -> DB Manager`. If you expand the `PostGIS` menu to the left, you should see all your PostgreSQL database connections listed.

Expand further and select a geometry table to preview, and you should be rewarded with a view of your data as shown in Figure 18.2.

Figure 18.2: DB Manager Preview

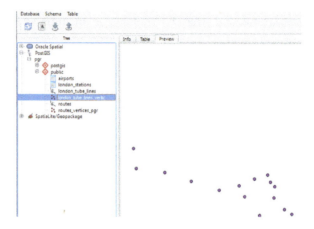

18.1   Features of DB Manager Plugin

The DB Manager Plugin offers the following features

1. Ability to define ad-hoc spatial queries and drag them to a map view. These spatial queries should output at least one geometry column and a field for primary key.
2. Ability to load in new spatial tables. It supports numerous formats since it utilizes GDAL for loading.
3. Ability to do basic maintenance such as create new schemas, create views, and delete tables and views.
4. Ability to drag any table or view with a geometry, geography, or raster column to a map view.

18.2   Using the SQL Query Window

The most useful feature for pgRouting purposes is the SQL window.

With this you can write a full SQL statement. Click the wrench icon and cut and paste the query from Listing 4.5, on page 51 as shown in Figure 18.3.

If you need help constructing your query, you can click the *SQL* icon button. The *SQL* button will pop open a window that will list tables, columns, and commonly used functions such as PostGIS functions.

For queries involving more than one table, such as those in pgRouting, you are better off just typing it in the query window.

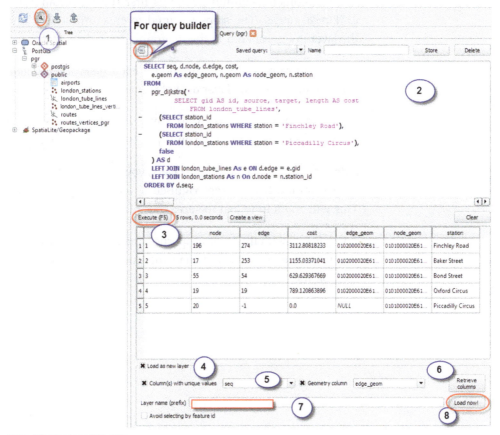

Figure 18.3: DB Manager SQL Window

The query you write should contain at least one geometry column. Clicking *Execute* will output the basic attribute detail of the query.

In order to have a map view of the query, select the column to use as spatial column and an identifier column (seq in this example). Make sure the *Column(s) with unique values* and *Geometry column* checkboxes are checked so you can select the appropriate values.

Give a layer name you want the query to use in your map view and click the *Load Now* button.

Figure 18.3, on the preceding page shows selected the edge_geom for the geometry column. For this first run we'll name the layer dijkstra_route. The steps required to create the query and load the layer are numbered in the diagram.

Repeat the same exercise but choose node_geom for the geometry column and name the layer dijkstra_node.

If you switch back to the Map View, you should see your query layers shown, along with the ability to toggle them on or off.

After you are done loading the layers, you can select the dijkstra_route layer from the *Layers Panel*, right-click, and choose Zoom To Layer. This will zoom in to just the area that fills your query extent.

If you fiddle with the layer properties, putting in labels and so forth, you should end up with a map that looks something like Figure 18.4, on the next page.

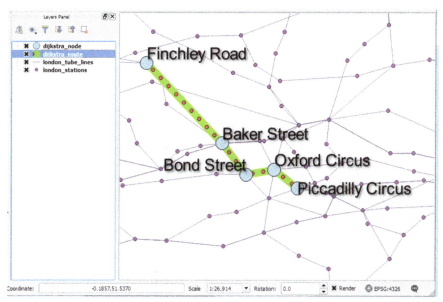

Figure 18.4: Map View zoomed to
query

19 *OpenLayers Plugin*

The OpenLayers Plugin utilizes OpenLayers web map scripting kit to allow you to overlay tile maps such as OpenStreetMap, Google Maps, MapQuest, Bing Maps and others. If it's installed, you'll find it listed under Web -> OpenLayers Plugin as shown in Figure 19.1.

Figure 19.1: OpenLayers Plugin

If you didn't see the OpenLayers Plugin on the menu, you can install it like any other plugin as we did in Figure 18.1, on page 219 for the DB Manager.

The OpenLayers Plugin layer you pick will show in the Layers Panel. In Figure 19.1 we chose the default OpenStreetMap tiles. If the layer ends up at the top, drag it down to the bottom of the layer list so that it gets drawn first and doesn't hide your database layers.

Note that when you add the OpenStreetMap layer, the projection of the map changes to web Mercator, denoted by EPSG:3857 in the lower right of the status bar. Since the OpenStreetMap layer is not reprojectable, QGIS reprojected your database tables to match the OpenStreetMap layer projection.

Figure 19.2, on the next page shows a portion of our query displayed over OpenStreetMap from the OpenLayers plugin.

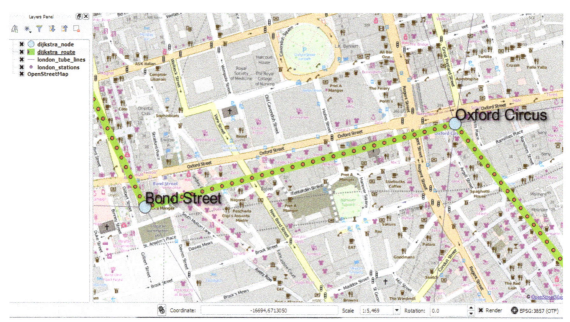

Figure 19.2:   OpenLayers Open-
StreetMap

pgRoutingLayer Plugin

The pgRoutingLayer plugin is designed to help you use pgRouting functions in your QGIS map without having to resort to writing the pgRouting query by hand.

You can think of it as a gui approach to writing the SQL done in Using the SQL Query window, on page 220.

The latest version of the pgRoutingLayer plugin available in the QGIS plugin repository, is version 2.1.0. This version has logic to detect the version of pgRouting installed in your database, and will only show you function options compatible with your version.

20.1   Using Latest Stable

You can always get the latest stable version from the standard QGIS repository. Currently this is version pgRoutingLayer 2.1.0.

If installed, you'll find it under the Database-> pgRouting Layer -> pgRouting Layer menu. If not, install it via the Plugins-> Manage and Install Plugins menu option.

> The pgRoutingLayer plugin is flagged as experimental in the QGIS plugin repository. In order to install it, Click on Settings in the Plugin Manager and check the Show also experimental plugins box. Click the Reload repository button to refresh the list to include pgRoutingLayer, then proceed with the install.

We'll repeat our ad hoc query shown in 18.4, on page 223, but instead of writing SQL, we'll use the pgRouting Layer plugin to write the query for us and click our way through the process.

Before we start, you should uncheck all other layers in the Layers Panel except the london_tube_lines and london_stations layers. You should also show the labels for london_stations using the name column as done in Figure 17.2, on page 218.

> pgRoutingLayer 2.1 plugin supports bigints unlike the older pgRoutingLayer plugin versions.

When you select the pgRoutingLayer Plugin, you should see a pgRouting Layer panel appear as shown in Figure 20.1.

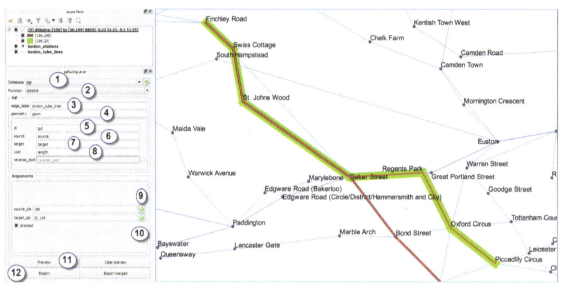

Figure 20.1: pgRoutingLayer Plugin (2.1+)

The steps to use the plugin are as follows and numbered in Figure 20.1.

1. Select your database
2. Select the pgRouting function you'd like to use. For this exercise, we have chosen dijkstra, but you will find many more routing functions in the list, such as aStar, drivingDistance, alphashape, ksp, etc. Depending on the function you pick, the panel of fields to fill in changes. Since we picked dijkstra, you should see the fields pretty closely mirror what we used in our spatial query.
3. Type the name of the edge table.
4. Type the name of the geometry column.

5. Type the name of the edge id column.

6. Type the name of the source column. Note it defaults to `source` so can be left as is.

7. Type the name of the target column. Note it defaults to `target` so can be left as is.

8. Type the name of the cost column.

9. Click the green button next to the `source_id` field and on the map, select the station you want to start at. You should see the node id for that station fill in.

10. *Click the green button next to the* `target_id` *field* and on the map, select the station you want to end at. You should see the node id for that station fill in. Click again if you want to select additional stations.

11. When you click the *Preview* button, the path should be drawn on the map.

12. If you like what you see, you can click the *Export* button which will save this run as a Layer on the map. In this case, the layer `dijkstra - from 196 to 199,20` was added to the map. Note that pgRoutingLayer 2.1 does a bounding box to limit the portion of the network that needs to be analyzed to solve the query.

Note that with the new features in pgRouting 2.2, we get the option of setting multiple trips. So instead of just Finchley To Piccadilly, we planned trips from Finchley with destinations to Piccadilly or Green Park. In this case dijkstra will return two solutions, which we can distinguish and style differently using the `path_name` field of the result. Note also that the newer version has an additional button called *Export Merged*. *Export Merged* will return each solution path as a single linestring, where as the regular *Merged* button will return the path segments of each solution with `path_name` denoting which solution the path segments are for.

We encourage you to explore the other pgRouting functions exposed by this tool.

Part 5

Integrating pgRouting in Web Applications

This part will cover building web applications with pgRouting. After this part you should know how to integrate pgRouting in your web applications and how to display results of pgRouting queries on a web map.

Basic Application Setup

We will create a web application that has a PostgreSQL stored function that makes calls to pgRouting, PostGIS, and PostgreSQL functions. The stored function will be called via a PHP server-side script. The format we'll be using for transporting data will be JavaScript Object Notation (JSON) and Geographic JavaScript Object Notation (GeoJSON)

http://json.org
http://geojson.org

GeoJSON is a common transport format for mapping client frameworks. The main difference between regular JSON and GeoJSON is that GeoJSON consists of an additional attribute called the geometry and formalizes how geometry type should be expressed. We'll be using the PostGIS function ST_AsGeoJSON for converting the geometry part into GeoJSON format.

Many modern web client frameworks are designed to push back inputs as JSON posts and accept data as JSON data objects via web services. Leaflet, the client side mapping framework we'll be using, can consume GeoJSON for display on the map.

http://leafletjs.com

In addition to Leaflet, we'll be using AngularJS in concert with Bootstrap for the client front-end. AngularJS is a popular open source JavaScript-based client framework developed by Google with very rich JSON support that we'll use to handle the requests from the user to our web service.

https://angularjs.org/
http://getbootstrap.com/

PostgreSQL 9.3+ has functionality for working with JSON, making it fairly trivial to keep most of the business logic in the database.

This app will require PostgreSQL 9.3+. PostgreSQL 9.4+ introduced many more functions for working with JSONB(binary JSON) and PostgreSQL 9.5 and 9.6 expanded the JSON function offering to include functions for editing JSON documents.

Requests will be passed from AngularJS to our PHP script as a JSON object and responses will be returned from our PHP script as a JSON object generated by our stored function.

BootStrap is a popular open source styling and UI component library developed by Twitter for building responsive web applications that scale well according to device size. It is commonly used for designing websites and in conjunction with frameworks like AngularJS.

When we are done, our application will look something like Figure 21.1. You can also check it out at http://www.postgis.us/demos/pgr_1e/leafletapp.html.

Figure 21.1: Web App with Leaflet map

Database Stored Functions to Support the App

Our app will consist of several database stored functions, but the only function that our web server will interact with will be a function, aptly named app shown in Listing 22.1. The app function will inspect the request provided as a JSON document and route it to another function if needed.

Listing 22.1: app function

```
CREATE OR REPLACE FUNCTION app(param_input jsonb) RETURNS json AS
$$
DECLARE var_result json;
BEGIN
  IF param_input->>'action' IN('edge_tables','edge_table_extent', 'node','route') THEN
            EXECUTE 'SELECT app_' || quote_ident(param_input->>'action')
                    || '($1)' INTO var_result USING param_input;
  ELSE
        var_result := '"invalid action '
            || COALESCE(param_input->>'action','') || '"'::json;
  END IF;
  RETURN var_result;
END;
$$
language 'plpgsql';
```

The input param_input is the form request we get from the user, which should contain an action property denoting the kind of request.

The ->> is a PostgreSQL operator supported for JSON and JSONB data types. It returns a named property value in the form of text. A similar operator you will find is -> which returns a property value as another JSONB or JSON value. The JSON/JSONB returning variant is useful for pulling out nested objects such as obj->'family'->>'name'.

We are going to support the following kinds of actions:

- edge_tables - Provides a listing of edge tables and available columns in each that can be used as geometry, costs, etc.
- edge_table_extent - Given a selected table and geometry column, will return the spatial extent of the table column as a 2-dimensional array. This information is used to set the map extent when the user changes the selected *Edge Table* and *Geometry Column*.
- node - Given a point location, edge table, and other things, will return the closest node id corresponding to the location clicked on the map as well as the actual location of the node
- *route - Given edge, start and end nodes, and other info, will return a Dijkstra route and accompanying data.*
  This will be used to draw the route on the map and populate a data grid.

Once the app function has determined the action is valid, it then pushes the request to another function specifically designed to handle that action. Our naming convention for the action functions is app_<name_of_action>.

22.1   *App Helper Functions*

There is a helper function we use across many functions to get specific details about a table like the primary key and to also split the table name into schema and table. This is called app_parse_table and is shown in Listing 22.2.

Listing 22.2: app_parse_table

```
CREATE OR REPLACE FUNCTION app_parse_table(param_table text,
    OUT e_table_schema text,
    OUT e_table_name text, OUT e_table_full_name text, OUT e_pk_column text)
    RETURNS record
AS
$$
    BEGIN
        SELECT quote_ident(NULLIF(split_part(param_table,'.',1),'')),
            quote_ident(split_part(param_table,'.',2))
                INTO e_table_schema, e_table_name;
        SELECT quote_ident(column_name) INTO e_pk_column
            FROM information_schema.key_column_usage AS cu
            WHERE (table_schema = e_table_schema or e_table_schema IS NULL)
                AND table_name = e_table_name
        --prefer gid over any other unique
            ORDER BY CASE WHEN column_name = 'gid' THEN 1 ELSE 2 END LIMIT 1;
                e_table_full_name := COALESCE(e_table_schema || '.','') || e_table_na
```

```
        RETURN;
    END;

$$ language 'plpgsql';
```

We standardize on input using PostgreSQL binary JSON type jsonb, since it's more efficient for querying elements. For output we are using json type which is plain text. Although jsonb is touted as the preferred JSON type, it has the side effect that data in it is re-sorted for binary efficiency. Since we'll be using JSON output for presentation on a grid, reordering of columns is not a desirable feature.

> The jsonb type was introduced in PostgreSQL 9.4. It has more functions and operators for it. If you are using 9.3, change all jsonb references in the code to JSON.

22.2 *App Action Functions*

Each action in the app has a corresponding PostgreSQL stored helper function. In this section, we'll go over the action functions app_edge_tables, app_edge_table_extent, app_node, and app_route.

app_edge_tables

The first feature of our app is to provide a list of edge tables to choose from, as well as relevant column names in each edge table. We get the list of edge tables by querying the PostGIS *geometry_columns* view as well as PostgreSQL *information_schema.columns* catalog view. We consider any table that contains LINESTRINGS or MULTILINESTRINGS as a possible edge table. The client sends this over as part of a JSON request that has attribute *action = edge_tables*. The code to deal with the *edge_tables* action is shown in Listing 22.3.

Listing 22.3: app_edge_tables function

```
CREATE OR REPLACE FUNCTION app_edge_tables(param_input jsonb) RETURNS json AS
$$
    SELECT json_agg(f)
        FROM (
            SELECT quote_ident(f_table_schema) || '.'
```

```
                          || quote_ident(f_table_name) As et,
                          array_agg(f_geometry_column) As gcols,
                      ARRAY(
                        SELECT c.column_name::text
                        FROM information_schema.columns As c
                        WHERE c.table_name::text = f_table_name
                            AND c.table_schema::text = gc.f_table_schema
                            AND c.data_type IN('double precision', 'numeric', 'float4')
                        ORDER BY c.column_name) As ccols,
                      ARRAY(
                        SELECT c.column_name::text
                        FROM information_schema.columns As c
                        WHERE c.table_name::text = f_table_name
                            AND c.table_schema::text = gc.f_table_schema
                            AND c.udt_name != 'geometry'
                        ORDER BY c.ordinal_position) As dcols
                  FROM geometry_columns AS gc
                      WHERE gc.type ILIKE '%LINESTRING'
                  GROUP BY et, gc.f_table_schema, gc.f_table_name
                  ORDER BY et) As f;
        $$
        language 'sql';
```

Once `app_edge_tables` has done it's work, it returns a JSON object consisting of an array where each element corresponds to an edge table and relevant info about this table such as name of table as et, which columns are suitable for cost columns as ccols, which columns contain linestrings (suitable for an edge geometry) as gcols, and all non-geometry columns as dcols.

1. This information is then used to populate the *Edge Table* drop down with the et field as the display.
2. When the user selects an edge table, the associated gcols is used to populate the *Geom Column* drop down options. The associated ccols is used to populate the *Cost Column* and *Reverse Cost* drop downs. The associated dcols is used to populate the *Display Columns* drop down.

app_edge_table_extent

When the user selects an entry from *Geom Column* drop down, a service call is made for the action *edge_table_extent* and passing along the selected *Edge Table* and *Geom Column*. This will trigger a call to the `app_edge_table_extent` stored function shown in Listing 22.4.

Listing 22.4: app_edge_table_extent function

```
CREATE OR REPLACE FUNCTION app_edge_table_extent(param_input jsonb)
    RETURNS json AS
$$
    DECLARE var_result json; var_et record; var_sql text; var_geom_col text;
        var_output_srid integer := 4326; var_edge_srid integer;
    BEGIN
        var_et :=  app_parse_table(param_input->>'edge_table');
        var_geom_col :=  quote_ident(param_input->>'geom_col') ;
        var_edge_srid := (SELECT srid FROM geometry_columns
            WHERE f_table_name = var_et.e_table_name
            AND f_table_schema = var_et.e_table_schema
            AND f_geometry_column = var_geom_col);
        var_sql := 'WITH e AS ( SELECT ST_Transform(ST_SetSRID(ST_Extent('
            || var_geom_col || '),$1),$2)::box2d AS ext FROM '
            || var_et.e_table_full_name || ')
    SELECT
        to_json(ARRAY[ ARRAY[ST_YMin(ext), ST_XMin(ext)],
            ARRAY[ST_YMax(ext), ST_XMax(ext)] ]) As bounds
FROM e' ;
        EXECUTE var_sql INTO var_result USING var_edge_srid, var_output_srid;
        RETURN var_result;
    END;
$$
language 'plpgsql';
```

ST_Extent is a PostGIS function that returns the bounding box of
a set of geometries. In this case we are doing it for the whole table. If you have data in the millions of rows, you may want to
replace ST_Extent(geom) with ST_EstimatedExtent(table_schema,
table_name, geometry_column) which will return an approximate
extent based on stats collected from the last table analyze. Use
ST_EstimatedExtent with caution. If you have never done something of the form vacuum analyze sometable or analyze sometable,
then there may be no stats for *sometable* and ST_EstimatedExtent
will result in an error. Also, since these stats are based on a sampling of data, they will deviate a bit from the actual extent of the
table, especially for large tables or frequently updated tables.

app_node

When the user clicks on the radio button next to *Start Vertex* or *End Vertex* and then clicks on the map, the *node* action is triggered and sends along the longitude/latitude location they clicked, as well as the *Edge Table* and *Geom Column*. This triggers the app_node database stored function shown in Listing 22.5.

Listing 22.5: app_node function

```
CREATE OR REPLACE FUNCTION app_node(param_input jsonb)
 RETURNS json AS
$$
    DECLARE var_result json; var_sql text; var_et record;
        var_output_srid integer := 4326; var_edge_srid integer;
    BEGIN
        var_et :=  app_parse_table(param_input->>'edge_table');
        var_et.e_table_name := var_et.e_table_name || '_vertices_pgr';
        var_et.e_table_full_name := quote_ident(var_et.e_table_schema) || '.'
        || quote_ident(var_et.e_table_name);
        var_edge_srid := (SELECT srid FROM geometry_columns
        WHERE f_table_name = var_et.e_table_name
        AND f_table_schema = var_et.e_table_schema
        AND f_geometry_column = 'the_geom');
        var_sql := 'SELECT row_to_json(fc)
            FROM (SELECT ''FeatureCollection'' As type, json_agg(f) As features
FROM (SELECT ''Feature'' As type
, ST_AsGeoJSON( ST_Transform(
    e.geom,' || var_output_srid::text || '))::json As geometry
, row_to_json(
    (SELECT l
        FROM (SELECT id As node) As l
    )) As properties
FROM (SELECT id, the_geom As geom
    FROM ' || var_et.e_table_full_name || ') AS e
        ORDER BY e.geom <-> $1  LIMIT 1)  As f) AS fc' ;

        EXECUTE var_sql INTO var_result
            USING  ST_Transform( ST_SetSRID( ST_Point(
                    (param_input->'loc'->>'lon')::float8,
                    (param_input->'loc'->>'lat')::float8),
                        var_output_srid),
                    var_edge_srid );
    RETURN var_result;
    END;
$$
language 'plpgsql';
```

app_node assumes there is a corresponding vertices table for the passed in edge that is of form *<edge_table_name>_vertices_pgr* which is the naming convention pgr_createTopology follows when creating a vertices table for a network. It then finds the closest node in the vertices table to the passed-in user point.

app_node returns a GeoJSON feature collection consisting of one point feature that has a property called node denoting the node id of the closest node. The geometry it returns is the location of the node in longitude/latitude units. Note that our table need not have geometry in longitdue/latitude srid=4326, but the output and input are in this spatial reference system and converted as needed.

app_route

The final function of our app is the routing function. This does the the job of calling a pgRouting routing function based on a request and returns a GeoJSON feature collection consisting of route information and display columns from the edge table selected by the user for display. The code is shown in Listing 22.6.

For brevity our routing only handles Dijkstra Point to Point.

Listing 22.6: app_route function

```
CREATE OR REPLACE FUNCTION app_route(param_input jsonb) RETURNS json AS
$$
    DECLARE var_result json; var_sql text; var_sql_route text; var_et record;
        var_output_srid integer := 4326; var_edge_srid integer;
        var_geom_col text; var_cost_col text; var_dcols text;
    BEGIN
        var_et :=  app_parse_table(param_input->>'edge_table');
        var_geom_col :=  quote_ident(param_input->>'geom_col');
        var_cost_col := quote_ident(param_input->>'cost_col');
        var_edge_srid := (SELECT srid FROM geometry_columns
        WHERE f_table_name = var_et.e_table_name
            AND f_table_schema = var_et.e_table_schema
            AND f_geometry_column = var_geom_col);
        var_sql_route := 'SELECT ' || var_et.e_pk_column
            || ' AS id, source, target, '
            || var_cost_col || '::float8 As cost '
            -- add reverse cost column if present
            || COALESCE(
                ', ' || quote_ident( NULLIF(param_input->>'rcost_col','') )
```

```
                        || ' As reverse_cost ', '')
                  || '
              FROM ' || var_et.e_table_full_name || ' AS e ';
              var_dcols := (SELECT string_agg( 'e.'
                      || quote_ident(replace(a::text, '"', ''))
                      , ',' )
                  FROM json_array_elements( (param_input->'display_cols')::json ) As a

              var_sql := 'SELECT row_to_json(fc)
                  FROM (
                      SELECT ''FeatureCollection'' As type, json_agg(f) As features
      FROM (SELECT ''Feature'' As type
    , ST_AsGeoJSON(
          ST_Transform(e.' || var_geom_col || ',4326))::json As geometry
              ,row_to_json((SELECT l FROM (SELECT r.* '
              || COALESCE(',' || var_dcols, '' ) || ') As l
      )) As properties
    FROM pgr_dijkstra(' || quote_literal(var_sql_route) || ', '
    || (param_input->>'start_vid')::bigint::text
          || ', ' || (param_input->>'end_vid')::bigint::text || ', false) '
    || ' As r INNER JOIN ' || var_et.e_table_full_name || ' AS e
          ON r.edge = e.' || var_et.e_pk_column || '
          ORDER BY r.seq) As f) AS fc' ;
          EXECUTE var_sql INTO var_result;
          RETURN var_result;
      END;
  $$
  language 'plpgsql';
```

The app_route stored function pulls from param_input the *edge_table,
geom_col, cost_col*, and *rcost_col* table and column names. It also uses
the start_vid and end_vid properties for source node and target
node. It then runs pgr_dijkstra using this information and joins
back with the edge table to get additional properties requested in
the param_input->'display_cols'. The result is passed back as
a GeoJSON feature collection where each feature is a row in the
Dijkstra solution and properties of each row from the edges table.

23 *Web Server-side*

We will have a light-weight server-side piece that passes our JSON post request to our core database function app and returns the result back to the user. We'll demonstrate how to achieve this with PHP.

Since the code just takes the raw input from the AngularJS client, passes it off to the database, and returns the result back to the client, all you need to achieve this in any Web server-side language is a PostgreSQL database connector and ability to read the raw web posted output.

23.1 *PHP Application Service*

PHP is a web server-side scripting language that runs under both Apache and Windows IIS, as well as several other web servers like Nginx. Although it's lost its hipness rating to newcomers like Go, Django, and NodeJS, it is still probably the most used and tested web server scripting language on the web, as well as probably having the most plugin libraries available of any web server scripting language.

Our server-side PHP code consists of two files:

- config.inc.php which contains the database credentials
- AppService.php which does the handling of getting a request from the client, passing it to the database, and returning the database response to the user.

The config.inc.php file looks like this:

Listing 23.1: config.inc.php

```php
<?php
$conn_str = 'dbname=pgr host=localhost port=5432 user=pgr password=Loc8pr3$$';?>
```

For this app, we created a postgres user called *pgr* with rights to execute our functions and query tables.

The AppService.php looks like this:

Listing 23.2: AppService.php

```php
1   <?php include_once('config.inc.php');
2   $sql = 'SELECT app($1);'; $params = array( file_get_contents('php://input'));
3
4   $dbconn = pg_connect($conn_str) or die("could not connect");
5
6   /** pass to our app function **/
7   $result = pg_query_params($dbconn, $sql, $params);
8   if ($result === false) return;
9
10  $row = pg_fetch_array($result);
11  pg_free_result($result);
12  if ($row === false) return;
13
14  echo $row[0];?>
```

AppService.php, takes the user request stream, which our AngularJS app will pass as a JSON formatted string, and stores this in
a variable called *$params* which is then passed in as an argument
to the core PostgreSQL app stored function aptly named *app*. The
app will return exactly one row with one column which consists of
a JSON formatted text containing all the data to fulfill the request.

Client Front-End

As noted, we are using AngularJS for much of the handling of the user interaction. We are using AngularJS 1.5 which is the last of the AngularJS series. Angular 2, as of this writing, is in beta release and contains considerable changes over 1.5. Since Angular 2 is a complete rewrite of AngularJS with completely different API the suffix JS is dropped leaving just Angular for the name.

24.1 The HTML Page

For the GUI representation we are utilizing BootStrap and HTML. The HTML page presented to the user has a structure shown in Listing 24.1.

Listing 24.1: Page Layout

```
1   <!DOCTYPE html>
2   <html ng-app="app">
3   <head>
4     <title>pgRouting App</title>
5     <meta charset="utf-8" />
6     <meta name="viewport" content="width=device-width, initial-scale=1.0" />
7     <link rel="stylesheet" href="https://maxcdn.bootstrapcdn.com/bootstrap/3.3.6/css/bootstrap.min.css" />
8   </head>
9   <body>
10    <div id="divApp" style="height:100%;width:100%" ng-controller="AppCtrl">
11    <!-- Map and form content go here -->
12    </div>
13    </body>
14
15    <script src="https://cdnjs.cloudflare.com/ajax/libs/angular.js/1.5.7/angular.min.js"></script>
16    <link rel="stylesheet" href="libs/angular-ui-grid/ui-grid.min.css"/>
17    <script src="libs/angular-ui-grid/ui-grid.min.js"></script>
18    <script src="js/app.js"></script>
19    <script src="js/services/AppService.js"></script>
20    <!-- Leaflet CSS and JS -->
21  </body>
22  </html>
```

Line 1, ng-app="app" initializes the whole page as being part of the AngularJS application module called *app*. *app* is defined in the code in the file app.js included in *line 18*. Our app has just a single class of type controller called *AppCtrl* which is defined in *app.js* and will control the code inside the div called *divApp* in *lines 10-12*. *Line 15* contains angular javascript library and helper functions.

For larger AngularJS 1 apps, you'll have more than one controller, and in Angular 2 and above, controllers no longer exist and have been superseded by things called "Components".

Lines 16-17 contain library code for *Angular UI Grid* which we'll be using to display results on a grid. *Angular UI Grid* is an open source grid for AngularJS you can download from http://ui-grid.info/. It contains features such as automatic display of JSON data, sorting, resizing columns, and filtering. It also has the convenient feature that for the grid header, it converts fields with underscores to spaces and proper cases. This is convenient for PostgreSQL tables that standardize on lower case underscore format as we do in this app. We are using a small subset of it's functionality.

Bootstrap also provides javascript as helpers for some of its controls, but we are not including the Bootstrap JS (which would require also including JQuery) because we won't be using any of that functionality aside from the Bootstrap Cascading Style Sheets (CSS) for our app. CSS is an HTML standard that allows use of named styles for widgets such as tables, buttons, and header text. The term cascading comes from the feature that if a style is defined in multiple CSS files, the last style to be included supersedes the earlier includes. Because of this, it's easy to include a default set of styles and have a user override with their own replacement styles simply by including an additional CSS file.

Line 18 contains an Angular Services class that will serve as a proxy for our calls to the server AppServices.php script. We could have just as easily made direct calls the the $http built-in service in Angular, but defining our own service allows us to inject additional logic (such as just having the URL specified in one place), and also later on provide a mockup class for testing if we choose.

Within the *divApp* section is where we place the form and map the user will interact with. The contents of the *divApp* section is shown in Listing 24.2.

Listing 24.2: Contents of the divApp div

```
<div id="map" class="col-md-8"></div>
<div class="col-md-4">
  <form>
    <div class="panel panel-info">
      <div class="panel-heading"><b>Dijkstra Point to Point</b></div>
      <div class="panel-body">
        <label>Edge Table</label>
          <select ng-model="selectedItems['selectedEdgeTable']"
            ng-options="et as et.et for et in edge_tables" >
          </select><br />
        <label>Geom Column</label>
          <select ng-model="formData.geom_col"
            ng-options="gc as gc for gc in selectedItems['selectedEdgeTable'].gcols"
            ng-change="commandEdgeTableExtent()">
          </select><br />
        <label>Cost Column</label>
          <select ng-model="formData.cost_col"
            ng-options="gc as gc for gc in selectedItems['selectedEdgeTable'].ccols">
          </select><br />
        <label>Reverse Cost Column</label>
          <select ng-model="formData.rcost_col">
            <option ng-selected="selected" value="">None</option>
            <option ng-repeat="gc in selectedItems['selectedEdgeTable'].ccols">{{gc}}</option>
          </select><br />
        <label>Start Vertex</label>
          <input type="text" ng-model="formData.start_vid" />
          <input type="radio" name="selectedNodeField" ng-model="selectedNodeField"
                value="start_vid" /> <br />
        <label>End Vertex</label>
          <input type="text" ng-model="formData.end_vid" />
          <input type="radio" name="selectedNodeField" ng-model="selectedNodeField"
                value="end_vid" /> <br />
        <label>Display Columns</label> (use Ctrl to select multiple) <br />
          <select ng-model="formData.display_cols" multiple
            ng-options="gc as gc for gc in selectedItems['selectedEdgeTable'].dcols">
          </select>
      </div>
    </div>

    <div class="panel-footer">
      <button class="btn-primary" ng-click="commandRoute()"
        ng-show="formData.cost_col != null">Route</button>
    </div>
  </form>
```

```
<div id="gridResults" ng-show="gridOptions.data"
  ui-grid="gridOptions"
```

The class tags such as class="panel panel-info" are CSS classes provided by BootStrap used to create the look of a panel. In the case of *class="panel panel-info"*, the class panel is used to layout a table around the content to look like a panel.

The *panel-info* controls the general look, giving the panel a blueish style. Other named panel classes in Bootstrap such as *panel-success* provide a greenish look.

AngularJS introduces new attributes to HTML. All attributes you see that start with *ng* are AngularJS attributes. The Angular 1 series supports two-way binding by default. This binding is done using a special tag *ng-model*. Note that all the form fields have an *ng-model* property that either bind to an element in *selectedItems* or *formData*. This means that if we set these elements in code, the form fields will automatically update, and similarly, if we change the form fields on the screen, the back end elements they are bound to will change accordingly.

Most of the drop down lists *select* in HTML, have a property called *ng-options*. This allows us to set the drop down list options to JavaScript (JSON) objects or arrays. The *edge_tables* variable is a variable we set on load of the page from contents returned by the app_edge_tables database stored function.

The *Edge Table* drop down, when a user selects an edge from the list, stores the whole selected edge object into the variable: *selectedItems['selectedEdgeTable']*. Note that *Geom Column*, *Cost Column*, and *Reverse Cost Column* all rely on a subelement of *selectedItems['selectedEdgeTable']* to populate their lists. As a result, when the user changes the selected edge, these lists automatically get refreshed as well as a result of the two-way binding.

24.2 AppService.js

AppService.js contains the service called *AppService* packaged in a module *app.services*. We'll use *AppService* to handle all our database requests and it in return will pass our request to AppService.php.

Listing 24.3: AppService.js

```
angular.module("app.services", [])
.service('AppService', ['$http', '$window', '$timeout',
function ($http, $window, $timeout) {
        this.rootServiceUrl = 'AppService.php';

        this.postData = function (formData, callback) {
                $http({
                        method: 'POST',
                        url: this.rootServiceUrl,
                        data: formData
                })
                .success(function (data, status, headers, conf) {
                        callback(null,data);
                })
                .error(function (data, status, headers, conf){
                        callback(data,null);
                });
        };
}])
```

AppService contains a single method called postData we will use to interact with the database.

The AppService.js code is pretty much the same regardless of the web server language you choose. The only thing that changes would be the *this.rootServiceUrl* setting.

24.3 app.js

The app.js file contains the definition of the AngularJS *app* module and *AppCtrl* controller. It responds to changes in the HTML page and also dynamically loads data in the page. The basic structure of our app module is shown in Listing 24.4.

Listing 24.4: app.js

```
var app = angular.module('app', ['app.services', 'ui.grid', 'ui.grid.resizeColumns'])
```

```
.controller('AppCtrl', ['$scope', '$window',  'uiGridConstants', 'AppService',
    function ($scope, $window,  uiGridConstants, AppService) {
        $scope.formData = {display_cols: []};
        $scope.selectedItems = {};
        $scope.selectedNodeField =  "start_vid";
        $scope.edge_tables = null;
        $scope.refresh = true;

        $scope.gridOptions = {
            data: null,
            enableRowSelection: true,
            multiSelect: false, showGridHeader: true, showGridFooter: true
        };

        AppService.postData({action: 'edge_tables'},
          function(err,data){
              if (data){
                $scope.edge_tables = data;
              }
          });

        /** form event functions go here **/

        /** bind $scope.onMapClick to the click event of Leaftlet map **/
         mymap.on('click', $scope.onMapClick);
    }]);
```

Listing 24.4, on the previous page:

1. Defines a module called *app*
2. The *app* module is stated to depend on modules *app.services*, *ui.grid*, and *ui.grid.resizeColumns*.
3. The *app* contains a single controller called *AppCtrl* which will include all the event functions needed by our form and map. Note that the controller consists of a list of objects, the last being the payload function that itself contains subfunctions. The list of objects being passed to the payload function are often referred to as *Dependency Injection* because we are injecting dependencies into the function.
4. On load of *AppCtrl*, it does a service call using the *AppService* service with action *edge_tables* which is used to populate the *$scope.edge_tables* variable. Note that behind the scenes, this call will make a call to `AppService.php` which in turn will call our database stored function app, which in turn will call `app_edge_tables` which then returns a JSON dataset consisting of a list of edge tables and associated properties of each.

Next we'll cover the event functions. These functions rely on the mapping toolkit you use, so will be different in Leaflet vs. Open-Layers.

25 *Web Mapping Client*

Two of the most popular open source JavaScript mapping frameworks are Leaflet and OpenLayers. In this part, we'll demonstrate how to use Leaflet to display results of your pgRouting queries.

Leaflet is a newer mapping toolkit than OpenLayers and strives to be a simpler solution. OpenLayers, now in the third version, provides a bit more out of the box than Leaflet without need of extra add-ons. Although OpenLayers is a much older project than Leaflet, the OpenLayers 3 series is a complete rewrite of older OpenLayers, so for sake of comparison can be considered just as new and without all the extra code to support older browsers as found in OpenLayers 2. Being vastly different from OpenLayers 2, version 3 with slightly different conventions can be considered as a completely different toolkit from it's predecessor.

That being said, we chose Leaflet over OpenLayers because we found it a little easier to hook in with AngularJS and Bootstrap and we didn't need any extensive functionality (*YMMV---Your Mileage May Vary*).

25.1   Leaflet

Leaflet was designed from the ground up as a tool for non-mapping web developers to integrate mapping features in their apps. While the base package of Leaflet is light, you can seek out the plethora of Leaflet extensions to get more features. Given its light-weight no-frills base, Leaflet tends to be a popular favorite for Web service providers such as CartoDb and ESRI, who have developed their own Leaflet extensions to work with the web services they provide.

You can download leaflet from `http://leafletjs.com/` as well as check out the documentation and some samples. Alternatively, you can link directly to the Leaflet JavaScript and CSS files from Leaflet website as we do.

In Listing 24.1, on page 247, we replace *<!-- Leaflet CSS and JS -->* with the following code:

```
<link rel="stylesheet"
  href="https://npmcdn.com/leaflet@1.0.0-rc.3/dist/leaflet.css" />
<script src="https://npmcdn.com/leaflet@1.0.0-rc.3/dist/leaflet.js">
</script>
<script>
  OSM_ATTR = 'Map data &copy;
    <a href="http://openstreetmap.org">OpenStreetMap</a> contributors, '
    '<a href="http://creativecommons.org/licenses/by-sa/2.0/">CC-BY-SA</a
  OSM_URL = 'http://{s}.tile.openstreetmap.org/{z}/{x}/{y}.png';
</script>

<script>
  var mymap = L.map('map').setView([38.904, -77.016], 13);
  L.tileLayer(OSM_URL, {
      attribution: OSM_ATTR,
      maxZoom: 18
    }).addTo(mymap);
</script>
```

This code will load in the Leaflet JavaScript and CSS support files as well as render a Leaflet map in the div called *map* that we have included in Listing 24.2, on page 249.

The JavaScript part adds a single Tile Layer to the map using the OpenStreetMap tile service and positions it in DC. This will serve as our basemap. Like many JavaScript mapping frameworks, Leaflet expects coordinates in latitude, longitude instead of the spatial database standard of longitude, latitude, so be very careful.

25.2 *Functions that Interface with the Map*

The next set of functions are Angular scope functions for the AngularJS AppCtrl controller that interact with the map. A scope defines what AngularJS considers area where it has control. In the scope it may cache data in properties of the scope as well as have functions available to other parts that makeup the scope.

commandEdgeTableExtent

When a user selects from *Geom Column* (HTML code shown in Listing 24.2, on page 249) it calls the `$scope.commandEdgeTableExtent` function in `app.js` shown in Listing 25.1.

The `$scope.commandEdgeTableExtent` triggers a call to the database stored function `app_edge_table_extent` shown in Listing 22.4, on page 241. The return is a JSON array with two arrays consisting of the latitude/longitude lower and upper bounds of the table. On return of the result this information is passed to *map.fitBounds* to set the extent of the map.

Listing 25.1: Leaflet commandEdgeTableExtent

```
$scope.commandEdgeTableExtent = function() {
    $scope.formData['edge_table'] = $scope.selectedItems.selectedEdgeTable.et;
    $scope.formData['action'] = 'edge_table_extent';
    if ($scope.formData['geom_col'] > '' ){
      AppService.postData($scope.formData,
       function(err,data){
            if (data){
              mymap.fitBounds(data);
              $scope.formData['start_vid'] = '';
              $scope.formData['end_vid'] = '';
          }
      });
    }
}
```

onMapClick

When a user clicks on one of the radio buttons beside the *Start Vertex* and *End Vertex* text boxes and then clicks on a location on the map, this triggers the click event of the map which in turn calls the `$scope.onMapClick` function passing along the location the user clicked on the map. This will cause a call to the `app_node` function listed in Listing 22.5, on page 242 and return the node id closest to where the user clicked. The `$scope.onMapClick` will store the returned node in the selected node field corresponding to one of the fields labeled *Start Vertex* or *End Vertex*.

Listing 25.2: Leaflet onMapClick

```
$scope.onMapClick = function(e){
  $scope.formData['edge_table'] = $scope.selectedItems.selectedEdgeTable.et;
  $scope.formData['action'] = 'node';
  $scope.formData['loc'] = {lon: e.latlng.lng, lat: e.latlng.lat};

  AppService.postData($scope.formData, function(err,data){
      if (data){
          L.geoJson(data, {
            style: function (feature) {
                return {color: 'red'};
            }, onEachFeature: function (feature, layer) {
                layer.bindPopup(feature.properties.node);
            }
          }).addTo(mymap).on('move', $scope.onPinMove);
          $scope.formData[$scope.selectedNodeField] =
            data.features[0].properties.node;
      }
  });
};

mymap.on('click', $scope.onMapClick);
```

commandRoute

The final feature of our application is to be able to route between
selected *Start Vertex* and *End Vertex* nodes This is done using the
function $scope.commandRoute shown in Listing 25.3.

Listing 25.3: Leaflet commandRoute

```
$scope.commandRoute = function(){
  $scope.formData['edge_table'] = $scope.selectedItems.selectedEdgeTable.et;
  $scope.formData['action'] = 'route';
  $scope.refresh = true;
  AppService.postData($scope.formData, function(err,data){
      if (data){
        gData = [];
        data.features.forEach(function(e) { gData.push(e.properties) } );
        /** force reset of columns and data **/
        $scope.gridOptions.columnDefs = null;
        $scope.gridOptions.data = gData;
        $scope.refresh = false;
          L.geoJson(data, {
            style: function (feature) {
                return {color: 'red'};
```

```
            }
        }).addTo(mymap);
      }
    });
};
```

When the user clicks the *Route* button on the screen, the `$scope.commandRoute`
function is called. `$scope.commandRoute` triggers a call to the stored
database function `app_route` shown in Listing 22.6, on page 243.
The result returned by `app_route` is a GeoJSON data set consisting
of all the columns returned by `pgr_dijkstra` in addition to geometry column from the selected *Edge Table* and columns checked in the
Display Columns list box. This data is used to both create a new map
layer as well as to populate the Angular UI grid.

Part 6

Appendix

Appendix A: Changes Between pgRouting 2.0 and 2.1

This appendix outlines differences between pgRouting 2.0 and 2.1 that are useful to know for migrating applications for the old function calls to the newer function calls.

26.1 Key Changes Between pgRouting 2.0 Syntax and 2.x Syntax

The key changes in calls between pgRouting 2.0 and pgRouting 2.1 are as follows:

- has_rcost argument is no longer used in the newer syntax. In pgRouting 2.1, if you pass in has_rcost, you are using the older syntax and will get the older output table structure. In the older syntax, you needed to pass in a true for has_rcost in order to be able to use reverse_cost column. In the new syntax, the assumption is made that if you pass in an SQL with reverse_cost column, then you want to use reverse cost in the computation.
- Functions no longer use the pgr_cost* family of result types, but instead have distinctive outputs with more descriptive column names.
- In pgRouting 2.0 syntax, the vertex numbers only supported integer. Newer 2.1+ syntax supports big integers as well.
- In newer syntax there is often an additional column output called agg_cost which is the cumulative cost of a path result.
- In newer syntax, the seq column output by many routing functions starts at 1 instead of 0.

Finding Optimal Routes with pgDijikstra - pgRouting 2.0 Syntax

The old syntax (pgRouting 2.0), used a helper PostgreSQL composite type called pgr_costResult. The pgr_costResult type has the following structure:

Column	Type	Purpose
seq	integer	sequential order of travel
id1	integer	usually the node id
id2	integer	usually the edge id
cost	double preci-sion	cost of this edge in total path

Using pgr_dijkstra for Shortest Path

In this example, we'll come up with lowest cost path to go from New York (node 1) to Mumbai (node 4). The query in its simplest form looks like this:

Listing 26.1: Dijkstra shortest path from New York to Mumbai

```
1  SELECT X.*
2  FROM pgr_Dijkstra(
3      'SELECT id, source, target, dist_km As cost FROM airport_routes',
4      1,
5      4,
6      FALSE,
7      FALSE
8  ) X
9  ORDER BY seq;
```

In this case we assume travel from A to B is same as from B to A in both cost and possibility, so we set that to false. *Line 7* is an argument called *has_reverse_cost* and is a Boolean denoting if cost is different from reverse cost of each edge. Note that if your graph is not directed, then having a reverse cost doesn't make sense. If you do have input of true for this, then it is assumed that you will provide a column in the SQL query called reverse_cost.

The key element of most routing functions in pgRouting is the SQL statement to define the network seen in *line 3*. In this example, we are feeding the whole airport_routes edges table into the function.

The output of this function is a set of pgr_costResult which looks like:

```
seq | id1 | id2 | cost
----+-----+-----+-------
  0 |  1 |  6 | 12544
  1 |  4 | -1 |     0
```

The above result tells us that the shortest path from our stop and start destination requires only one hop. The last record id2 of any `pgr_dijkstra` call has an edge value of -1 since it refers to our target.

Listing 26.2: Dijkstra joined with other tables

```
1  SELECT X.seq, N.city, ST_AsGeoJSON(E.geom) As gson
2  FROM pgr_dijkstra(
3      'SELECT id, source, target, dist_km As cost FROM airport_routes',
4      (SELECT id FROM airports WHERE icao = 'KJFK'),
5      (SELECT id FROM airports WHERE icao = 'VABB'),
6      FALSE,
7      FALSE
8  ) X   INNER JOIN airports AS N ON X.id1 = N.id
9    LEFT JOIN airport_routes AS E ON X.id2 = E.id
10 ORDER BY seq;
```

Listing 26.3: Dijkstra using dynamic costs

```
1  SELECT X.seq,
2      N.city || COALESCE('-' || lead(N.city) OVER(ORDER By seq),'') As route, X.cost
3  FROM pgr_dijkstra(
4      'SELECT id, source, target,
5         dist_km/1000 + (dist_km - 1000)/2000*4 + (dist_km - 2000)/4000*10 As cost
6         FROM airport_routes',
7      (SELECT id FROM airports WHERE icao = 'KJFK'),
8      (SELECT id FROM airports WHERE icao = 'VABB'),
9      FALSE,
10     FALSE
11 ) X   INNER JOIN airports AS N ON X.id1 = N.id
12 ORDER BY seq;
```

The output of our revised query looks like:

```
seq |      route      | cost
----+-----------------+--------
  0 | New York-London | 23.756
  1 | London-Dubai    | 23.074
  2 | Dubai-Mumbai    | 3.5875
  3 | Mumbai          |      0
```

Using pgr_kDijkstraCost to Compute Total Cost of Shortest Path

Listing 26.4: kDijkstra comparing trip costs

```
1  SELECT seq, id1 AS source, id2 AS target, cost
2    FROM pgr_kDijkstraCost(
3      'SELECT id, source, target,
4          dist_km/1000 + (dist_km - 1000)/2000*4 + (dist_km - 2000)/4000*10 AS cost
5          FROM airport_routes',
6        (SELECT id FROM airports WHERE icao = 'KJFK'),
7        ARRAY(SELECT id FROM airports WHERE icao IN('VABB', 'EGLC') ),
8        false, false
9    );
```

Using pgr_kDijikstraPath to Compute Paths for Each Destination

In pgRouting 2.0, the function that returned trip paths for a single node, multi-target was called pgr_kDijkstraPath. In pgRouting 2.1, the old function still exists, but you should use the new overloaded pgr_dijikstra that takes an array as target and returns more meaningful edge/node columns and also agg_cost.

The path function gives you a row for each segment in your trip and the associated cost with that segment. Since it is giving you multiple rows with complete path for each answer, it returns a result set where each row has a similar structure to pgr_costResult, except the fields have different meaning and there is an additional field to denote the destination path node. The destination path node you'll need if you want to regroup the results into a single row per path solution.

Since it is giving you multiple rows with complete path for each answer, it returns a set of objects of type pgr_costResult3 which has a similar structure to pgr_costResult, except the fields have different meaning and there is an additional field to denote the destination path node. You'll need the destination path node to regroup the results.

So in context of pgr_kDijkstraPath, the output fields mean the following:

Column	Type	Purpose
seq	integer	sequential order of results
id1	integer	destination node id (call it path id since all records with same id1 are segments in the same trip path)
id2	integer	the node id of start of segment
id3	integer	the edge id of the segment
cost	double precision	cost of this segment of trip in total path

pgr_ksp pgRouting 2.0 Syntax

pgr_ksp, similar to *pgr_dijkstra*, solves the problem of given a source and destination node, what edges need to be traversed to accomplish the task. Unlike *pgr_dijkstra* it returns multiple answers to the question, and as a result needs to output pgr_costResult3 type rows to denote which segments belong to which answer. Note that pgr_costResult3 is also used by pgr_kDijkstra, except instead of asking multiple questions and expecting one solution per question, with pgr_ksp we are asking one question and expecting multiple solutions to the question.

Listing 26.5: pgr_ksp 2.0 to find multiple solutions

```
1   SELECT k.id1 As solution,
2       CASE WHEN r.city_1 = n.city THEN
3            r.city_1 || '-' || r.city_2
4       ELSE r.city_2 || '-' || r.city_1 END As route
5   FROM pgr_ksp(
6     'SELECT id, source, target,
7             dist_km AS cost, dist_km As reverse_cost
8          FROM airport_routes',
9       (SELECT id FROM airports WHERE icao = 'KJFK'),
10       (SELECT id FROM airports WHERE icao = 'VABB'),
11     3,
12      true
13   ) As k INNER JOIN airports As n On (k.id2 = n.id)
14       INNER JOIN airport_routes As r ON (k.id3 = r.id)
15   ORDER BY solution, k.seq;
```

The format of `pgr_ksp` is very similar to *pgr_dijkstra* except `pgr_ksp` always assumes directed and only computes the path in the direction of the edges, except if you set the `has_reverse_cost` argument to `true` as denoted in *line 12* and specify a `reverse_cost` column in your query. We also need to tell the function how many answers we want back as denoted in *line 11*. Since we asked for three solutions we got solutions numbered from `0-2` where each set denotes and answer to the question and the lowest numbered solution is the best answer.

Appendix B: Installation Extras

This appendix outlines specific details about where to get binaries, instructions for compiling pgRouting and extras, and installation of extra software covered in this book.

27.1   Where to get Binaries

Microsoft Windows

The EnterpriseDb and BigSQL PostgreSQL offerings for windows are listed here: https://www.postgresql.org/download/windows/.

In addition, the PostGIS windows build-bot, affectionately called, Winnie, builds the PostGIS and pgRouting development versions for each PostgreSQL version whenever there is a change in the pgRouting or PostGIS code-base. These are packaged separately as stand-alone pgRouting binary zip for each version of PostgreSQL supported and are compatible with both the PostgreSQL EDB and BigSQL Windows distributions. For pgRouting 2.3, you'll find binaries for PostgreSQL 9.3-9.6. So if you want to work with the development version, just copy the files into the same named folders of your PostgreSQL install, overwriting existing files. More details can be found on the PostGIS Windows download page http://postgis.net/windows_downloads.

PostgreSQL EDB also offers both 32-bit and 64-bit PostgreSQL/-PostGIS packages for desktop Mac and Linux, however these packages do not include pgRouting.

The BigSQL distribution also offers 64-bit PostgreSQL/PostGIS/o-grfdw packages for Windows, Linux (Deb and rpm packages), and Mac. These include install for PostGIS, but not pgRouting.

PostgreSQL EDB Distribution

For PostgreSQL Windows EDB Distributions, pgRouting 2.3 is packaged in the PostGIS Windows Bundles via the PostgreSQL EDB Application Stack Builder for PostgreSQL 9.3-9.6. This means when
you install the PostGIS Bundle via Application Stack Builder, you
are also installing pgRouting and ogrfdw binaries as well.

When you install PostgreSQL, you should see the Application Stack
Builder as a menu option as shown in Figure 27.1.

Figure 27.1: PostgreSQL menu on
Windows 2012R2

Once you launch the Application Stack Builder, you should see a
menu with a Spatial Extensions subsection as shown in Figure 27.2,
on the next page.

If you are on Windows 64-bit, you'll be offered both the 32-bit and
64-bit options. If you installed PostgreSQL 64-bit, choose the 64-bit
option and if you installed 32-bit, choose the 32-bit option.

The Windows installers are also available as a standalone detailed
on `http://postgis.net/windows_downloads`.

You can have both PostGIS 2.2 and PostGIS 2.3 installed on your
system. If you choose to install both, make sure to install PostGIS
2.3 last so that the newer dependency libraries from the PostGIS 2.3
install are used.

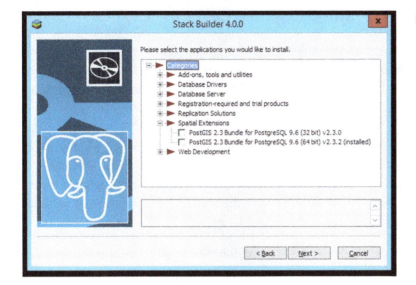

Figure 27.2: Application Stack Builder

BigSQL Distribution

BigSQL is a distribution with PostgreSQL/PostGIS binaries available for 64-bit Windows, Linux, and MacOSX which you can download from `https://www.bigsql.org/postgresql/installers.jsp`.

The distribution includes a command line and web-based package installer that you can use to install PostGIS and ogrfdw. On Windows, make sure to launch command line as an administrator.

To get help run:

```
pgc --help
```

At the time of writing, the BigSQL distribution does not include a package for pgRouting, however there are plans to provide this in the near future. To update your local list of packages and see a list of packages:

```
pgc update
pgc list
```

To install a package such as PostGIS, run:

```
pgc install postgis23
```

To upgrade all installed package binaries, use the `upgrade` command as shown below. Make sure that you have the PostgreSQL and BigSQL services turned off if you are upgrading PostgreSQL.

```
pgc upgrade
```

The Windows pgRouting binaries available at `http://postgis.net/windows_downloads/` can be used with the BigSQL distribution. When using the pgRouting binaries, if there is a corresponding `postgresql` folder, you'll want to copy the files into the `postgresql` subfolder instead of the same named folder.

For example if you are installing for PostgreSQL 9.6 the zip folder files `share/extension` go into `pg96/share/postgresql/extension` and `lib` files go into `pg96/lib/postgresql`, but `bin` files go into `pg96/bin` since there is no `postgresql` subfolder in the `bin` folder.

For other operating systems, pgRouting is often available as a separate binary package, and not necessarily from the same source that you got your PostGIS and PostgreSQL.

CentOS, RedHat EL, Scientific, Fedora, Oracle Linux

The PostgreSQL development group (PGDG), runs a yum repository `http://yum.postgresql.org` for both released PostgreSQL and development versions of PostgreSQL. This repository, in addition to having packages for PostgreSQL, PostGIS, and ogrfdw also includes pgRouting. We authored a guide that details using this repository to install PostgreSQL 9.5, PostGIS 2.2, pgRouting 2.1, and ogrfdw: `http://loc8.cc/pgr/poyum`.

MacOSX

Although there are many binary sources for PostGIS on Mac (PostgresApp.com, EDB, KyngChaos), KyngChaos `http://loc8.cc/pgr/kyngchaos` to our knowledge is the only binary package that includes pgRouting and that is for 9.4 and pgRouting 2.0.

Sadly Mac distributions do not play well together, so you can't install PostGIS from one distribution and grab pgRouting from another.

For a fairly modern pgRouting experience on Mac, HomeBrew seems to be the best.   https://brew.sh/

Latest HomeBrew scripts covering PostGIS 2.3, pgRouting 2.3, osm2pgrouting 2.2, and PostgreSQL 9.6 can be found at `http://loc8.cc/pgr/pghomebrew`

Ubuntu and Debian

The PostgreSQL development group (PGDG) also runs an apt repository for Ubuntu and Debian users. This repository contains packages for PostgreSQL 9.5, 9.6, PostGIS 2.2-2.3, and pgRouting 2.1-2.3. Instructions for installing these are documented in the PostGIS wiki at `http://loc8.cc/pgr/aptinstall`.

27.2   *ogr_fdw Installation*

- The PostgreSQL Yum repo already comes packaged with ogrfdw, but if you want to compile your own to get latest changes, these instructions, while specific to CentOS, should work for most any Linux distribution: *Compiling and Installing OGR_FDW on CentOS after Yum install PostgeSQL PostGIS* - `http://loc8.cc/pgr/ogrfdwcentos`
- *Windows ogr_fdw - distributed as part of PostGIS bundle (from version 2.2 on).*
  Also available in the extras folder in the experimental section as standalone (can be used for PostGIS lower than 2.2): `http://postgis.net/windows_downloads/`.

Books from Locate Press

Be sure to visit http://locatepress.com for information on new and upcoming titles.

QGIS Map Design

USE QGIS TO TAKE YOUR CARTOGRAPHIC PRODUCTS TO THE HIGHEST LEVEL.

With step-by-step instructions for creating the most modern print map designs seen in any instructional materials to-date, this book covers everything from basic styling and labeling to advanced techniques like illuminated contours and dynamic masking.

See how QGIS is rapidly surpassing the cartographic capabilities of any other geoware available today with its data-driven overrides, flexible expression functions, multitudinous color tools, blend modes, and atlasing capabilities. A prior familiarity with basic QGIS capabilities is assumed. All example data and project files are included.

Written by two of the leading experts in the realm of open source mapping, Anita and Gretchen are experienced authors who pour their wealth of knowledge into the book. Get ready to bump up your mapping experience!

The PyQGIS Programmer's Guide

EXTENDING QGIS JUST GOT EASIER!

This book is your fast track to getting started with PyQGIS. After a brief introduction to Python, you'll learn how to understand the QGIS Application Programmer Interface (API), write scripts, and build a plugin. The book is designed to allow you to work through the examples as you go along. At the end of each chapter you'll find a set of exercises you can do to enhance your learning experience.

The PyQGIS Programmer's Guide is compatible with the version 2.0 API released with QGIS 2.x. All code samples and data are freely available from the book's website. Get started learning PyQGIS today!

Geospatial Power Tools

EVERYONE LOVES POWER TOOLS!

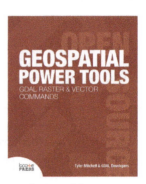

The GDAL and OGR utilities are the power tools of the GIS world, and best of all, they're free.

The utilities include tools for examining, converting, transforming, building and analysing data. This book is a collection of the GDAL and OGR documentation, but also includes substantial new content designed to help guide you in using the utilities to solve your current data problems.

Inside you'll find a quick reference for looking up the right syntax and example usage quickly. The book is divided into three parts: *Workflows and examples*, *GDAL raster utilities*, and *OGR vector utilities*.

Once you get a taste of the power the GDAL/OGR suite provides, you'll wonder how you ever got along without them. This book will get you on the fast track to becoming more efficient in your GIS data processing efforts.

Discover QGIS

GET MAPPING WITH DISCOVER QGIS!

Get your hands on the award winning GeoAcademy exercises in a convenient workbook format. The GeoAcademy is the first ever GIS curriculum based on a national standard—the U.S. Department of Labor's Geospatial Competency Model—a hierarchical model of the knowledge, skills, and abilities needed to work as a GIS professional in today's marketplace.

The GeoAcademy material in this workbook has been updated for use with QGIS v2.14, Inkscape v0.91, and GRASS GIS v7.0.3. This is the most up-to-date version of the GeoAcademy curriculum. To aid in learning, all exercise data includes solution files.

The workbook is edited by one of the lead GeoAcademy authors, Kurt Menke, a highly experienced FOSS4G educator.

www.ingramcontent.com/pod-product-compliance
Lightning Source LLC
Chambersburg PA
CBHW080358060326
40689CB00019B/4052